MILITARY UNIFORMS
OF THE WORLD

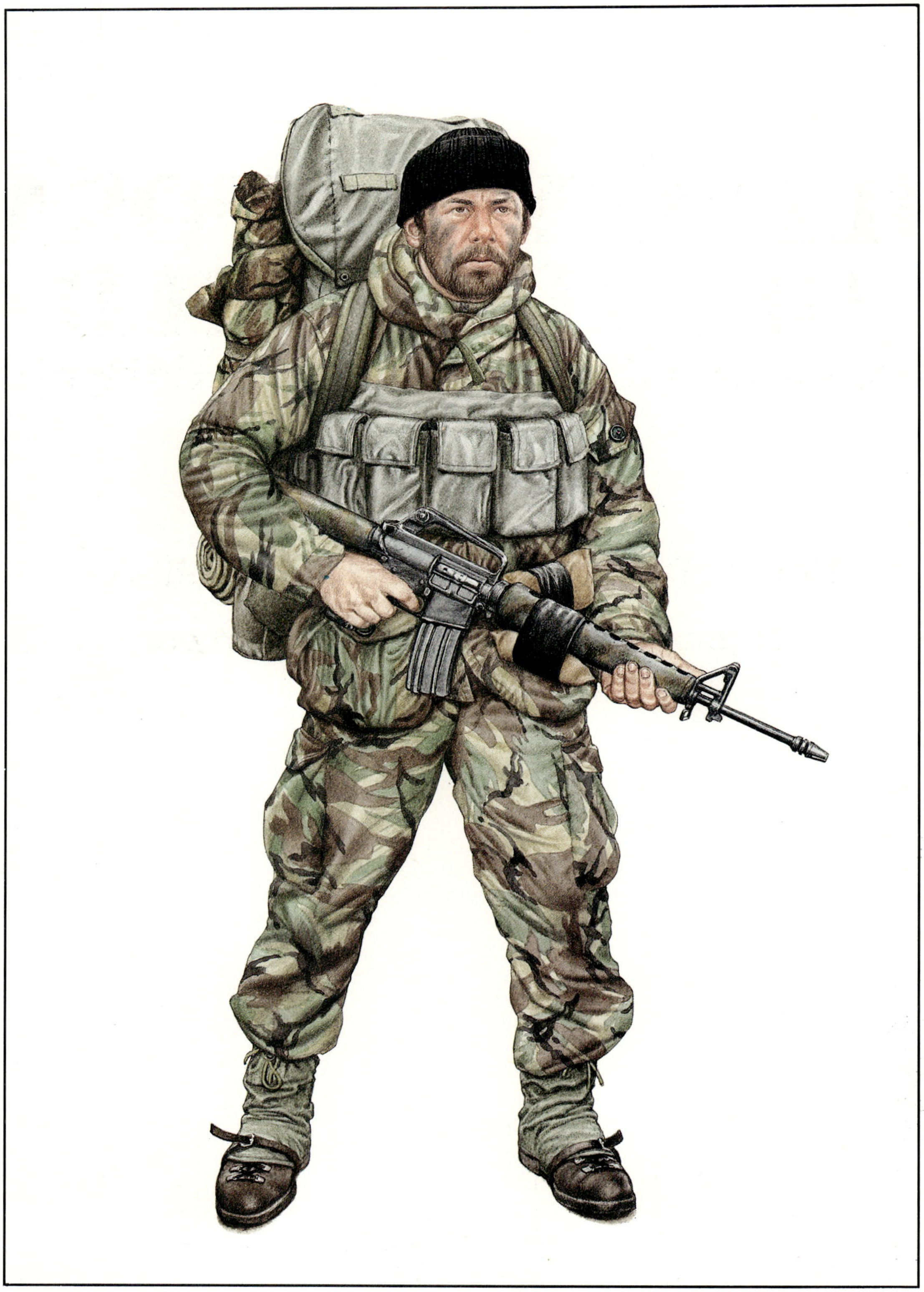

MILITARY UNIFORMS OF THE WORLD
Uniforms and equipment since World War II

Editors Dr John Pimlott & Adrian Gilbert

Illustrations by Malcolm McGregor

Crescent Books
New York

Acknowledgments

Photographs were supplied by:
Amena Pictures, Black Star, Camera Press, C.O.I., M.Flament, John Hillelson Agency, Robert Hunt Library, I.W.M., Bureau Maritieme Den Haag, M.O.D., New Zealand Army, New Zealand House, P.A., Photo Source, Photri, Popperfoto, Rapho, The Research House, Rex Features, Soldier Magazine, Frank Spooner Pictures, John Topham Picture Library, United Nations, US Army, US Navy, Peter Young.

Production editor Richard Williams
Designer Michael Moule

First published in Great Britain by
Orbis Book Publishing Corporation
A BPCC plc company

1986 edition published by Crescent Books,
distributed by Crown Publishers, Inc.

© Orbis Publishing Limited, 1983, 1984, 1985
Compilation © Orbis Book Publishing Corporation 1986

All rights reserved. No part of this publication may be reproduced, stored in a retrieval system, or transmitted, in any form or by any means, electronic, mechanical, photocopying, recording or otherwise, without the prior permission of the publisher. Such permission, if granted, is subject to a fee depending on the nature of the use.

Printed in Italy

ISBN 0-517-62003-0

h g f e d c b a

Title page: Marine, Special Boat Squadron, Falklands 1982

CONTENTS

Introduction	6
The United States	**8**
The US Army in Korea	10
US Airborne Forces	12
The US 1st Air Cavalry Division	14
The US Marines	16
US Special Forces	18
The US Marines on Grenada	20
Britain and the Commonwealth	**22**
The Royal Australian Regiment in Korea	24
The Gloucestershire Regiment	26
The British Army in Kenya	28
The Parachute Regiment	30
The Royal Regiment of Artillery	32
The Brigade of Gurkhas	34
The New Zealand Army	36
The Argyll and Sutherland Highlanders	38
The SAS in Oman	40
The Parachute Regiment in Northern Ireland	42
The Royal Marines	44
The SAS in the Falklands	46
The Blues and Royals	48
Western Europe	**50**
The Dutch Army	52
The Greek Democratic Army	54
The Greek National Army	56
French Foreign Legion Paras	58
The Swedish Army	60
The French Army in Algeria	62
The Belgian Army in the Congo	64
The Portuguese Army in Africa	66
The Turkish Army in Cyprus	68
French Foreign Legion Paras in Kolwezi	70
The Italian Army in Lebanon	72
Latin America	**74**
The Cuban Revolutionary Army	76
The Cuban Army in Angola	78
The Salvadorean Army	80
The Argentinian Army	82
Argentinian Special Forces	84
Africa	**86**
The Algerian National Liberation Army	88
Mercenaries in the Congo	90
The Biafran Army	92
The Nigerian Federal Army	94
The Chadian Army	96
The Angolan National Liberation Front	98
The Rhodesian African Rifles	100
The Selous Scouts	102
The Patriotic Front	104
The Eritrean Liberation Movement	106
The South African Army	108
The Middle East	**110**
The Palmach	111
The Egyptian Army in the 1948 War	112
The Arab Legion	114
The Israeli Army	116
The Israeli Armoured Corps	118
The Egyptian Army 1954–80	120
The Jordanian Army	122
Dhofari Guerrillas	124
Egyptian Armoured Forces in the 1973 War	126
The Syrian Army in the 1973 War	128
The Palestine Liberation Organisation	130
The Iranian Army	132
The Iraqi Army	134
Israeli Airborne Forces	136
The Lebanese Army	138
South Asia	**140**
Azad Kashmir Forces	142
The Indian Army	144
The Pakistani Army	146
The Indian Army in 1971	148
The Pakistani Army in 1971	150
The Mukti Bahini	152
Southeast Asia	**154**
The Malayan Races Liberation Army	156
The North Vietnamese Army	158
The Indonesian Marines	160
The Viet Cong	162
The South Vietnamese Army	164
The Khmer Rouge	166
East Asia	**168**
The Chinese Nationalist Army	170
The People's Liberation Army	172
The North Korean Army	174
The People's Liberation Army in Korea	176
The South Korean Army	178
The Soviet Bloc	**180**
The Soviet Army in Hungary	182
Soviet Armoured Forces	184
Afghan Guerrillas	186
The Afghan Army	188
The Soviet Army in Afghanistan	190
Further Reading	**192**

Introduction

We live in a violent world, in which individuals, dissident groups and states all too often resort to the weapons of war to solve their problems or satisfy their grievances. Since 1945 there has not been a year – indeed, there has probably not even been a day – when a war has not been taking place somewhere in the world, and although none has yet grown to the proportions of World War II, to the people involved they have been just as devastating and, in many millions of cases, just as final.

In the two superpower blocs, dominated by the United States and Soviet Union respectively, the possession of nuclear weapons has created a state of heavily-armed peace, but elsewhere the violence has taken many forms under a variety of different pressures. The most obvious is direct invasion of a state's territory by an enemy force, as occurred in Korea in 1950 and the Falklands in 1982, and this produces 'conventional' war of a familiar type, involving the full range of modern weapons systems – armour, artillery and airpower – and the fighting of predictable campaigns by organised, regular armies. Elsewhere, as in Malaya in 1948 or Algeria in 1962, the disturbance has been provoked by small groups of revolutionaries, intent upon independence from an alien (often colonial) form of government. In these insurgencies regular armies invariably find the going tough against guerrilla forces who do not stand and fight in the expected way. Finally, some dissident groups, such as those of Biafra in 1967 or Angola in 1975, may be strong enough to field organised armies, producing civil or secessionist wars, fought within the boundaries of the state using conventional weapons and tactics. Whatever the cause, the level and destructiveness of the fighting will depend on the size of the forces involved, their access to (and ability to use) modern weapons, and their contacts with outside powers. Such outside interference, particularly if it involves the two superpowers, can often alter the nature of the war, not only because it enables the combatants to deploy the latest technology, but also because it increases the risk of escalation to higher and more devastating levels of conflict.

It is within this complex and dangerous environment that the modern fighting man is expected to operate, and his job is not an enviable one. Although each army or guerrilla force is different, reflecting the ideology, organisation and aims of its particular state or group, the individual soldiers face certain common problems. Chief among these is the inescapable fact that war at all levels is now a political affair, forcing the soldier to be aware of the 'public relations' aspect of his actions. Gone are the days when organised bodies of troops met on the field of battle to decide a particular issue by force of combat alone: since the advent of politico-military ideologies such as communism and Muslim fundamentalism, and the invention of nuclear weapons, wars are fought within the framework of political rather than purely military policies. Guerrillas fight to secure political aims and are opposed by armies that are more effective if their personnel are aware that they are countering political beliefs as much as military techniques. In the same way, conventional wars cannot be allowed to take their own course, for they must be kept 'limited' by politicians fearful of escalation to uncontrollable levels that may involve the use of nuclear arsenals. Such political awareness can have its dangers – not least that armies, frustrated by such close control, may be tempted to take over political power within the state for themselves – but it also means that individual soldiers (and particularly their officers) must understand why they are fighting. The age of the educated soldier has dawned.

Nor is such education confined to the political awareness of the fighting man, for in an age of rapidly improving technology, he must also in many cases have a detailed practical knowledge of how his weapons work and what their effect will be. Soldiers of all types now have access to weapons of far greater destructive capability than ever before, ranging from automatic smallarms and manportable anti-tank or anti-aircraft missiles to long-range artillery pieces and main battle tanks of bewildering complexity. Moreover, the modern soldier is much better informed on the battlefield than his World War II counterpart, receiving information from satellites, reconnaissance aircraft and remotely piloted vehicles, relayed via improved communications to data-processing and battlefield computers. He can therefore expect to achieve a far greater kill-ratio over longer distances. A single soldier, adequately armed with modern weapons, can do as much damage now as a company or even a battalion of 40 years ago.

The result is a confused and frightening battlefield, regardless of the level of combat. The modern fighting man has to be prepared to face anything from a hail of bullets to a silent shroud of chemical agents, and he must expect to fight for long periods without respite. In counter-insurgency campaigns, he must endure the constant threat of being attacked by people he cannot see in terrain that is alien to him; in conventional battles, he must expect to fight 24 hours a day until he drops (a period of about 72 hours if the Israeli experience of October 1973 is typical). At the same time he must endure the normal stress of war – the constant fear of death, the loss of comrades, the problems of disrupted lines of supply – and, in a highly mobile or low-level campaign, he must be able to make decisions on his own, without the benefit of direct orders. It is a difficult ideal to achieve, but if it is even approached, the fighting man will be an effective instrument of policy; if it is not, he will be nothing more than a member of an armed and dangerous horde. It is a thin dividing line.

Although the superpowers seem to be settling some of their differences, and although the process of decolonisation was virtually complete by 1980, war continues to be, for the foreseeable future, a constant of the international situation.

Right: A sergeant of the British Parachute Regiment, face streaked with camouflage cream, adopts an heroic pose. He is carrying a 9mm Sterling L2A3 sub-machine gun and sports parachute-qualification wings for the British and French armies, on the arm and above the breast pocket respectively.

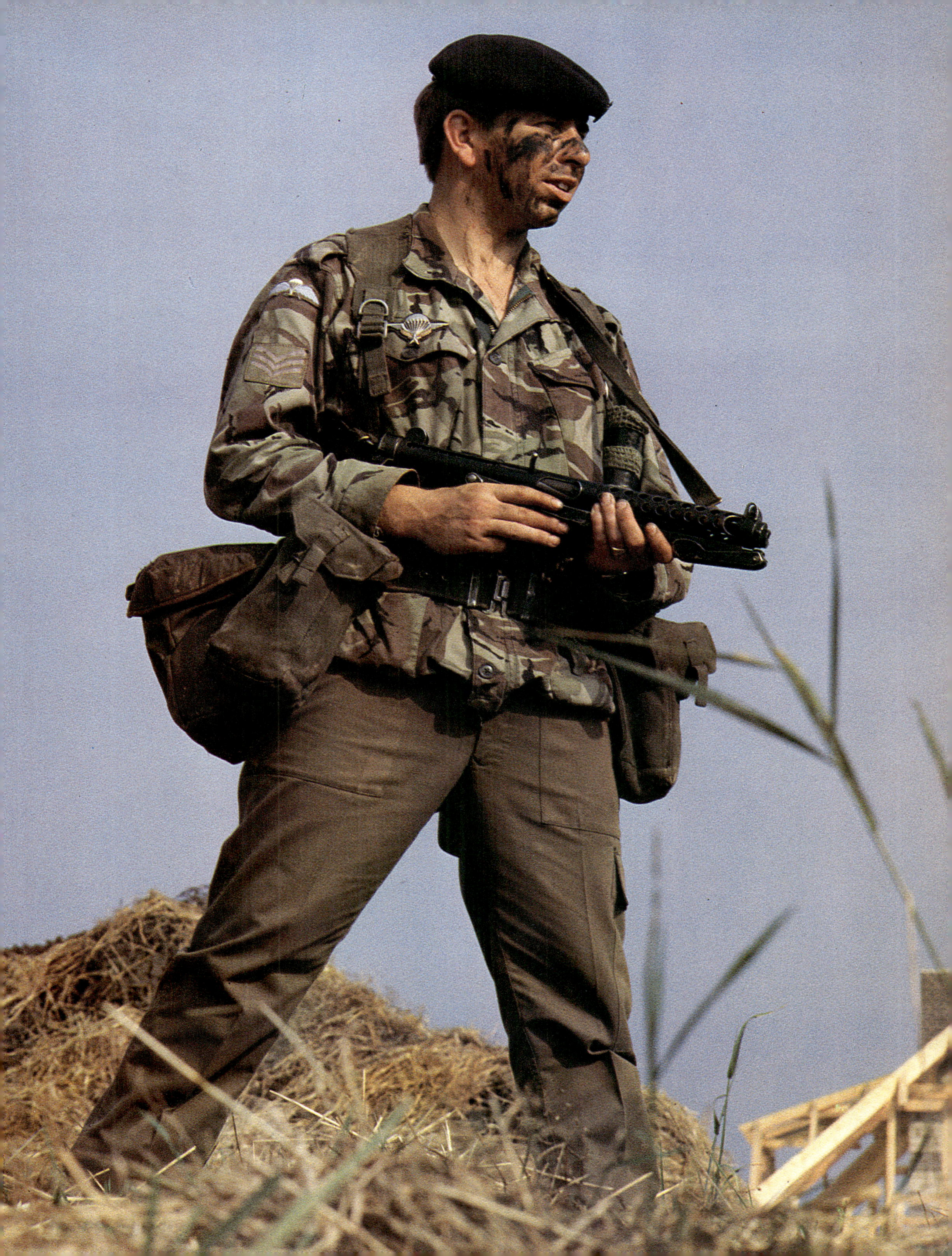

The United States

When World War II ended in September 1945 the United States, in common with most of its Western allies, immediately began to reduce the size of its armed forces, returning conscripts to civilian life and scrapping vast quantities of equipment. The process was accelerated by the recent display of atomic power at Hiroshima and Nagasaki, for the awesome potential of the new technology suggested to US policy-makers that future security lay not with large armed forces but with a small, nuclear-capable air force. By early 1947 the US Army had been cut from eight million to less than 700,000 men, and the development of weapons and tactics had virtually ceased. Stretched over a huge area including the United States, Western Europe and Japan, the army had no alternative but to make do with World War II weapons such as the M1 carbine and the vulnerable M4 Sherman tank.

The North Korean invasion of the South in June 1950 therefore caught the Americans unprepared for conventional war, particularly against an enemy well-versed in the tactics of the Red Army and supplied with Soviet weapons. At first, as troops softened by five years of occupation duty were deployed to Korea from Japan, it looked as if the Americans and their hastily-mobilised United Nations allies would be defeated; only after General MacArthur's brilliant outflanking move at Inchon in September did the tide begin to turn. This coincided with a return to selective conscription in the United States – a policy that was to result in an army of over two million men by 1953. In October 1950, however, hordes of Chinese troops swept into North Korea to overwhelm the UN positions, and the situation was only saved by the introduction of new tactics, based firmly upon US-supplied technology. By 1951 the US Army had been re-equipped with large numbers of artillery pieces as well as the latest M26 and M46 main battle tanks (MBTs), and had access to virtually unlimited air support. This favoured the development of an attritional 'meatgrinder' strategy, designed to counter large enemy forces with massive barrages and air attacks. It proved successful enough to ensure the survival of South Korea, but it led the Americans towards a dependence on technology that proved too often to be a substitute for efficient manpower.

This was shown in the next major commitment of US forces to war, when in March 1965 President Johnson deployed elements of the army, air force and navy to support the flagging South Vietnamese against communist pressure. The US Army had not been drastically reduced at the end of the Korean War and, by the early 1960s, had received the next generation of military hardware, including M60 MBTs and tactical helicopters. The enduring belief in firepower, however, proved dangerously inappropriate to the problems of Vietnam. Despite apparent success against North Vietnamese regulars trying to infiltrate the border down the Ia Drang Valley or across the Demilitarised Zone, the real threat came from the Viet Cong guerrillas in the countryside, and the US Army was neither equipped nor prepared to deal with a politico-military insurgency. Some elements of the army did adapt to the new environment, notably the 'Green Berets' or US Special Forces, who created an anti-guerrilla force from the Montagnard tribesmen of the Central Highlands and took on the Viet Cong with squad-sized patrols. The majority, however, clung obstinately to the Korean War belief in firepower, using the new generation of smallarms (including the M16 automatic rifle and M60 machine gun), artillery and armour to conduct massive 'search and destroy' operations. Far from defeating the guerrillas, such tactics actually alienated the ordinary people of South Vietnam, undermining the combined American/South Vietnamese war effort and leading to a deep frustration among the soldiers. Some success was achieved when the helicopter was adapted from utility transport to troop-carrier and gunship – a process which culminated in the creation of an entire airmobile division (the 1st Air Cavalry) – but even this did little to halt the spread of the insurgency. By 1968, when the Viet Cong's Tet offensive exploded the myth that the Americans were winning in Vietnam, the army was beginning to suffer the demoralisation and public alienation that were to lead to its less-than-honourable withdrawal five years later.

The period since 1973 has seen a gradual and often painful recovery of military confidence in the United States, significantly helped by the return to all-regular recruitment and the evolution of improved tactical doctrines. Despite a marked reluctance by successive governments to commit armed forces to foreign adventures that might lead to a 'second Vietnam', the military has reasserted its professionalism, demonstrated in recent years by its involvement in the Multi-National Force (MNF) keeping the peace in Lebanon (1982–84), and the invasion of Grenada (October 1983). The latter operation was a timely example of rapid deployment, involving Marines and airborne troops whose speed of action and tactical flexibility did much to restore military pride. However, firepower remains a central feature of US military doctrine, and although the new technology of the 1980s – ranging from battlefield computers and sophisticated night-sights to the M1 Abrams MBT and the latest helicopter gunships – does enjoy the advantage of improved accuracy, it still tends to dictate tactics to a potentially worrying extent. The tactical doctrine developed in the early 1980s, known as the AirLand Battle Doctrine, with its intrinsic belief in the ability of small groups of technological armed forces to survive and prevail on a modern battlefield, is a case in point; with an army of less than 800,000 men (and women) at its disposal, the Americans may still be substituting weapons for manpower at a time when, with continuing global commitments, the latter is more useful.

Right: Soaked with spray thrown up at the stern of his craft, a US soldier armed with an M60 machine gun scans the river bank in South Vietnam for signs of communist activity. Such patrols on inland waterways and along the coast contributed to lessening the supply of war material to the Viet Cong.

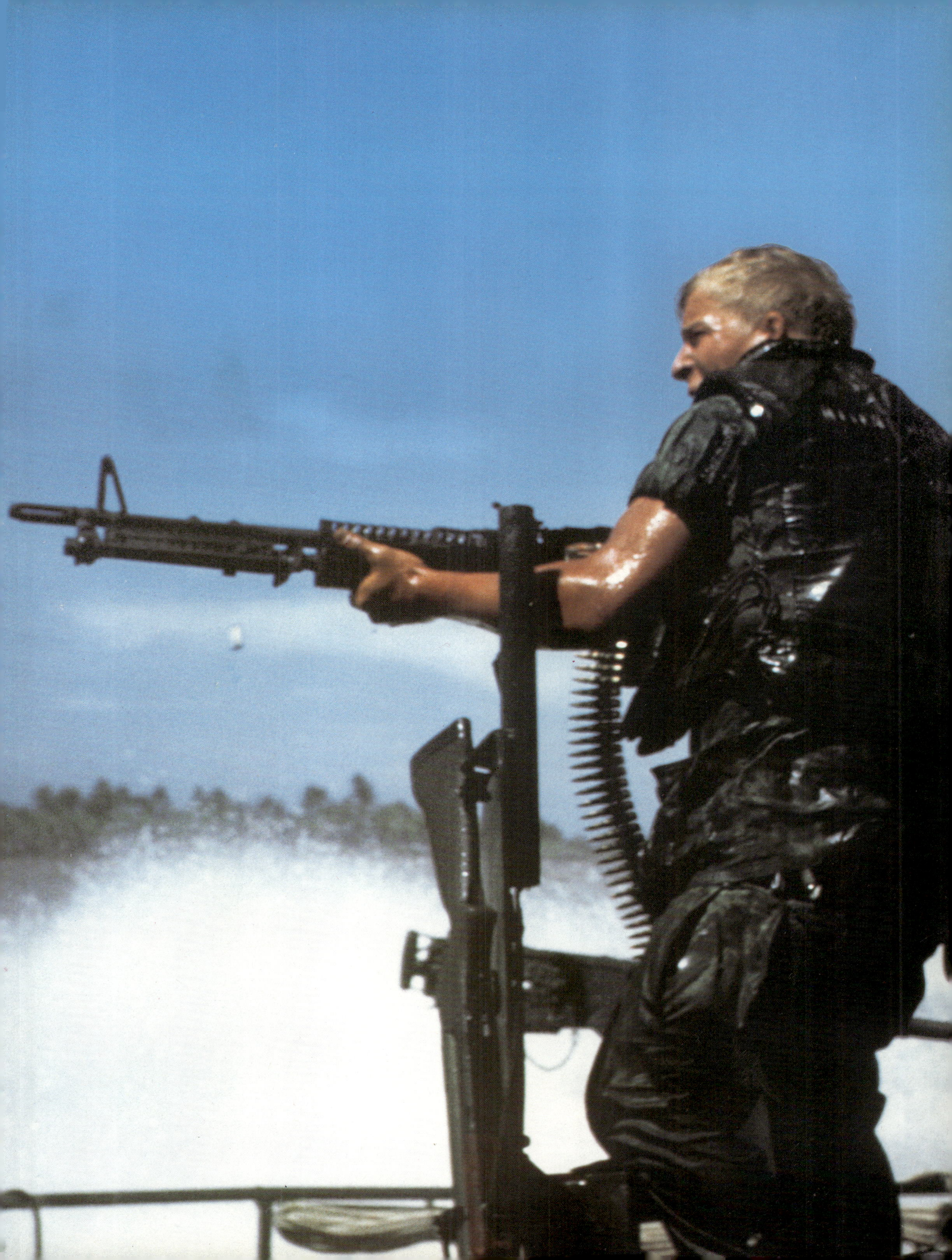

THE UNITED STATES

The US Army in Korea

When the armoured columns of the North Korean People's Army crossed the border on 25 June 1950 South Korea was caught unprepared and her forces collapsed under the weight of the communist onslaught. South Korea appealed to America for help and received a prompt response: American units in Japan were quickly mobilised and on 1 July the first US troops landed in South Korea, the advance guard of the 24th Infantry Division. During July two further divisions arrived (with a number of independent units) so that by 4 August some 47,000 US troops were in Korea.

Initially, high hopes were placed upon the American presence as a means of stiffening the wavering South Korean forces and halting the communist advance. The Americans underestimated the North Korean Army, however, as their own troops were in a poor state of combat readiness, softened by years of occupation duties in Japan, dangerously understrength and lacking in armaments and many other items of essential equipment.

An attempt to hold the strategically important city of Taejon failed and the Americans and South Koreans were flung back to Pusan at the southernmost tip of the Korean peninsula. Although the US Army was criticised for not holding the North Koreans – and in some instances unit morale was severely lacking – the blame was largely unjustified as the Americans were very short of arms and equipment. The North Koreans made good use of their T34/85 tanks while the Americans, without tanks of their own in the early stages of the war, were unable to stop the communists as their infantry anti-tank weapons (2.36in rocket launchers) had little effect on the North Korean armour.

Holding prepared positions around the Naktong River – the Pusan Perimeter – the Americans made a determined stand and beat off the North Korean attacks. Reinforcements began to arrive and a US counter-attack was prepared. In mid-September a daring amphibious assault was launched against Inchon on the west coast. The landings were a complete success, the South Korean capital of Seoul was retaken and North Korean supply lines severed. Faced by a northward assault from Pusan the North Koreans' offensive rapidly changed to a disorderly retreat. By early October the Americans had crossed the 38th parallel – the old dividing line between the two Koreas – and were heading northward towards the Yalu River, which formed the border between China and North Korea.

In part, the sudden American success was due to inspired leadership by the US commander, General MacArthur, but more important was the commitment of hardened army and Marine units and the arrival of improved arms, including 3.5in rocket launchers and the generous allocation of modern tanks, notably M26 Pershings and M46 Pattons, and heavy artillery which could break up North Korean formations at long range.

As the American Army drove north it was organised into three corps: I and IX Corps came under the control of the Eighth US Army while the X Corps, operating semi-independently on the eastern side of the Peninsula, came under MacArthur's direct control. However, the complex command structures employed by the American Army in Korea and a growing over-confidence on the part of the US commanders was to lead to near disaster.

Over-extended and badly strung out, the Americans were caught completely off-balance when the communist Chinese Army launched a massive offensive across the Yalu River in October 1950. The United Nations forces were swamped by the Chinese attack and hurriedly fell back south across the 38th parallel. American morale plummeted; not only had the victories of the summer been completely overturned but the entire position of the American Army lay in jeopardy. The fall in morale was characterised by a lack of combat willingness which became known as 'bugout' fever. Only the firm resolve of the new Eighth Army commander, General Matthew Ridgway, brought the situation under control.

By the end of January 1951 Chinese supply lines were over-stretched and American firepower and determination halted the communists. A static war of attrition resulted where Ridgway pitted US material superiority against Chinese manpower. Adopting a deliberate policy of slowly and relentlessly bombarding the Chinese from a series of strong points he denied them their basic advantage of greater manoeuvrability. These 'meatgrinder' tactics held the Chinese and a stalemate resulted until the armistice on 27 July 1953.

At its peak, the American contribution to the war in Korea stood at over 300,000 men and during the course of the conflict 34,000 were killed and a further 105,000 wounded. Although the American Army failed to defeat the communists outright it at least prevented them from annexing South Korea, preserving the status quo in divided Korea.

Above: US troops watch the progress of an action well-equipped with Mk 2 fragmentation grenades and bandoliers of smallarms ammunition. As in World War II the Americans placed great value upon firepower, so that the opposing communist advantages in manpower could be nullified by American material superiority.

US Infantryman
— Korea 1951 —

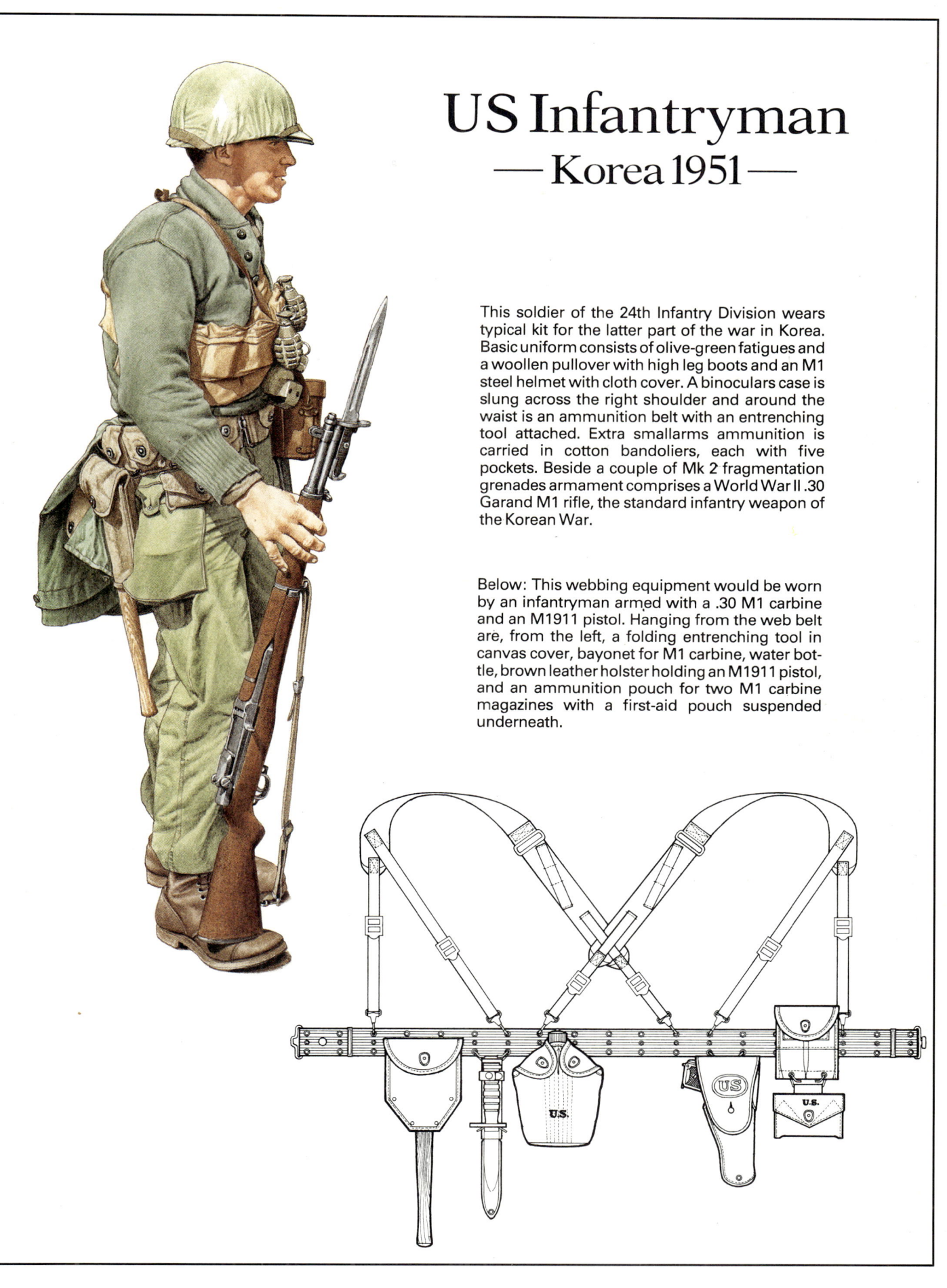

This soldier of the 24th Infantry Division wears typical kit for the latter part of the war in Korea. Basic uniform consists of olive-green fatigues and a woollen pullover with high leg boots and an M1 steel helmet with cloth cover. A binoculars case is slung across the right shoulder and around the waist is an ammunition belt with an entrenching tool attached. Extra smallarms ammunition is carried in cotton bandoliers, each with five pockets. Beside a couple of Mk 2 fragmentation grenades armament comprises a World War II .30 Garand M1 rifle, the standard infantry weapon of the Korean War.

Below: This webbing equipment would be worn by an infantryman armed with a .30 M1 carbine and an M1911 pistol. Hanging from the web belt are, from the left, a folding entrenching tool in canvas cover, bayonet for M1 carbine, water bottle, brown leather holster holding an M1911 pistol, and an ammunition pouch for two M1 carbine magazines with a first-aid pouch suspended underneath.

THE UNITED STATES

US Airborne Forces

United States airborne troops evolved around the time of America's entry into World War II in 1941, and during the course of the war they came to be regarded as amongst the best troops in the US armed forces. After serving in the Mediterranean and North Africa in the latter stages of 1942, the crack 82nd Airborne Division took part in Operation Husky – the invasion of Sicily in July 1943 – and was later employed in Italy during the summer to apply vital pressure against the Axis southern flank in Italy. The 82nd Airborne was then despatched to Britain to be joined by 101st Airborne Division; the two formations played a vital role during the Normandy invasion, being para-dropped behind enemy lines to secure key German strong points in support of the main landings. As part of Operation Market Garden – which culminated in the battle for Arnhem – the two US airborne divisions once again proved their worth by gaining their objectives, despite the operation's lack of overall success.

After the cessation of hostilities in 1945 several units of paratroops were included in the UN forces occupying Japan, while others remained in training in the USA. At the outbreak of the Korean conflict in 1950 the American ground forces found themselves seriously outnumbered by their communist opponents, and US-based formations were rushed to the war zone. In spite of being fully trained, the 82nd was held back as a strategic reserve, backed by the 11th Airborne, which was, however, completing its divisional training cycle. As an emergency measure, the 187th Airborne Regimental Combat Team was formed from men of the two airborne divisions, again kept in reserve but used as a back-up for emergencies.

One of the 187th's first roles in the war was a somewhat bizarre one, namely to quell rioting by communist prisoners of war at the United Nations camp on Koje-do island. Using a minimum of force the 187th suppressed the disturbance at Koje-do and were then returned to base. In June 1953, under the command of Brigadier-General William C. Westmoreland, they were parachuted in to reinforce the beleaguered 2nd US Division at the battle of Kumsong Bulge, an engagement which marked the end of the fighting in Korea.

The Korean War saw the first significant use of the helicopter, and during the 1950s its importance in the sphere of military operations continued to increase. However, the helicopter posed special problems for the paratroop forces: the concept of employing parachute-dropped soldiers had always been controversial, and paratroop critics claimed that helicopters were far more effective in carrying out an airborne assault than a parachute drop.

Advances in helicopter technology and the advent of the war in Vietnam only served to extend further the helicopter's importance within the US armed forces, with the result that whole units were equipped with helicopters, eventually up to divisional level. Nonetheless, these airmobile formations did not signal the end of the paratrooper – a full-strength battalion of the 173rd Airborne Brigade was successfully para-dropped during Operation Junction City in 1967 – though, increasingly, paratroop units assumed a new role of helicopter-equipped airmobile troops, which at least ensured their survival as airborne soldiers as opposed to being swallowed up by the infantry.

Despite the increasingly hostile environment of the modern battlefield, which makes large-scale parachute drops exceedingly hazardous, the need for a picked unit of troops that can be transported by air over vast distances, and can be parachuted onto a target area with a minimum of delay, still remains. And in the 1970s, the development of the concept of the Rapid Deployment Force – capable of being despatched to trouble spots throughout the globe – has helped ensure that the US paratrooper has a future as a parachute-borne soldier.

Above: Before making a high-altitude drop, two paras of the 82nd Airborne hook-up to their aircraft's oxygen supply. The paratroopers' reserve parachutes and altimeters can be seen attached on the front of their parachute harnesses. High-altitude drops are typically carried out by small select groups wishing to avoid detection from the ground. Left: A para of the 187th RCT prepares to make a jump over Korea in November 1951. Tucked into the parachute harness is a .30 M1A1 carbine, fitted with the folding stock especially manufactured for airborne forces.

US Paratrooper
— Korea 1951 —

Above: A unit of the 82nd Airborne prepares to board a C-130 transport aircraft as part of a para-drop field-training exercise. These paratroopers are equipped with a main parachute – worn on the back – and a front-mounted reserve parachute.

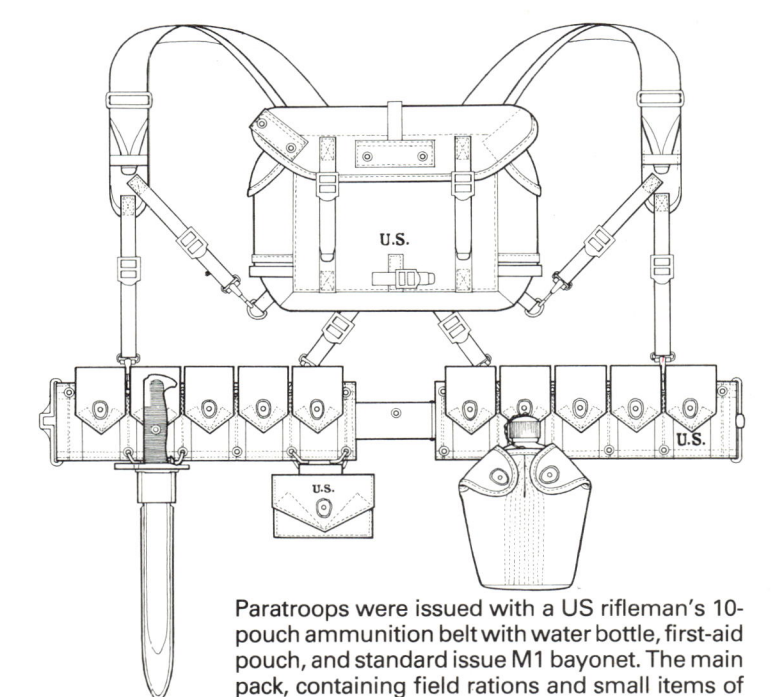

By the end of the 1940s the US special airborne suit of World War II was being phased out in favour of the harder-wearing infantry field uniforms. This paratrooper wears the regular M1 helmet rather than the airborne version, with an M41 field jacket and M43 waterproofed trousers, tucked into 'Corcoran' paratroop boots. He carries a wrapped first-aid dressing clipped to his left shoulder strap as well as a first-aid pouch below on his belt. His main armament is a .30 Garand rifle, with a combat knife and a .45 M1911 A1 pistol as side arms. The thonged holster is for strapping the Colt to the thigh, 'Western' style.

Paratroops were issued with a US rifleman's 10-pouch ammunition belt with water bottle, first-aid pouch, and standard issue M1 bayonet. The main pack, containing field rations and small items of equipment, was designed to hang down on the front of the thighs below the reserve parachute during the drop.

13

THE UNITED STATES

The US 1st Air Cavalry Division

The Vietnam War proved to be a testing ground for both new military equipment and new types of military formations. The 1st Cavalry Division (Airmobile) was raised in July 1965 as an experiment in integrating helicopters into a full division-level formation. Although helicopter-equipped units had been used before, the 1st Cavalry represented a unique experiment in deploying a large and completely autonomous airmobile formation.

The 1st Cavalry had a complement of 16,000 men organised along the lines of a standard US infantry division but with the ability of its men and weapons to be airlifted into combat by the 400 aircraft at the division's command. Air transport was provided by the division aviation group, organised into three helicopter battalions which could airlift three of the division's eight infantry battalions at any one time. Battlefield reconnaissance duties were undertaken by the heliborne air cavalry squadron whose prime function was to seek out the Viet Cong and direct the main infantry force to engage them in combat. An elite within an elite, the troops of the air cavalry squadron were invariably the first into combat and their ability to pin down the elusive guerrilla enemy was vital to the success of mobile counter-guerrilla operations.

The cornerstone of the airmobile concept was instant and continuous mobility but if the 1st Cavalry was to operate as an effective divisional formation its own organic artillery was essential. Yet the task of transporting the weight and volume of artillery pieces and their ammunition was a major problem for the 1st Cavalry, undermining the basic philosophy of airborne tactical flexibility. The mobility-firepower equation was neatly resolved, however, through the enterprising use of helicopter technology. The lightweight 105mm howitzers were easily carried by the Chinook transport helicopters, and once in Vietnam it was discovered that 155mm howitzers – the crucial heavyweight backbone of divisional artillery – could be airlifted by CH-54 Sky Cranes.

Utilising the helicopter further, an aerial artillery battalion was formed, divided into three batteries, each of 12 helicopters armed with 2.75in rocket launchers. When used at battery and battalion level these airborne artillery platforms were able to deploy a devastating firepower capacity against a range of targets outside the capability of conventional ground-based guns. The aerial artillery battalion was particularly useful when acting in a ground-suppression role, creating a safe landing zone for infantry units committed to ground combat.

No sooner had the 1st Cavalry arrived in Vietnam than they were sent to battle, to destroy a strong NVA force in the Ia Drang Valley in the Central Highlands. Despite fierce enemy resistance the 1st Cavalry broke the NVA attack, inflicting nearly 2000 casualties for the loss of only four helicopters. The battles of the Ia Drang Valley proved the worth of the airmobile division and established an *esprit de corps* of rugged professionalism which guaranteed the 1st Cavalry its position as one of the top units which served in the Vietnam War.

During Tet elements of the 1st Cavalry performed interdiction missions around Hue while the whole division acted as the spearhead for the relief of Khe Sanh. Later in the year the 1st Cavalry's helicopters launched attack after attack against NVA strongholds in the A Shau Valley, playing a major role in the destruction of communist supply bases. The 1st Cavalry's last major operation in Vietnam was the invasion of Cambodia in May 1970 when it acted as the airborne vanguard for the South Vietnamese ground assault. The 1st Cavalry's ability to locate and destroy enemy formations in difficult circumstances was a further vindication of the airmobile division.

Above: Two men of the 1st Air Cavalry Division with a captured Viet Cong. The soldier on the left is wearing his poncho over his fatigue shirt and his boots are the field pattern, not the tropical. The band around the helmet was designed for attaching foliage but it was often used to hold cigarettes.

US 1st Air Cavalry Trooper
—Vietnam 1966—

This soldier's kit is fairly typical of that carried by American combat troops during the Vietnam War. A simple cotton fatigue uniform is worn along with US nylon and leather jungle boots and an M1 steel helmet with camouflage cover; two bottles of insect repellent are held in the helmet band. Web equipment is of the M56 pattern and attached to it are M26A1 fragmentation grenades and boxes containing belts of M60 machine gun ammunition. The firearm being carried is the M16A1, which was first seriously tested in Vietnam and after a few initial setbacks proved itself a highly effective weapon. An interesting feature is the snap ring – fixed to the left shoulder strap – for abseiling from helicopters.

Below: US M56 web equipment as worn by the 1st Air Cavalry in Vietnam. Attached to the centre of the web belt is a small 'butt' pack (with bed roll slung underneath) and on each side are water bottles and ammunition pouches for M16 magazines. The M7 knife bayonet is for the M16 rifle.

THE UNITED STATES

The US Marines

Formed in 1775, the United States Marine Corps has had a long and distinguished history as one of the world's premier fighting forces. The Marines gained special prominence during World War II when they spearheaded the American campaign in the Pacific and earned themselves a 'gung-ho' reputation for combat eagerness. During the war the size of the Marine Corps expanded enormously to just under half-a-million men, organised into an all-arms service complete with its own armoured, naval and air support units.

The prime role of the Marines has been to act as a 'rapid deployment force' ready to be sent into action at a moment's notice – and since 1945 the Marines have seen no shortage of action. In the Lebanon in 1958 and in San Domingo in 1965 US Marines were active in coming to the aid of pro-US governments faced by internal instability.

The Korean War was the first major conflict to involve American forces since World War II, and the Marines were among the first to enter the fray as part of the force holding the Pusan Perimeter in July 1950. In the landings at Inchon in September the assault was spearheaded by the 1st Marine Division. When the Chinese came to the aid of their North Korean allies in the winter of 1950 the 1st Marine Division was again in the thick of action. The speed of the Chinese advance caught the Americans by surprise and the 1st Division was cut off at the Chosin Reservoir; but despite being vastly outnumbered it carried out a fighting retreat of epic proportion, breaking through the lines of the 60,000-strong Chinese Ninth Army Group and reaching the safety of the harbour at Hungnam.

Following the Korean conflict the next occasion of full-scale US military involvement occurred in 1965, when the Marines found themselves fighting a remorseless infantry war against the Viet Cong and North Vietnamese Army in the jungles and paddy fields of South Vietnam. The Tet offensive of 1968 saw a massive flare-up of the guerrilla war and the Marines were soon engaged in the fight – most notably at Khe Sanh and in Hue. At the end of January the isolated Marine fire-base at Khe Sanh came under close siege from more than 20,000 North Vietnamese troops, who maintained a constant artillery barrage against the beleaguered Marines for over 10 weeks until the siege was lifted in April. In the imperial city of Hue, the Viet Cong managed to secure the Citadel area, and the Marines were allotted the task of flushing them out. A 24-day street battle developed, as the Marines fought the VC in grim house-to-house combat that left 5000 enemy dead in the ruins of the Citadel.

Despite these victories, America had little heart for the war, and after 1968 began the process of disengagement from Vietnam, which entailed a progressive reduction of Marine numbers.

Since Vietnam the Marine Corps has proved its value on a number of occasions, most notably during the war in the Lebanon in 1982 where the Marines acted as part of a peace-keeping force which was intended to restore order to the war-torn streets of Beirut.

US Marines regroup under fire during the fighting for the Citadel at Hue. By 1968 the Marines were armed with the M16 rifle, an automatic weapon that proved more effective in close combat than did its predecessor the M14. Beside their M16s, these Marines were well equipped with a multitude of infantry-support weapons, including machine guns, mortars and grenades – the latter a highly effective weapon in the house-to-house fighting that characterised the battle for Hue.

US Marine Private 1st Class
— Vietnam 1968 —

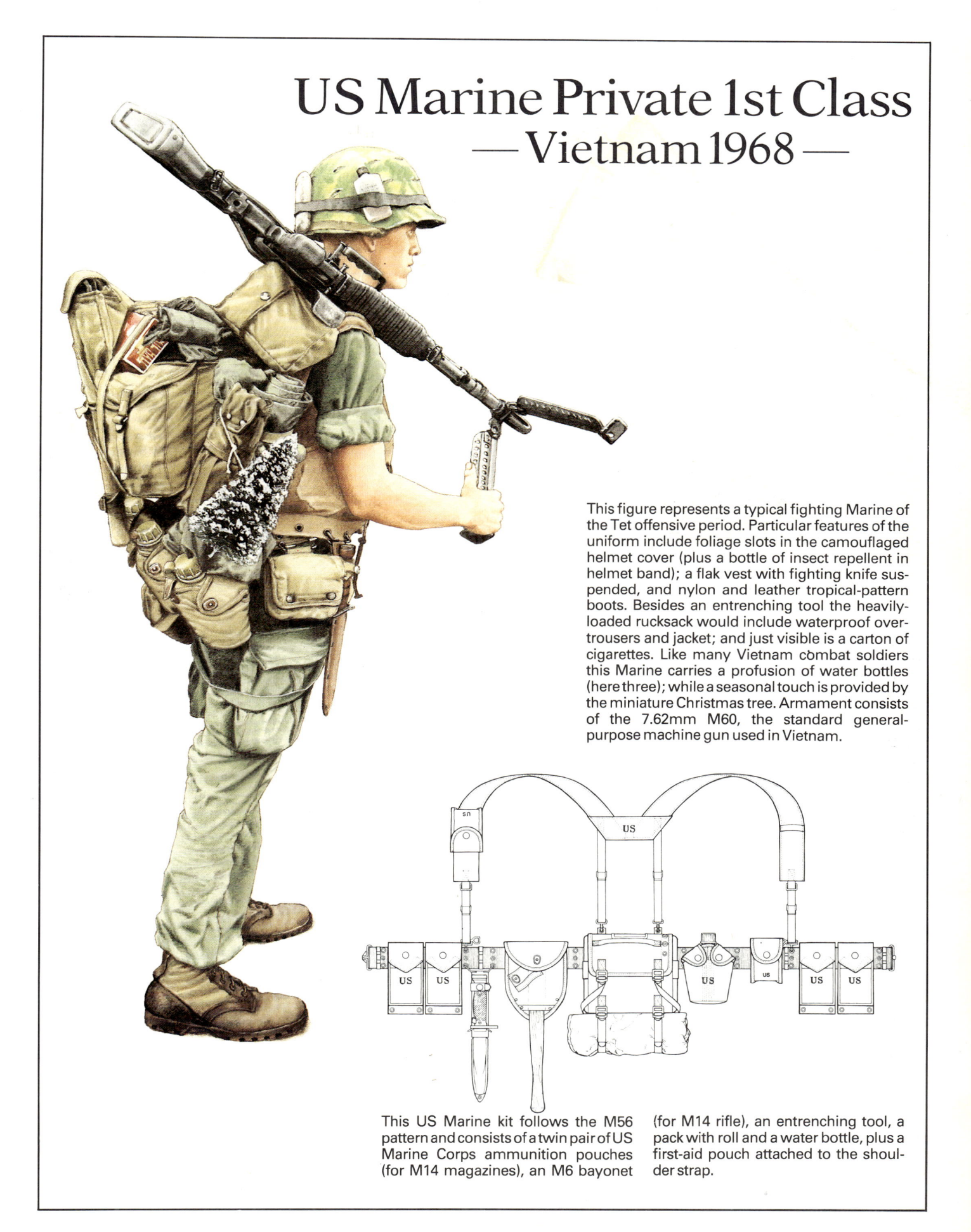

This figure represents a typical fighting Marine of the Tet offensive period. Particular features of the uniform include foliage slots in the camouflaged helmet cover (plus a bottle of insect repellent in helmet band); a flak vest with fighting knife suspended, and nylon and leather tropical-pattern boots. Besides an entrenching tool the heavily-loaded rucksack would include waterproof over-trousers and jacket; and just visible is a carton of cigarettes. Like many Vietnam combat soldiers this Marine carries a profusion of water bottles (here three); while a seasonal touch is provided by the miniature Christmas tree. Armament consists of the 7.62mm M60, the standard general-purpose machine gun used in Vietnam.

This US Marine kit follows the M56 pattern and consists of a twin pair of US Marine Corps ammunition pouches (for M14 magazines), an M6 bayonet (for M14 rifle), an entrenching tool, a pack with roll and a water bottle, plus a first-aid pouch attached to the shoulder strap.

THE UNITED STATES

US Special Forces

The US Special Forces were constituted as a unit on 20 June 1952 at Fort Bragg, North Carolina, when the 10th Special Forces Group was set up. It consisted of one officer, one warrant officer and eight enlisted men. A year later, in September 1953, the second unit, the 77th Special Forces Group, was set up. By 1961 the total strength of the Special Forces was 800 men and they were an established part of the US Army.

The US Special Forces were, however, the subject of vigorous debate within the US military establishment from the time of their creation. Many military theorists were opposed to the creation of small elite units, but in the early 1960s the argument was tipped decisively in the Special Forces' favour by President John F. Kennedy, who saw them as an ideal weapon to use against communist-supported guerrilla movements in the developing world. He wanted the US to establish effective, flexible counter-insurgency units, and pressed for the expansion and development of the Special Forces. In October 1961 he visited the Army's Special Warfare Center at Fort Bragg and soon numbers were expanded to 5000 personnel.

The obvious area in which the Special Forces were to be employed in their counter-insurgency role was Vietnam, where the Viet Cong insurgents had been steadily gaining ground since the late 1950s. Special Forces soldiers had, in fact, been in Vietnam since 1957, when training elements from the 1st Special Forces Group in Okinawa had begun instructing South Vietnamese troops. But from 1961 US Special Forces were committed to a more active counter-insurgency role, working among the Montagnards in the Central Highlands, creating Civilian Irregular Defense Groups (CIDG) to inhibit Viet Cong operations in this strategically vital area.

The basic Special Force unit was the A Team, or A Detachment, consisting of two officers and 10 enlisted men. All the men were volunteers and had to be airborne-qualified. They were then trained in five speciality areas – weapons, communications, combat medicine, intelligence and engineering – and given further courses in escape and evasion, survival, and land navigation. The A Teams were controlled by the B Detachments, which in turn were under the operational command of a C Detachment. The 5th Special Forces Group was set up in 1964 to run Special Force operations in Vietnam.

There were three main layers to Special Forces work. The first was in the creation of the CIDG in the Central Highlands, a task which was swiftly converted into the formation of more aggressive anti-communist forces in the area; and, as the fighting in the Central Highlands increased in intensity in the mid-1960s it shifted its focus towards the frontier with Laos and Cambodia, enabling the Special Forces to monitor and check the movement of men and supplies from North Vietnam into the South. These operations continued to increase in scale until after the Tet offensive of 1968, when the Special Forces began to hand over their responsibilities to South Vietnamese Special Forces.

The second main set of operations was in the so-called 'alphabet' projects, reconnaissance units used to infiltrate enemy-held areas. These too used Vietnamese and Montagnard troops in conjunction with Special Forces personnel. The results of these operations were of extremely high quality.

The final general set of operations carried out by the Special Forces in Vietnam is still shrouded in mystery. These are the activities of the 'Studies and Observation Group' (SOG) that was set up in January 1964, and eventually included 2000 US and 8000 indigenous personnel. SOG was organised into three regional commands, and carried out clandestine cross-border operations, including trying to rescue downed US aircrew.

The other main involvement of the Special Forces was in Latin America. Faced with the growth of guerrilla movements there in the 1960s, the US expanded the activities of the School of the Americas in Panama to train selected Latin American army officers in counter-insurgency. The instructors at the School were Special Forces personnel, who also themselves underwent training there in jungle warfare and survival. As well as training Latin American military personnel to fight insurgency in their own countries, the Special Forces intervened directly in a series of top-secret missions. It is believed that in the 1960s they operated in Guatemala, Colombia and Bolivia – two Special Forces personnel were rumoured to have been present with the Bolivian Rangers unit which captured and shot Che Guevara in 1967.

Special Forces have not been so extensively involved in combat operations since the 1960s, but they have continued to develop counter-insurgency and special operations techniques, ready for the next Vietnam-style emergency.

Below: Special Forces troops discuss an exercise over the bonnet of a jeep. Special Forces personnel undergo the most rigorous and comprehensive of training programmes, designed to prepare them for the diversity of problems to be encountered on active service.

US Special Forces Soldier
— Vietnam 1968 —

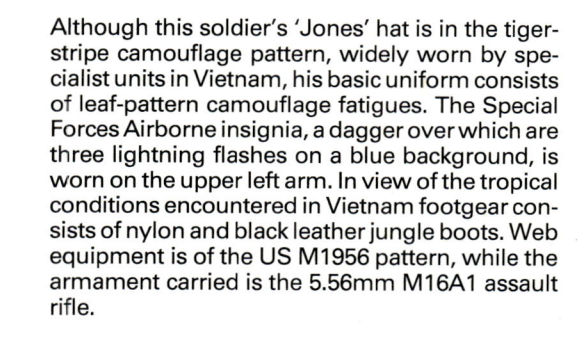

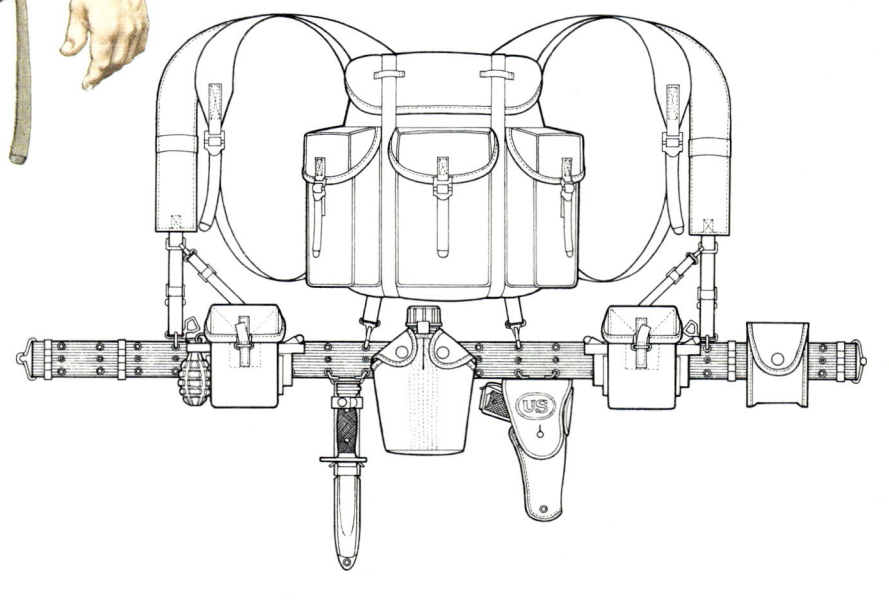

Although this soldier's 'Jones' hat is in the tiger-stripe camouflage pattern, widely worn by specialist units in Vietnam, his basic uniform consists of leaf-pattern camouflage fatigues. The Special Forces Airborne insignia, a dagger over which are three lightning flashes on a blue background, is worn on the upper left arm. In view of the tropical conditions encountered in Vietnam footgear consists of nylon and black leather jungle boots. Web equipment is of the US M1956 pattern, while the armament carried is the 5.56mm M16A1 assault rifle.

Above: On this Special Forces soldier's M1956 web belt are, from the left: an M16 ammunition pouch with grenade attached, M16 bayonet, water bottle, leather holster for a .45 pistol, a second M16 pouch and a first aid pouch. The tropical rucksack was popular with Special Forces troops in Vietnam and featured a steel X-frame that lay flat against the back, and three large outside pockets.

THE UNITED STATES

The US Marines on Grenada

The United States Marine Corps – comprising nearly 200,000 men and women – is organised and equipped to carry out seaborne assaults at short notice anywhere in the world. Its three ground force combat divisions – the 1st Division at Camp Pendleton, California, available for commitment to the Rapid Deployment Joint Task Force/Central Command (RDJTF/Centcom), the 2nd at Camp Lejeune, North Carolina, responsible for operations in the Atlantic, Caribbean and Mediterranean, and the 3rd on the island of Okinawa, committed exclusively to the Pacific – are self-contained fighting formations, mustering about 50,000 personnel each, backed by integral armour, artillery, engineers, helicopters, tactical aircraft and naval support vessels. They can be deployed in their entirety as Marine Amphibious Forces (MAFs), but this is unlikely in peacetime, when smaller formations are more suited to US security needs. Two Marine Amphibious Brigades (MABs), each of about 12,000 personnel, are currently maintained – one at Camp Pendleton for the RDJTF and the other in Hawaii for Pacific operations – while both the Mediterranean and Pacific fleets deploy Marine Amphibious Units (MAUs). The latter, each of about 1900 Marines, are centred upon composite infantry battalions with their own M60 battle tanks, LVTP-7 amphibious personnel carriers, 155mm M198 towed howitzers, Sea Knight and Sea Cobra helicopters, with Marine Corps Phantoms in support. Small enough to be carried on board a single assault ship, the MAU is the ideal formation for rapid response to low-level crises.

Above: As Grenadians watch, US Marines, led by their officer, go out on patrol of the island. These men are carrying full packs and are wearing PASGT (personal armour system, ground troops) 'bullet-proof' vests. Below: This Marine carries his flag folded in the correct order; his M16A1 has an M203 grenade launcher attached.

In October 1983 the Mediterranean-based MAU was acting as America's contribution to the Multi-National Force in the Lebanon and was about to be relieved. The 22nd MAU, commanded by Lieutenant-Colonel Ray Smith, had left the USA on board the assault ship USS *Saipan* and joined a US Navy task force under Rear-Admiral Joseph Metcalf III, flying his flag aboard the helicopter assault ship USS *Guam*, for passage across the Atlantic. After only a few days at sea, however, Metcalf was ordered to turn back, rendezvous with the aircraft carrier USS *Independence* and proceed to the Caribbean island of Grenada. Arriving offshore on 21 October, the Marines were immediately prepared for an assault landing as part of an invasion force. President Reagan, alarmed at recent political developments on the island (on 19 October the prime minister, Maurice Bishop, had been overthrown by a Revolutionary Military Council under General Hudson Austin) and aware of Cuban involvement, particularly in the building of a new international airport at Point Salines to the south of the capital, St George's, was determined to prevent Grenada from becoming a communist base, perilously close to the flash-point areas of Central America. It was the sort of operation for which the Marines had been trained, and for which they were ideally suited.

The invasion began at 0500 hours on 25 October, when a small detachment of Marine SEAL (Sea, Air, Land) specialists went ashore to the north of St George's, advancing rapidly to seize Government House and the person of Sir Paul Scoon, the pro-Western governor-general. Their operation was a success, although they were soon pinned down by sniper fire from elements of the Grenadian Army, a force hitherto dismissed as inefficient by US intelligence. An hour later, helicopters from the *Guam* and *Saipan* brought the bulk of the MAU ashore on the east coast of the island, where the airport at Pearls was taken against minimal opposition. At much the same time US Rangers, backed by men of the 82nd Airborne Division, were assaulting Point Salines, but here progress was slow against Cuban and Grenadian opposition. As a result, elements of the 22nd MAU were moved by helicopter and assault craft around the island, landing to the north of St George's at 0400 hours on 26 October to take the enemy in the rear. Approaches to the capital were blocked by M60s and Colonel Smith sent a detachment of his Marines to capture Fort Frederick, a dominant feature of the town. Under air and ground attack, Grenadian opposition melted away, and although desultory fighting was to continue for another four days, the Marines' task was complete. As they withdrew, they could congratulate themselves on having done the job for which they were organised efficiently and with great skill. Their flexibility and mobility had outmanoeuvred the enemy force and, at least in purely military terms, it was an impressive interventionary operation.

US Marine
— Grenada 1983 —

During the Vietnam War, the US Marine Corps issued its troops in the field with a jungle-pattern camouflage uniform, and this served as a basis for a new uniform adopted in the late 1970s. This man is wearing one of the two varieties: the 'woodland' pattern (there is also a 'leaf' pattern). The stars-and-stripes patch on the sleeve became popular during overseas deployments in the 1980s. Although a new model of helmet (nicknamed 'Fritz' because of its resemblance to the German 'coal-scuttle' helmet) was in service with the US Army on Grenada in 1983, the Marines were still using the M1. This man's 7.62mm M60 GPMG has a box attached for the ammunition belt.

The 'ALICE' (All-purpose Lightweight Individual Carrying Equipment) webbing worn by this Marine and shown below was introduced in the late 1970s, for use by all US forces. The pouches at the ends are for 30-round M16 magazines and there are attached side pockets for grenades. The water bottle's cover has a small pocket for purifying tablets and a wound dressing is contained in the pouch attached to the shoulder strap. The bayonet is for an M16 and to its right is a plastic case for a three-way folding shovel.

Britain and the Commonwealth

The British Army is one of the most experienced and consistently successful armed forces in the modern world. Since 1945 it has fought conventional campaigns in Korea (1950–53), Suez (1956) and the Falklands (1982), contributed actively to the defence of Europe, principally through the Nato (North Atlantic Treaty Organisation) alliance, intervened in support of friendly states (as in Jordan in 1958 and East Africa in 1964), participated in United Nations and multinational peacekeeping operations (as in Cyprus since 1964 and Lebanon 1983–84), and helped to supervise truce or disengagement agreements (as in Zimbabwe in 1980 and Sinai since 1982), while at the same time ensuring the security of the home islands and of the dwindling remnants of Empire. But by far its most impressive achievement has been its record of success in the notoriously difficult field of counter-insurgency, and it is this role that has contributed most to the army's reputation for professionalism and skill.

Counter-insurgency operations began as soon as World War II ended, as British troops faced Jewish guerrillas in Palestine (1945–48). This campaign was followed closely by similar experiences in Malaya (1948–60), Kenya (1952–60) and Cyprus (1955–59). During this period the army was sustained by a policy of conscription (known as 'National Service'), but even when that was phased out after 1960, leaving Britain with armed forces of little more than 350,000 men, counter-insurgency remained a major role. Throughout the 1960s, in Brunei and Borneo (1962–66), Radfan and Aden (1964–67) and, from 1969, Northern Ireland, elements of the army were kept busy opposing guerrillas and urban terrorists.

Not all the campaigns of the past four decades have been a complete success – the withdrawal from Aden, for example, occurred before the insurgents had been defeated – but compared to the record of other Western powers in similar operations, that of Britain is impressive. The British-inspired and British-led campaign in Dhofar (1970–75) is a classic example of a counter-insurgency victory, and the lessons and principles of the British response have been absorbed by other forces such as the Australian, New Zealand, South African and (until 1980) Rhodesian armies, which all experienced similar campaigns or contributed to those being fought by the British. Indeed, when Australian and New Zealand units fought in South Vietnam in the 1960s, their degree of success, albeit rather localised, was highlighted by the concurrent failure of their US allies.

The reasons for this record of success are not difficult to find. The British Army, and its offshoots in the white Commonwealth, was raised and organised primarily as a colonial policing force, and although modern insurgency may be more sophisticated than the tribal revolts of a hundred years ago, the techniques of response are little different. As long ago as the Boer War (1899–1902), when Boer commandos mounted hit-and-run attacks on British forces on the South African veldt, the army recognised the importance of isolating the enemy, denying him the sanctuary of a sympathetic population, and of fighting him with small units engaged in long patrols. In more recent times, these aims may have been pursued using a wider range of techniques, including propaganda, intelligence gathering and collation, and helicopter mobility, but the basic principles remain the same.

The British Army has absorbed and adhered to a crucial factor in counter-insurgency: if the aim of the revolt is essentially political, then the response must also be political, accepting the pre-eminence of civilian policy and persuading the broad mass of the people to support the government instead of the guerrillas. It is a principle that reflects one of the most important characteristics of the modern army – its subordination to the politics of a democratic state. At no time has the British Army, nor indeed its white Commonwealth counterparts, tried to interfere with civilian rule, even in an age of constant, often frustrating, economic pressure. This is a priceless asset in a turbulent world where the military coup is a more frequent method of changing governments than the ballot box. In this regard it is interesting to compare British experience with that of France where the army became highly politicised by counter-insurgency campaigns.

But the British Army is under pressure. In the mid-1980s it remains a force responsible for a wide range of duties – from Nato and Northern Ireland to international peacekeeping and 'Fortress Falklands' – and its limited resources are stretched even further by periodic force-level cuts. At the same time, the lack of extensive funds affects the development and issue of new equipment, for although the army is by no means ill-equipped, it is beginning to struggle to maintain its foothold in the confusing world of new technology. The force that fought in Palestine in the 1940s, dressed and armed in ways that had been familiar for a generation, has changed considerably. Not only has it adopted camouflage dress and semi-automatic rifles, but it is also learning to use such things as battlefield computers, satellite data links and a new generation of more accurate and effective weapons. This is clearly of crucial importance in connection with Nato, lest the army find itself lagging behind at a time when the alliance is adopting new tactical doctrines based firmly on the technological revolution.

Nevertheless, the army retains one thing that is unlikely to be lost easily – its professionalism. Regardless of the problems of finance and under-manning, the fact that the British Army can react as quickly and effectively as it did in the Falklands in 1982, shows that good training, *esprit de corps* and basic military skills still count for much. So long as that remains true, the British Army is likely to preserve its enviable reputation.

Right: A Royal Marine Commando waits patiently during landing drill on board the liner Canberra, on the voyage to the South Atlantic, April 1982. He is carrying a PRC 350 radio set – the normal means of radio communication at section and platoon level in the British forces – and is fitted with a throat microphone for maximum flexibility. His 7.62mm SLR has been wrapped in hessian as protection against the elements.

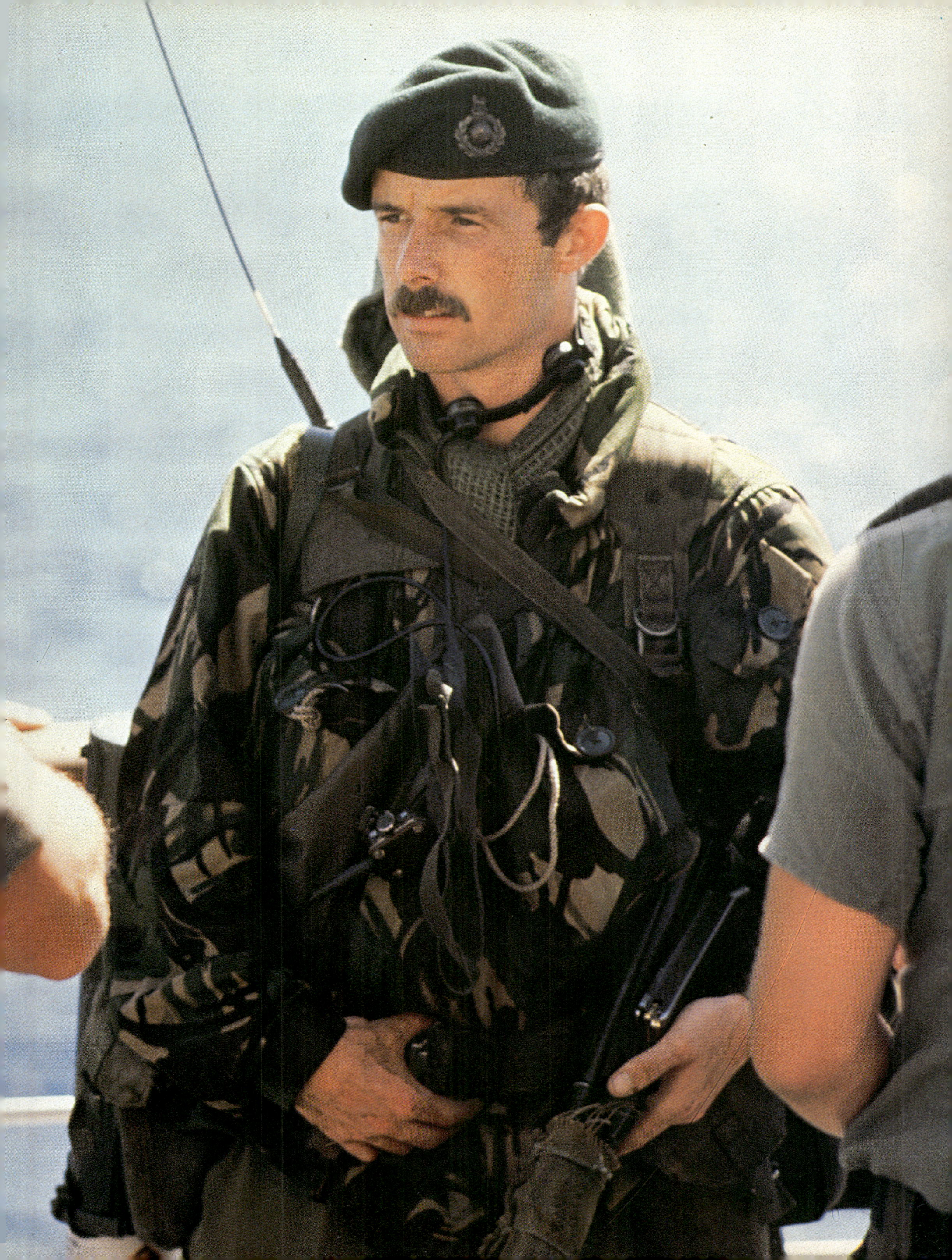

BRITAIN AND THE COMMONWEALTH

The Royal Australian Regiment in Korea

In June 1950, when the armed forces of communist North Korea streamed south to invade the Republic of Korea, the Australian government responded promptly to the UN Security Council's appeal for support in repelling the communist invasion by ordering her ground, air and naval forces (based in Japan) to mobilise immediately.

The first element of the Australian ground forces contingent – the 3rd Battalion of the Royal Australian Regiment – arrived in Korea on 28 September 1950. At that point in the war the United Nations forces had been forced back to the Pusan Perimeter where they were fighting a desperate battle for survival; it was not long before the Australians were in the thick of the fighting as part of the newly formed Commonwealth Brigade. Over the next few weeks the Battalion played its part in the United Nations' counter-offensive, and on 17 October it scored a notable victory at the battle for Sariwon where nearly 2000 North Koreans were captured.

The Chinese counter-attack was as much a surprise for the Australians as it was for the other UN forces, and on 5 November the 3rd Battalion fought its first encounter with the Chinese Army. As part of the general withdrawal southwards during the winter of 1950-51 the dogged resistance displayed by the Australian troops won the respect of friend and foe alike. Once the UN line had stabilised the Australian infantry were engaged in a defensive role, safeguarding the UN positions against Chinese attacks. The communist spring offensive in April 1951 saw some of the toughest fighting of the war, and in the battle north of Kapyong the 3rd Battalion – with other British and Commonwealth units – particularly distinguished itself, to the extent of winning a coveted US Presidential citation for outstanding gallantry.

From the summer of 1951 the fighting settled down to a static war of trenches and barbed wire. The rough terrain and bitter climate did little to aid morale, but as an all-volunteer force the Australian contingent was able to maintain its battle efficiency. The men were drawn from sections of the regular Australian Army and from recently demobbed veterans of World War II. As in other armies, the weapons used were those of World War II, which for the infantry were Bren light machine guns, SMLE rifles and the distinctive Australian Owen sub-machine guns.

By July 1951 the numbers of Commonwealth troops had increased so that the 3rd Battalion became a part of the Commonwealth Division. The previous month the Australian contingent had itself been reinforced by the arrival of the 1st Battalion, the Royal Australian Regiment, which like its sister battalion was involved in the positional fighting that characterised the latter stages of the Korean War. In March 1953 the 1st Battalion was replaced by the newly arrived 2nd Battalion, though the 3rd still continued to fight on in the line. But at this stage the war was drawing to a close and on 27 July the armistice agreement was signed. During the course of the war a total of 10,557 Australian ground troops had been deployed in Korea and had suffered 1396 casualties. As in World War II, the Australians proved themselves to be an effective and successful fighting force, achieving results out of all proportion to the numbers engaged.

Above left: Troops of the 3rd Battalion, Royal Australian Regiment, give covering fire to one of their sections which has been pinned down in front of communist positions. Above: Members of the same battalion rest during a break in action near Koemek-tong in March 1951.

Australian Infantryman
— Korea 1951 —

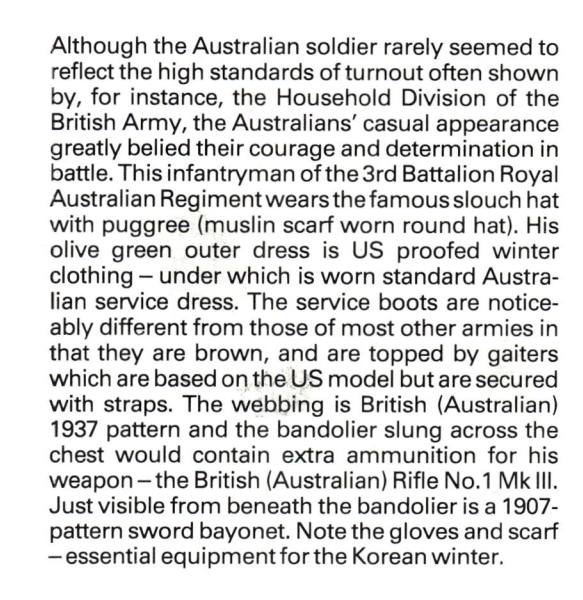

Although the Australian soldier rarely seemed to reflect the high standards of turnout often shown by, for instance, the Household Division of the British Army, the Australians' casual appearance greatly belied their courage and determination in battle. This infantryman of the 3rd Battalion Royal Australian Regiment wears the famous slouch hat with puggree (muslin scarf worn round hat). His olive green outer dress is US proofed winter clothing – under which is worn standard Australian service dress. The service boots are noticeably different from those of most other armies in that they are brown, and are topped by gaiters which are based on the US model but are secured with straps. The webbing is British (Australian) 1937 pattern and the bandolier slung across the chest would contain extra ammunition for his weapon – the British (Australian) Rifle No.1 Mk III. Just visible from beneath the bandolier is a 1907-pattern sword bayonet. Note the gloves and scarf – essential equipment for the Korean winter.

The Australian version of British 1937-pattern webbing (later superseded by British 1958-pattern – which is still in use in the British Army today). Battle order is shown here. On the belt itself, equipment comprises from the left, an ammunition pouch for the British (Australian) Rifle No.1 Mk III, a 1907-pattern sword bayonet (a World War I weapon looking decidedly anachronistic by the 1950s), an entrenching tool helve with carrier (head inside), a 1.13 litre (two pint) enamelled steel water bottle, and to the right of that a further ammunition pouch. In the centre is a small pack which would probably be used to carry such essentials as light rations and mess tins. The 'L' straps of Australian webbing differ slightly from the British pattern.

25

BRITAIN AND THE COMMONWEALTH

The Gloucestershire Regiment

The Gloucestershire Regiment of today can trace its ancestry to March 1694 when Colonel John Gibson was authorised to raise a regiment of foot. Over the next hundred years the regiment evolved into the 28th Foot and saw service throughout the globe, playing an active part in colonial and 'dynastic' wars of the 18th century. The 28th Foot gained one of its greatest distinctions during the Napoleonic Wars when it was despatched to Egypt as part of a force charged with the overthrow of the French Army then in occupation. On 28 March 1801 – at the battle of Alexandria – the 28th Foot found itself simultaneously attacked from the front and the rear, whereupon the rear rank about faced and coolly repulsed the French attack. To honour their bravery under fire the 28th was granted the right to wear their regimental number to the rear of their head-dress (the 'back badge') as well as the standard cap badge to the fore.

Late in the 19th century the 28th began its association with the English county of Gloucestershire and in 1881 – as a result of the Cardwell reforms – the 28th was combined with another Gloucestershire regiment, the 61st, to become the Gloucestershire Regiment. The Glosters (as they were called) played an important role in World War I, their strength being massively expanded to 24 battalions which saw service in all the important theatres of operation, and which suffered over 8000 men killed in the process. World War II also saw a large increase in the regiment's size, with battalions fighting in Europe, North Africa and the Far East. But it was in Korea that the Glosters won their greatest fame when they fought a defiant holding action against the Chinese 63rd Army on the Imjin River.

On the evening of 22 April 1951 a forward patrol of a company of the 1st Glosters engaged elements of the 63rd Army's vanguard, and by the following day the Chinese had overwhelmed the UN forces and cut off the Glosters from their supporting units. Under constant attack, all four companies of the Gloster battalion redeployed on Hill 235 where they determined to make a last ditch stand.

Throughout 24 April, under orders to hold their position and with the promise of resupply and reinforcement, the now half-strength Glosters put up a spirited resistance, maintaining their line on Hill 235. Early on the morning of 25 April UN forces were ordered to withdraw but for the Glosters this was no easy matter as they were now surrounded by the Chinese at close-quarters. At 1030 hours, the Glosters' commander, Lt-Colonel Carne, ordered that each company should attempt to break out individually and that all weapons and equipment were to be destroyed. Of the four companies, three were destroyed; only D Company succeeded in getting through and then only 39 men of the company made it to UN lines. Their stand had not been in vain, however: the Glosters had not only helped to break the back of the Chinese advance but allowed the US I Corps to secure the Han River line and protect Seoul. The Glosters' heroic fight earned them the rare honour of a US Presidential citation and a reputation as one of Britain's foremost fighting units.

The men of the Glosters had displayed the most remarkable courage in resisting attacks by an enemy that was vastly superior in strength, and in continuing to fight on even when it seemed that they must be overwhelmed and that any further resistance was hopeless.

After Korea the Glosters returned to Britain but were soon in action in Kenya in 1955, helping put down the Mau Mau uprising. The British Army's main post war role was in overseeing Britain's withdrawal from Empire and so the Glosters were involved in a number of policing operations – Aden and Bahrain (1956), Cyprus (1957 and 1963) – as well as playing their part in Britain's Army of the Rhine.

In 1969 the Glosters were almost amalgamated with the Royal Hampshire Regiment but in 1970 they were reprieved just before the merger was due to take place. In 1969 the Glosters had carried out a tour of duty in strife-torn Northern Ireland. This was the first of a number of tours of Northern Ireland; stationed in Belfast the regiment gained a considerable reputation for intelligent resourcefulness and for their tact in dealing with this difficult situation. The Glosters have a regimental history stretching back nearly three centuries and like other English 'county' regiments they seem to embody the essential character of the British Army – a quiet professionalism combined with a deep pride in their regimental tradition.

Below: On their return from Korea the Glosters were given the task of acting as demonstration battalion at the School of Infantry in Wiltshire, where they gave territorials and reservists lessons in basic infantry tactics. In this photograph troops disembark from turretless Kangaroos, which have been assigned the function of acting as armoured personnel carriers.

British Infantryman
— Korea 1951 —

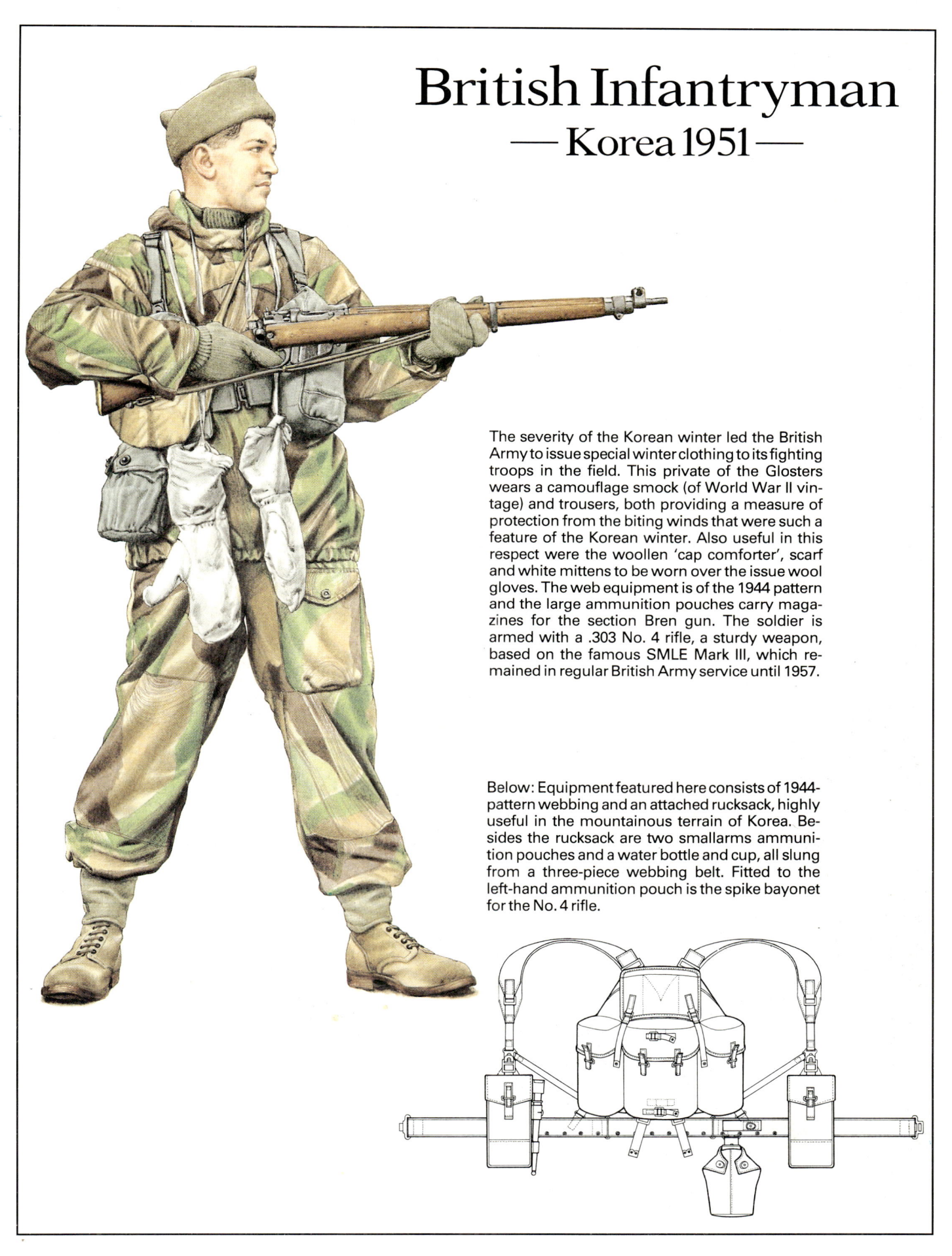

The severity of the Korean winter led the British Army to issue special winter clothing to its fighting troops in the field. This private of the Glosters wears a camouflage smock (of World War II vintage) and trousers, both providing a measure of protection from the biting winds that were such a feature of the Korean winter. Also useful in this respect were the woollen 'cap comforter', scarf and white mittens to be worn over the issue wool gloves. The web equipment is of the 1944 pattern and the large ammunition pouches carry magazines for the section Bren gun. The soldier is armed with a .303 No. 4 rifle, a sturdy weapon, based on the famous SMLE Mark III, which remained in regular British Army service until 1957.

Below: Equipment featured here consists of 1944-pattern webbing and an attached rucksack, highly useful in the mountainous terrain of Korea. Besides the rucksack are two smallarms ammunition pouches and a water bottle and cup, all slung from a three-piece webbing belt. Fitted to the left-hand ammunition pouch is the spike bayonet for the No. 4 rifle.

27

BRITAIN AND THE COMMONWEALTH

The British Army in Kenya

Kenya during the Emergency was not the worst posting a British soldier might expect. Over the entire length of the campaign less than 70 white members of the security forces were killed and a similar number wounded. Many of these casualties were police and Kenyan reservists and they were spread out between October 1952, when the first British battalion arrived, and the end of 1956 when Mau Mau resistance collapsed. The rate of attrition was so low that personal danger was hardly a morale problem for the British troops who served in the colony during the Mau Mau rebellion.

Although the risk was fairly one-sided (over 11,000 Mau Mau were presumed killed) this did not mean that the campaign was not physically arduous. While British soldiers performed guard duties in the congenial climate and surroundings of the areas settled by white colonists, their major task was the domination of the jungle areas around Mount Kenya and the Aberdare Mountains. A great deal of patrolling took place in this terrain of steep ridges and gullies clothed in dense woods and bamboo. Slogging through this inhospitable country in massive but often ineffective drives was not popular among British troops, wary of the unfamiliar environment. Indeed, although they were well trained enough in some respects they were not ideally equipped for counter-insurgency operations in jungle conditions.

Some of their problems derived from the fact that National Service was in force throughout the Emergency. The military qualities of conscripts who serve for a long period, as the British did, is usually quite high and the units that were sent overseas were, in any case, heavily weighted with professional soldiers, but conscription threw a burden on an army's training resources. The constant induction of raw recruits meant that much effort was spent in basic training and more advanced instruction suffered. There is no doubt that the British troops in Kenya did not have the advantage of the intense jungle training which their successors were given in Borneo more than a decade later.

The result was a shortage of jungle craft and of the right weapons. Too often, patrolling soldiers washed with soap, wore laundered clothes or even smoked so that their scent alarmed jungle fauna whose calls alerted the Mau Mau. Besides this the British Army had not come with really satisfactory jungle warfare weapons for its regular infantry, relying on the old Lee Enfield Number 5 rifle and the inaccurate Sten sub-machine gun. A number of experimental Belgian-made FN rifles were issued to British troops after 1954 and although an excellent weapon in most respects it was not ideal for jungle warfare. It was all a long way from the pump action shotguns and Owen sub-machine guns being used by the SAS in Malaya

Top: Armed with the new Belgian FN FAL rifle and kitted-out for jungle warfare British soldiers advance towards suspected Mau Mau positions. Above: Mau Mau guerrillas are searched by British troops shortly after their capture. The British are armed with the standard weapons of the Kenyan Emergency: a Sten sub-machine gun and Number 5 rifles.

and, perhaps, was indicative of the fact that British military planners had failed to understand that soldiering in Kenya would take place in a jungle environment.

But if the British troops in Kenya were not carefully enough prepared for their task, they revealed their qualities in the manner by which they overcame circumstances. At any one time there were only five British battalions (with six battalions of King's African Rifles) in Kenya and the sheer size of the area of operations meant that units were often very thin on the ground, but this gave British junior commanders the opportunity to show their ability to take on additional responsibility. Besides this, the standard of jungle craft improved as the campaign went on. And it should be remembered that, whatever the political consequences, the Kenyan Emergency resulted in a British military victory.

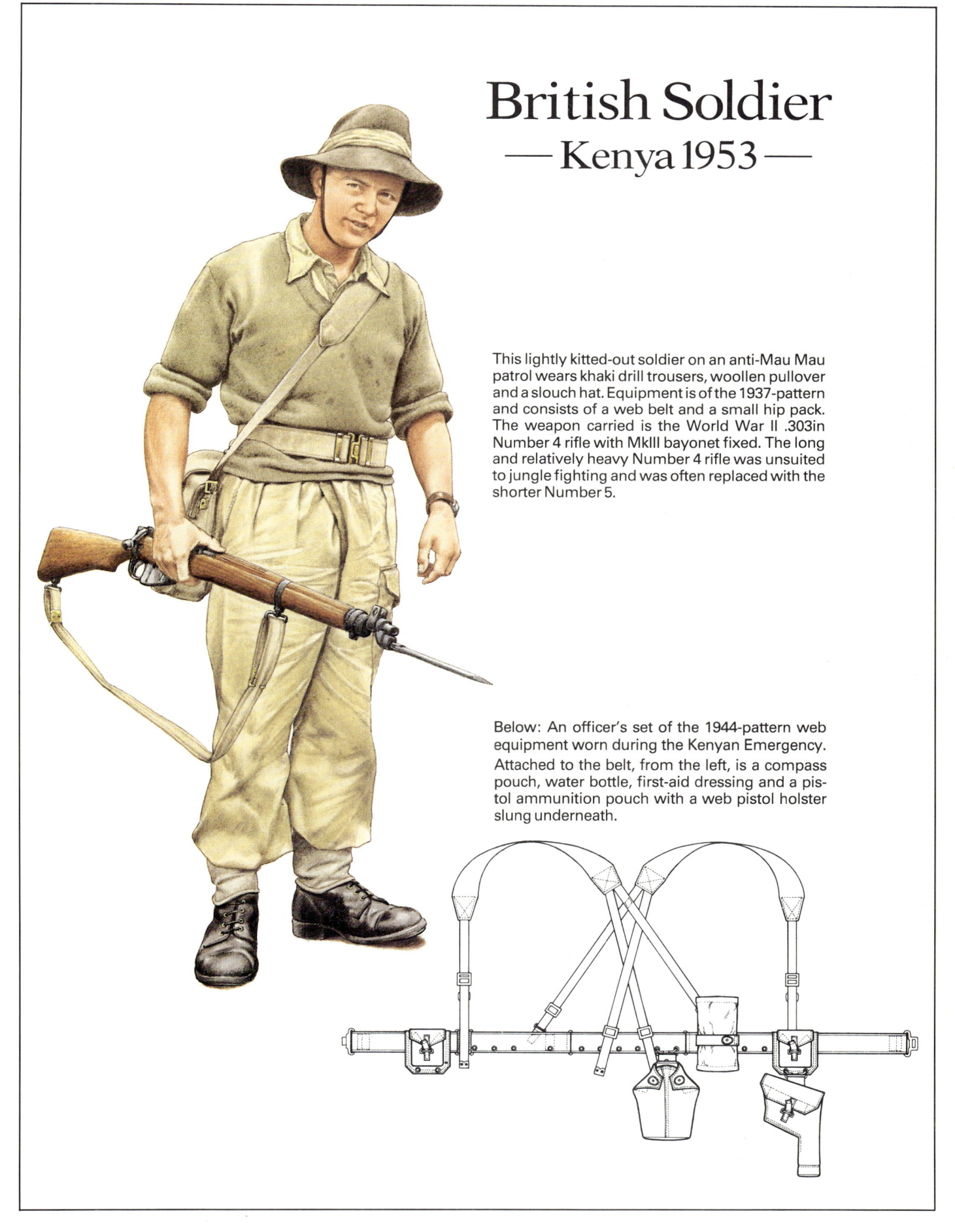

British Soldier
— Kenya 1953 —

This lightly kitted-out soldier on an anti-Mau Mau patrol wears khaki drill trousers, woollen pullover and a slouch hat. Equipment is of the 1937-pattern and consists of a web belt and a small hip pack. The weapon carried is the World War II .303in Number 4 rifle with MkIII bayonet fixed. The long and relatively heavy Number 4 rifle was unsuited to jungle fighting and was often replaced with the shorter Number 5.

Below: An officer's set of the 1944-pattern web equipment worn during the Kenyan Emergency. Attached to the belt, from the left, is a compass pouch, water bottle, first-aid dressing and a pistol ammunition pouch with a web pistol holster slung underneath.

BRITAIN AND THE COMMONWEALTH

The Parachute Regiment

Impressed by the exploits of German paratroopers during the invasion of Holland and Belgium in 1940, British military authorities authorised the formation of an airborne force capable of landing behind enemy lines either by parachute or through the use of gliders. The first parachute jump was made on 13 July 1940 and volunteers were soon raised to form the units which were to become the Parachute Regiment.

Although parachute troops had been successfully used in the Normandy landings in June 1944, it was in September of that year that their big test came when the newly formed 1st Airborne Division was allotted the task of carrying out an airborne attack on Arnhem. On this occasion British intelligence proved faulty and the Airborne Division found itself surrounded by strong German units who reacted to the surprise British attack with characteristic promptness. Totally surrounded by superior German forces, the paratroops put up a heroic defence and suffered heavy casualties – only some 2200 survivors were able to fight their way to safety leaving 7000 men killed, wounded or captured. Their red berets and resolute fighting qualities won them the title of the Red Devils, a name that has stuck over time.

After World War II the size of Britain's airborne forces contracted, but the value of such troops was realised and the Parachute Regiment found itself involved in the many small wars that marked Britain's withdrawal from Empire.

Paratroops were assigned an important role in the Suez expedition and were prominent in the fighting in Malaya, Aden and Cyprus, as well as playing their part in Britain's Nato commitment to Germany. The Parachute Regiment has also carried out several tours of duty in Northern Ireland.

Although trained for airborne warfare, the Parachute Regiment does have an infantry capacity. Since the formation of 5 Airborne Brigade in 1983, two battalions operate in the jumping role, and one operates in the infantry role, in rotation. Partly this is because of defence economies, but it is also because of a growing doubt as to the effectiveness of parachute drops in the increasingly hostile environment of the modern battlefield. While remaining an infantry force, the Paras maintain a jealously-guarded reputation for combat efficiency that places them among the elite of the British Army.

Naturally enough the Parachute Regiment was in the thick of the fighting during the conflict to regain the Falkland Islands in 1982. The 2nd and 3rd Battalions formed part of the landing force that took San Carlos Bay, and then 2 Para went on to carry out a brilliant assault on Argentinian positions at Goose Green. Although outnumbered and forced to attack well dug-in troops holding fortified positions, 2 Para gained its objective taking over 1400 Argentinian prisoners in the process. The fighting tradition of the Red Devils continues.

Above: A senior NCO conducts a last-minute check of parachute packs as members of 3 Para prepare to emplane in Cyprus for their assault on Gamil airfield, Egypt, November 1956. The lack of smallarms is apparent: unlike the French, who carried weapons with them at all times, the British Paras in 1956 packed them away in separate containers. On landing, the Paras were effectively unarmed until the containers had been found and broken open.

British Paratrooper
— Suez 1956 —

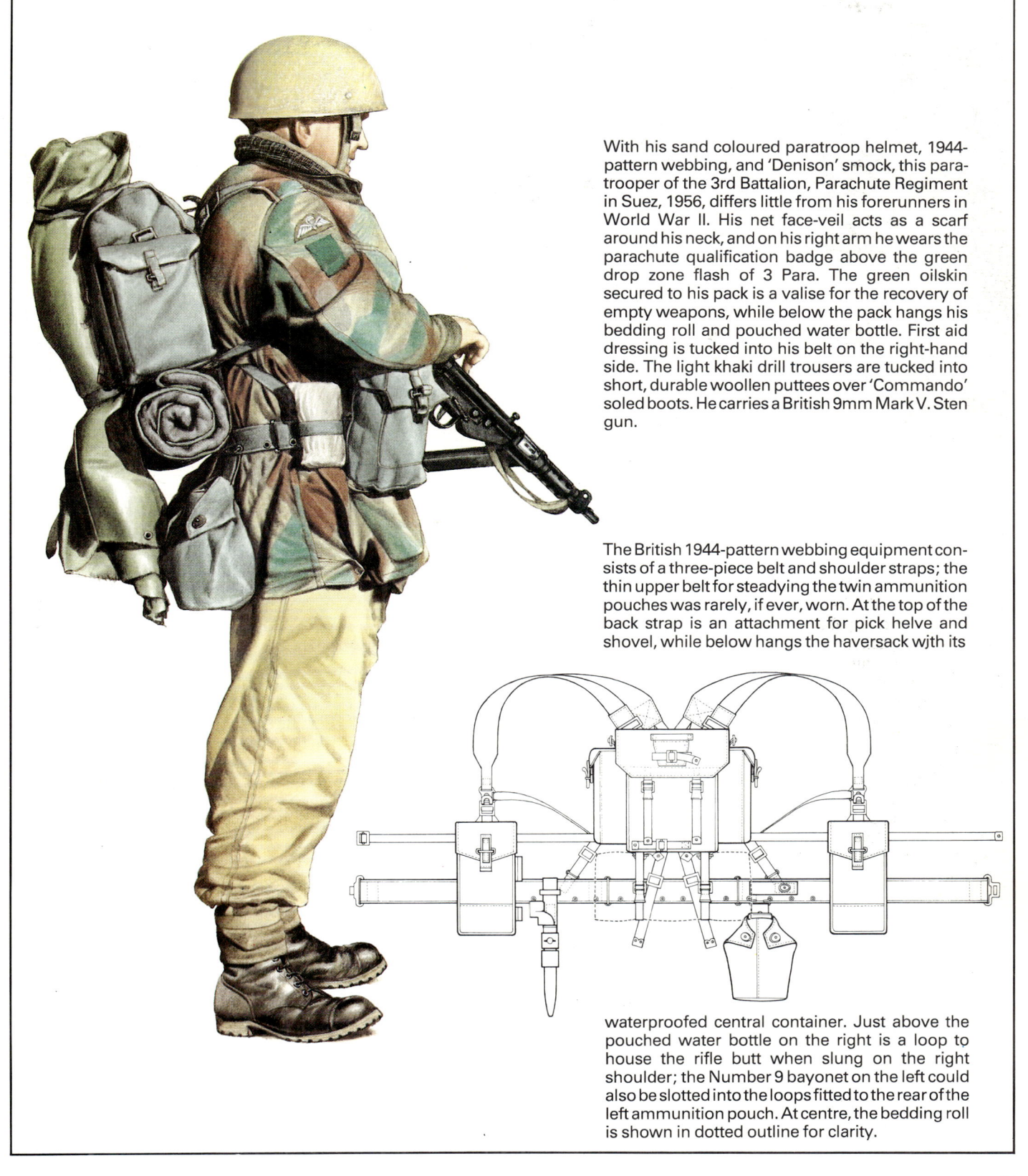

With his sand coloured paratroop helmet, 1944-pattern webbing, and 'Denison' smock, this paratrooper of the 3rd Battalion, Parachute Regiment in Suez, 1956, differs little from his forerunners in World War II. His net face-veil acts as a scarf around his neck, and on his right arm he wears the parachute qualification badge above the green drop zone flash of 3 Para. The green oilskin secured to his pack is a valise for the recovery of empty weapons, while below the pack hangs his bedding roll and pouched water bottle. First aid dressing is tucked into his belt on the right-hand side. The light khaki drill trousers are tucked into short, durable woollen puttees over 'Commando' soled boots. He carries a British 9mm Mark V. Sten gun.

The British 1944-pattern webbing equipment consists of a three-piece belt and shoulder straps; the thin upper belt for steadying the twin ammunition pouches was rarely, if ever, worn. At the top of the back strap is an attachment for pick helve and shovel, while below hangs the haversack with its waterproofed central container. Just above the pouched water bottle on the right is a loop to house the rifle butt when slung on the right shoulder; the Number 9 bayonet on the left could also be slotted into the loops fitted to the rear of the left ammunition pouch. At centre, the bedding roll is shown in dotted outline for clarity.

31

BRITAIN AND THE COMMONWEALTH

The Royal Regiment of Artillery

Although artillery had existed in the English Army from the 14th century – Edward III had three cannon at Crecy in 1346 – the Royal Artillery or, more precisely, the Royal Regiment of Artillery, was not formally constituted until 1716, and received its title in 1722. Since that time the regiment has been involved in practically every battle fought by the British Army, to the extent that in 1822 it was granted the motto 'Ubique' (Everywhere) on its cap-badge in place of a nominal battle honour. By the end of the 19th century the Artillery had two components – field and garrison – and during the 1914-18 war the garrison artillery, used in the siege role, was extensively involved in field operations in Flanders. In addition, the regiment also assumed responsibility for railway guns and anti-aircraft artillery. The massive artillery bombardments of the Western Front, made in preparation for massed infantry assaults, often demanded the services of six gunners for every infantryman involved in the actual attack. During World War II the addition of anti-tank artillery had expanded the size of the regiment and at one stage of the war it constituted one-third of the entire British Army. Opponents of the British during this conflict – most notably the officers and men of the German Army – had the greatest respect for the British artillery and considered it by far the most effective element among Britain's ground forces.

After 1945 the size of the regiment was reduced, but its technical scope was increased, employing guided missiles in anti-aircraft, ground bombardment and anti-tank roles, deploying sophisticated electronic equipment for detecting and registering targets, as well as utilising the latest towed and self-propelled guns and howitzers. Individual units have served in Korea, Malaysia, Borneo, and other trouble spots, and gunners have also been posted to Aden, Oman, Belize, British Guiana, Cyprus and Zimbabwe, as well as forming an important component of Nato forces in Germany. In addition to their normal duties, the Royal Artillery have been trained in internal security, and have done tours in Northern Ireland.

Today the Artillery is closely employed in conjunction with the other fighting elements within the army, and is correspondingly organised to work at a number of levels to suit the differing requirements made of it. In Germany the 1 (Br) Corps has its own artillery division which consists of a regiment of 175mm M107 self-propelled guns (SPGs) for counter-battery fire, a missile regiment armed with Lance missiles (capable of carrying a nuclear warhead, and normally kept in reserve), a 'locating' regiment responsible for meteorological, survey and other intelligence information, and two air defence regiments armed with Rapier anti-aircraft missiles. At the divisional level artillery support typically might comprise a regiment of 105mm Abbot SPGs and a regiment of 155mm M109A1 or M109AZ SPGs (both regiments consisting of three eight-gun batteries), plus a battery of long-range anti-tank weapons such as the Swingfire missile.

One of the most distinctive features of the recent changes in the weaponry of the Royal Artillery has been the widespread introduction of missiles. Advances in technology go hand-in-hand with other improvements, most notably the BATES fire control system which will dramatically increase the effectiveness of artillery action on the battlefield.

Above: A Royal Artillery gun crew, especially flown to Sardinia, fires the FH 70, the Anglo-German-Italian 150mm howitzer, during trials in 1974.

British Gunner
— British Guiana 1964 —

Despite the tropical location, this Royal Artilleryman wears the shirt from his temperate uniform, though khaki-drill trousers are worn with short puttees. Notable features of dress are the dark blue beret, with the Royal Artillery badge, and 1937-pattern web equipment, here blackened and polished. The firearm carried is not the usual SLR but a 9mm L2A3 Sterling sub-machine gun with bayonet fixed. The Sterling was adopted by the army in 1954 as the replacement to the old Sten sub-machine gun and is used primarily by those troops needing a handy lightweight weapon such as tank crew members and artillerymen. (Note the gunner is left handed.)

Below: Keeping a good lookout for possible signs of ambush, a British gunner armed with a 9mm L2A3 SMG leads a patrol through jungle in British Guiana.

BRITAIN AND THE COMMONWEALTH

The Brigade of Gurkhas

That today's British Army should be able to call upon the assistance of four regiments of Gurkha Rifles made up of tribesmen from the mountains of Nepal is a powerful reminder of Britain's colonial heritage. The British first came across the Gurkhas as enemies during the Nepalese War of 1814-16, but during the conflict a deep bond of mutual respect developed between the two opponents so that following the cessation of hostilities the Gurkhas offered their services to the British as soldiers. Although the British were slow in taking up the offer, by the late 19th century the Gurkha battalions were a highly regarded element of Britain's military forces.

In both world wars the Gurkhas furthered their reputation as determined infantry fighters – on the Western Front, at Gallipoli and in Mesopotamia and Palestine in World War I, in the Western Desert and in Italy and later in Burma during World War II.

Despite the many battle honours they won during World War II, the future of the Gurkhas looked uncertain when they returned from the battlefields of that conflict. The special relationship of the Gurkhas to India and to Britain was unique and seemed to be threatened by the onset of the Partition of 1947. Rather than being disbanded the Gurkha units were divided between India and Britain; six regiments went to India and the other four – 2nd King Edward VII's Own Goorkha Rifles or Simoor Rifles (two battalions), 6th Queen Elizabeth's Own Gurkha Rifles, 7th Duke of Edinburgh's Own Gurkha Rifles and 10th Princess Mary's Own Gurkha Rifles – remained in service with the British.

The four regiments of the Gurkha Brigade were shipped to Malaya where they established their headquarters in 1948, only to find themselves involved in putting down the communist uprising. The jungle skills refined during the 12-year war against the Chinese communists in Malaya were put to good use again during the fighting in Borneo, where the Gurkha Brigade was involved in defending the territory against Indonesian expansion. In 1965, while serving in Borneo, Lance-Corporal (later Sergeant) Rambahadur Limbu of the 10th Gurkha Rifles successfully rescued two wounded men of his section despite heavy enemy fire, for which he won the Victoria Cross.

In 1982 the Gurkhas were back in action, when the 1/7th Gurkha Rifles found themselves as part of the Task Force charged with regaining the Falkland Islands from Argentinian control. During the conflict the Gurkhas were mainly involved in mopping-up operations, though they did capture Mount William as part of the final battle to secure Port Stanley.

Despite the end of Empire, the Gurkhas remain very much a part of the British military scene, both as fighting men and as ceremonial soldiers when they take their occasional place alongside the Guards outside Buckingham Palace. Based now in Hong Kong, the Gurkhas have their own engineers, signallers and transport corps.

Above: Armed with an M16 assault rifle a Gurkha rifleman acts as 'point' for a patrol taking place in the jungles of Malaya. Left: Parading in Number 2 Service Dress a Gurkha proudly displays his Kukri fighting knife.
A distinctive feature of the Gurkha regiments is the flat-brimmed hat worn with a light khaki puggree and with the regimental badge worn on the left side.

Gurkha Rifleman
—Borneo 1966—

Above: Gurkha riflemen apply camouflage cream prior to setting out on a combat patrol during the conflict in the Falklands in June 1982.

A veteran of tropical warfare, this Gurkha wears jungle-green trousers and shirt, over which is British 1944-pattern web equipment. Attached to the jungle hat is a cloth company sign – worn on both front and rear of hat – which served as a recognition sign with the intention of preventing the riflemen from shooting each other when patrolling through thick jungle. The anti-mosquito face veil is worn as a neckscarf, and a further tropical feature of dress is the pair of British rubber and canvas jungle boots. Smaller in stature than other troops in the British Army, the Gurkhas preferred the lightweight US 5.56mm M16 assault rifle carried here.

Right: This is the 1944-pattern battle-order equipment that would have been worn by men of the 7th Gurkha Rifles operating in Borneo in the mid-1960s. On the three-piece belt are slung two ammunition pouches, modified to be carried lower on the belt and worn well to each side so as not to get in the soldier's way when crawling through jungle. On the left is a straight machete for clearing away vegetation, and on the right is a Kukri, the curved fighting knife made famous by the Gurkhas. Between the two knives are a bayonet frog and a British 1944-pattern water bottle. To the right of the Kukri is a loop for strapping the butt of a rifle when carried slung.

BRITAIN AND THE COMMONWEALTH

The New Zealand Army

During World War II the armed forces of New Zealand made a major commitment to Britain and the Empire, with large numbers of ground forces seeing active service in North Africa and Italy as well as the Far East. After the war the New Zealand Army was run down to a modest peace-time level, and when the decision was made to join Australia in support of the UN forces in Korea only a regiment of field artillery was despatched to the war zone. Some 1100 men strong, the New Zealand contingent arrived in Seoul in 1951 and known as 'Kayforce' played its part in restoring the military fortunes of the UN forces.

During the 1950s New Zealand troops were involved in the long campaign to suppress communist activity in Malaya. The jungle fighting skills gained in Malaya were put to good use in 1962 when a detachment of New Zealand SAS men served alongside American Special Forces in operations in Thailand. Three years later the New Zealand SAS squadron was engaged in fighting the Indonesians in Borneo, carrying out armed reconnaissance and ambush missions.

By the end of the 1950s it had become clear to New Zealand that the old relationship with Britain was coming to a close. The gradual break-up of the Empire ensured a withdrawal of the British from the Far East; their presence was largely replaced by a new American interest in the region, expressed in a series of anti-communist alliances with pro-American countries. Thus during the 1960s New Zealand began to develop closer ties with the US and so an announcement that New Zealand was to send troops to Vietnam came as no surprise.

In 1965 the first combat unit arrived in Vietnam – a battery of artillery – and over the next couple of years regular infantry and SAS units were also sent in. Altogether nearly 4000 New Zealanders served in Vietnam, fighting alongside the Australians in a joint ANZ task force. The ANZ troops gained a good reputation in Vietnam, where in contrast to the ARVN and some US units they were prepared to go out into the jungle or bush and fight it out with the Viet Cong and NVA forces.

The New Zealanders were armed and equipped from both British and US sources so that a typical infantry patrol might be transported to its destination in a US M113 APC (armoured personnel carrier), and would fight with a combination of M16 rifles, FN SLRs and Sterling sub-machine guns with M60 machine guns and M79 grenade launchers as the support weapons. The withdrawal of US troops from Vietnam in the late 1960s, however, also signalled the end of the New Zealand Army's participation in the war, and in 1971-72 the bulk of the men had returned to New Zealand.

The regular New Zealand Army is around 5500 men strong, divided into two infantry battalions, one artillery battery, a small armoured detachment consisting of M41 light tanks and Ferret scout cars, and logistical support. This small force is supported by reserve troops – both regulars and territorials – who make up two brigade groups composed of one regular and six territorial infantry battalions, three batteries of field artillery, one armoured squadron, one SAS squadron, and engineer and signals units. Very much a peace-time force the New Zealand Army could, nonetheless, be dramatically expanded in the event of war.

Top: New Zealand troops prepare to set off on a patrol, having disembarked from their M113 APC. Above: Armed with an SLR this New Zealand soldier questions a Vietnamese farmer with the help of an interpreter from the South Vietnamese Army.

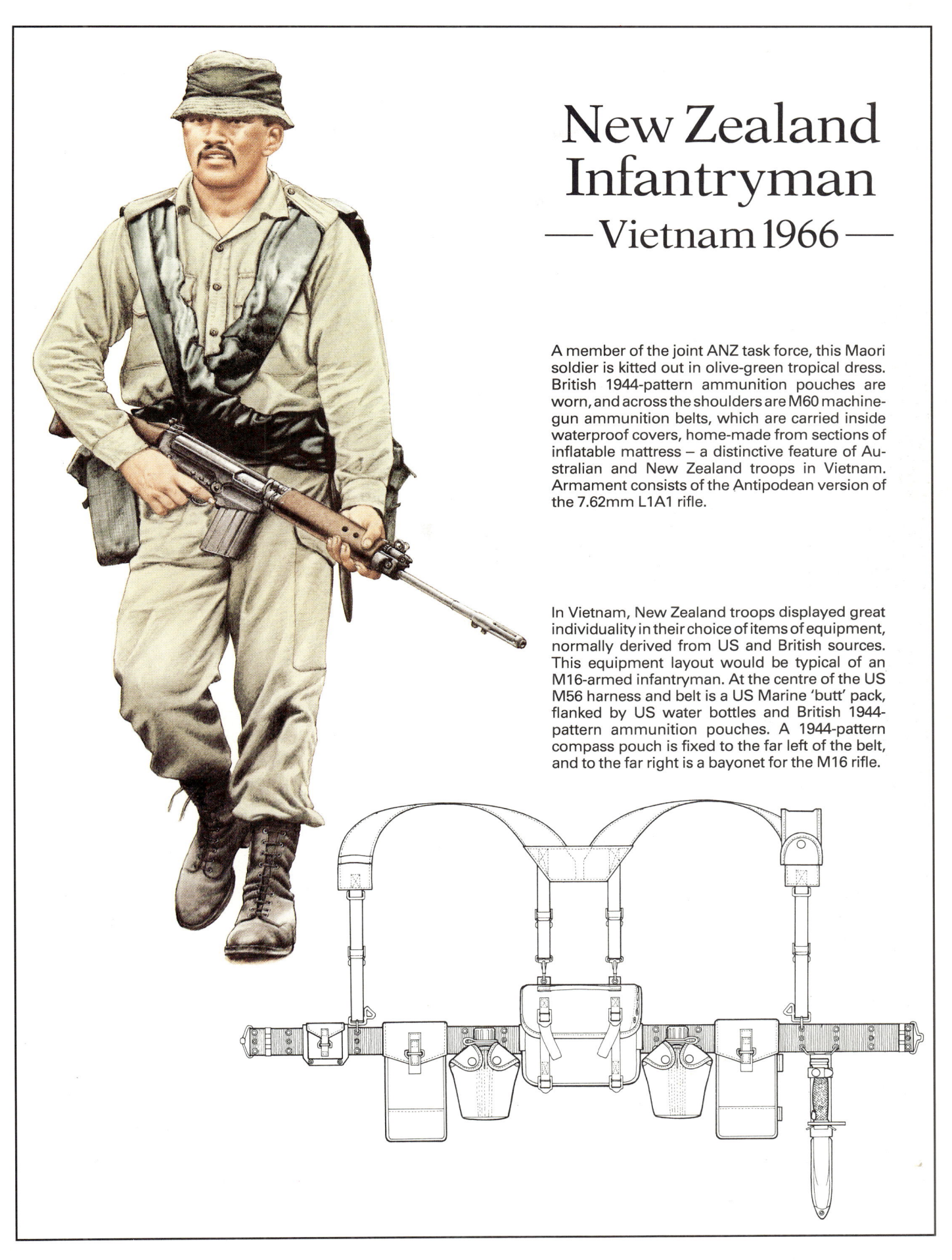

New Zealand Infantryman
—Vietnam 1966—

A member of the joint ANZ task force, this Maori soldier is kitted out in olive-green tropical dress. British 1944-pattern ammunition pouches are worn, and across the shoulders are M60 machine-gun ammunition belts, which are carried inside waterproof covers, home-made from sections of inflatable mattress — a distinctive feature of Australian and New Zealand troops in Vietnam. Armament consists of the Antipodean version of the 7.62mm L1A1 rifle.

In Vietnam, New Zealand troops displayed great individuality in their choice of items of equipment, normally derived from US and British sources. This equipment layout would be typical of an M16-armed infantryman. At the centre of the US M56 harness and belt is a US Marine 'butt' pack, flanked by US water bottles and British 1944-pattern ammunition pouches. A 1944-pattern compass pouch is fixed to the far left of the belt, and to the far right is a bayonet for the M16 rifle.

BRITAIN AND THE COMMONWEALTH

The Argyll and Sutherland Highlanders

One of the most famous of Scotland's many famous regiments, the Argyll and Sutherland Highlanders' ancestry dates back to 1794 when the 98th (Argyllshire Highlanders) Foot Regiment was raised to combat the armies of the French Revolution then sweeping across Europe. Renumbered the 91st Foot, the regiment fought with distinction in Spain, after acting as the rearguard in the epic retreat to Corunna in 1808. In 1854 the 93rd Highlanders distinguished themselves by their defence of the British base camp at Balaclava during the Crimean War.

In the army reforms introduced by Lord Edward Cardwell in the 1870s the Argylls were combined with the 93rd Sutherland Highlanders, and as the Argyll and Sutherland Highlanders took part in the Zulu and Boer Wars. World War I saw a massive increase in the size of the regiment so that a total of 17 battalions were raised, though in the bloodbath of the Western Front casualties were correspondingly high: 431 officers and 6475 other ranks killed. In World War II nine battalions came into being, seeing service in several theatres of war, most notably Malaya and Italy.

In the years after 1945 the Argyll and Sutherland Highlanders were mainly engaged in the many peacekeeping operations around the globe that characterised Britain's withdrawal from Empire. After service in Palestine the regiment was again in action in Korea where it gained a considerable reputation for its dogged fighting qualities (its decorations included a Victoria Cross won by the battalion adjutant). In common with other British regiments the Argylls did tours of Cyprus, Kenya, Borneo and Aden, the last of which brought the regiment into the public eye during the troubles of June–July 1967.

The town of Crater had fallen into the hands of Arab nationalist guerrillas, and, under the command of Lieutenant-Colonel Colin Mitchell, the Argylls were ordered to retake it. In a brilliantly conducted text-book operation the Highlanders slipped into the town at nightfall and swiftly dealt with the guerrillas. By the morning the entire area was once again under British control.

Mitchell's extrovert style of leadership and 'no-nonsense' approach to the guerrillas made him highly popular with the press – who dubbed him 'Mad Mitch' – but his criticisms of government policy and his courting of the limelight made him unpopular in establishment circles. And when disbandment of the Argylls was put forward as part of a package of defence economies it was construed as a government conspiracy to silence Mitchell and discredit the regiment, although in fact the decision was based on reasons of regimental seniority. A highly enthusiastic public campaign was consequently mounted around the slogan, 'Save the Argylls', and a petition of a million signatures was presented to the government. The disbandment order was duly countermanded, and the Argyll and Sutherland Highlanders gained a new lease of life, albeit in reduced form.

The Argylls in Crater, 1967: (top) keeping guard with a GPMG; (above) Mitchell firmly in the driving seat.

Argyll and Sutherland Highlander Corporal
—Aden 1967—

The Argyll and Sutherland Highlanders played an important part in the British Army's containment role in Aden during the 1960s. Although distinguished by a number of exclusive Scots features this soldier wears standard British Army khaki-drill bush jacket and trousers. Footwear consists of rubber-soled boots and short woollen puttees, and webbing equipment is of the 1958 pattern. Of special interest is the blue glengarry cap with—for Argyll and Sutherland Highlanders—a red and white diced band. NCO chevrons are worn on the right arm with the brassard in the regimental tartan. The A&SH cap badge is being worn illegally—it should be that of the Highland Brigade—and is set upon a black silk cockade. A&SH brass titles are worn on the shoulder; and the rifle is the ubiquitous 7.62mm L1A1.

Below: The British Army Respirator No. 4 Mk2 was carried by British troops in Aden during the 1960s, being widely employed in teargas attacks against the local populations during crowd control operations. The lightweight respirator case was worn on the back of the 1958 pattern belt—horizontally as shown.

BRITAIN AND THE COMMONWEALTH

The SAS in Oman

By 1970 Britain's 22nd Special Air Service Regiment (22 SAS) had come a long way from its roots in World War II. Far from being an exclusively clandestine force dedicated to infiltration and sabotage, it had gradually evolved into an elite formation trained and immensely experienced in the delicate art of counter-insurgency. Having fought in Malaya (1950-59), Borneo (1962-66) and Aden (1964-67), the regiment was a repository of techniques designed to isolate and destroy insurgent groups using a typically British 'mix' of propaganda, intelligence collection and collation, 'hearts and minds' policies and hard fighting skills. But in 1970 areas of potential deployment seemed few – Britain was in the process of pulling out of global commitments and Northern Ireland was felt to be too politically delicate to allow SAS-style operations – and it was with some relief that the regiment took on the task of aiding the Sultan of Oman in his campaign against communist-backed rebels in the western province of Dhofar.

Elements of 22 SAS had served in Oman on two previous occasions – in 1958-59 two squadrons had successfully stormed a rebel stronghold on the Jebel Akhdar and as recently as 1969 a small assault team had landed on the Musandam peninsula, overlooking the strategically-vital Strait of Hormuz, to put down a guerrilla group – and the regiment was well aware of the nature of the current threat. Early in 1970 the commanding officer of 22 SAS, Lieutenant-Colonel John Watts, had visited Dhofar and come away convinced that a properly structured counter-insurgency campaign, based upon propaganda, intelligence and specialised military tactics, was the only way to contain the Popular Front for the Liberation of the Occupied Arabian Gulf (PFLOAG). Thus when the repressive Sultan Said bin Taimur was overthrown by his more enlightened son Qaboos in July 1970 and British aid was formally requested, the SAS was in a good position to respond.

At first the commitment was small – a number of SAS-manned BATTs (British Army Training Teams) were deployed into the towns of the government-controlled Salalah plain, offering medical and military aid – and the emphasis was firmly upon propaganda and intelligence. A 'hearts and minds' policy was quickly initiated, with SAS specialists setting up a government radio station, newspaper and information service and helping to organise Civil Action Teams (CATs) whose task it was to provide material benefits such as medicines, wells, mosques and schools to the people. The overall aim was to give Dhofaris tangible proof of new policies of reform.

But this could only work if such techniques were extended into rebel-controlled areas in the mountains of the Jebel, beyond the Salalah plain, and this led the SAS into a second, more extensive, commitment. The process began in late 1970, when a group of rebels on the eastern Jebel, reacting to the anti-Islamic policies of the PFLOAG leadership, surrendered to the Sultan. Instead of punishing them it was decided, on SAS advice, to organise them into special anti-guerrilla forces known as *firqat*, which could then be sent back into the mountains to hunt down their erstwhile colleagues. Initially the intention seems to have been to restrict the SAS to training alone, but it soon became apparent that combat leadership would also be needed. As early as February 1971 an SAS/*firqat* force liberated the eastern town of Sudh, and this was followed up later in the year by a major advance into the mountains to the south of Jibjat, carving out a government-controlled base at Medinat Al Haq and introducing a CAT to the area.

This set the pattern for future operations, and although the Sultan's Armed Forces (SAF) gradually assumed responsibility for offensive sweeps onto the Jebel, the SAS/*firqat* partnership continued to play a crucial role in the campaign. The fighting was occasionally hard – in July 1972, for example, a small BATT/*firqat* group, commanded by Captain Mike Kealy of 22 SAS, survived an assault at Mirbat by over 200 well-armed rebels – but the less dramatic tasks of propaganda and intelligence were continued throughout. By the time the campaign reached a successful conclusion in late 1975, the SAS had yet again proved itself the foremost counter-insurgency organisation in the world.

Above: SAS troopers mending their broken Land Rover. They are wearing berets and the tropical hat and are armed with FN FAL rifles. Below left: SAS troopers breaking camp in Oman. The camp beds are raised to keep the sleeper off the ground, preventing scorpions or snakes from getting into the sleeping bag.

SAS Trooper
— Oman 1973 —

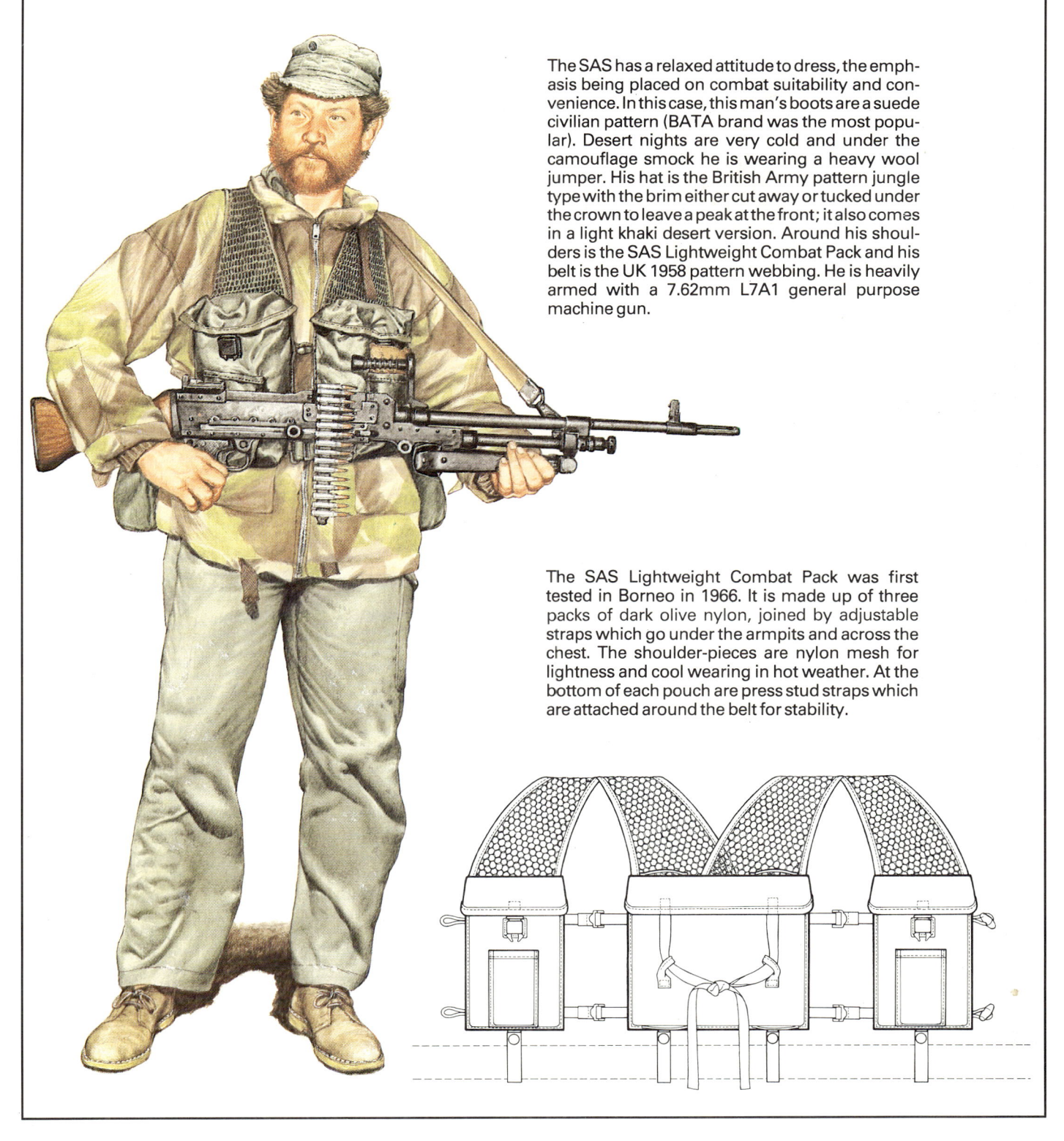

The SAS has a relaxed attitude to dress, the emphasis being placed on combat suitability and convenience. In this case, this man's boots are a suede civilian pattern (BATA brand was the most popular). Desert nights are very cold and under the camouflage smock he is wearing a heavy wool jumper. His hat is the British Army pattern jungle type with the brim either cut away or tucked under the crown to leave a peak at the front; it also comes in a light khaki desert version. Around his shoulders is the SAS Lightweight Combat Pack and his belt is the UK 1958 pattern webbing. He is heavily armed with a 7.62mm L7A1 general purpose machine gun.

The SAS Lightweight Combat Pack was first tested in Borneo in 1966. It is made up of three packs of dark olive nylon, joined by adjustable straps which go under the armpits and across the chest. The shoulder-pieces are nylon mesh for lightness and cool wearing in hot weather. At the bottom of each pouch are press stud straps which are attached around the belt for stability.

BRITAIN AND THE COMMONWEALTH

The Parachute Regiment in Northern Ireland

As one of the United Kingdom's premier military units, the Parachute Regiment faced special problems in Northern Ireland. Britain's Paras are trained for offensive action and the maximum application of force on the battlefield, while tours of duty in Northern Ireland have called for the sophisticated skills of counter-insurgency. Moreover, since the conflict is on Britain's very doorstep, it calls for an unusual measure of restraint in the application of military pressure. The limitations of operating in a 'domestic' landscape have forced the Paras to acquire new skills in dealing with the IRA, INLA and the Loyalist paramilitaries.

Like other units in the British armed forces, all three battalions of the Parachute Regiment have undertaken regular tours of duty since the escalation of the 'Troubles' in 1969 forced the authorities to deploy the army on the streets of Northern Ireland. Each battalion spends a period of four months in a given region before returning to England or being posted elsewhere. The soldiers have to be prepared to operate in two completely different environments – town and country – and have faced increasing military sophistication from their paramilitary opponents.

The two main urban areas, Belfast and Londonderry (or Derry, as it is known to the Republicans), call for close cooperation with the Royal Ulster Constabulary in keeping the level of guerrilla activity down.

Above: Armed with an SLR, a corporal of the Parachute Regiment takes up position on a street corner in Northern Ireland. Features of interest are the parachutist wings on the right arm; an earpiece for a lightweight two-way radio; and a flak jacket. Constructed from several layers of a synthetic fibre material called 'Kevlar', the flak jacket provides a considerable degree of protection from smallarms projectiles.

From their bases in fortified barracks, patrols of Paras are sent out into the streets to make the army's presence felt, while other smaller units are kept in semi-hiding, to cover particular trouble spots. Here the main problem is one of intense boredom as the Paras spend hour after hour scanning possible areas of enemy activity, usually with no action at all.

By adopting a high profile the Paras act as representatives of the British government, but on the other hand they also make themselves vulnerable to attack. Their uncompromising attitude towards the local population has singled the Paras out as special targets for IRA action. One example was the well-planned double bomb attack at Warrenpoint in 1979 in which 18 men of the second battalion were killed.

Since there is little love lost between the population in Republican areas and the Parachute Regiment, the Paras are forced into the role of an occupying force which in its turn does nothing to solve the complex military-political situation in the divided province of Ulster. Much of the Paras' reputation rests upon the 'Bloody Sunday' incident in 1972 in which 13 civil rights marchers were shot and killed by a unit of the Parachute Regiment. The Paras were exonerated by an official inquiry (although it was noted that some individuals had been 'reckless' in the use of their weapons), but Republican elements have successfully portrayed the Paras as especially bloodthirsty agents of 'British oppression'. As a result little help is provided by the local people and good intelligence of enemy activity is necessarily limited.

Out of the towns the main areas of activity are the largely Catholic and rural Fermanagh and south Armagh – termed 'bandit country' by the troops on the ground. The Paras have again been faced by a population hostile to the British Army, with the added problem of fighting an opponent who can quickly slip over the border after a raid to the relative safety of the Irish Republic.

In an effort to deny the IRA control over these border areas the Paras mount constant patrols, often spending days travelling across the hill countryside of south Armagh on the lookout for signs of enemy activity. Again, a major problem is lack of intelligence of IRA movements, although the army's modern, sophisticated surveillance equipment goes some way to rectifying this weakness.

The Parachute Regiment, in particular, as a prime target for terrorists, has to cope with problems greater than those facing many other regiments. Yet it can be argued that the quality of the British Army has been raised by the need to operate for long periods in an environment in which often complex decisions about the precise weight of force to be used have to be made on a daily basis.

After nearly two decades of conflict the solution to Northern Ireland's troubles remains as elusive as ever. For the present, therefore, the battalions of the Parachute Regiment will stay in the province.

British Paratrooper
— Northern Ireland 1980 —

Immediately recognisable by his red beret, this Para in Northern Ireland wears standard British kit for the conflict: olive-green trousers and a DPM smock over which is worn the now almost ubiquitous flak jacket. A 'skeleton' webbing belt is worn, consisting of ammunition pouches and two water bottles. Ease of communication is essential for the type of operations carried out by the British Army in Northern Ireland and this Para is suitably equipped with a two-way radio attached to his jacket collar. As a soldier on a combat patrol a matt-black plastic badge is worn on the beret and no sling is carried on the rifle – the 7.62mm SLR L1A1 – in order to prevent hostile civilians from pulling the rifle from a patrolling soldier's grasp. The British version of the Belgian FN FAL rifle, the SLR came into service in the late 1950s and since then has become the standard British infantry weapon, although it is due to be replaced by the small-calibre, automatic 'Individual Weapon' sometime in the 1980s. Popular with the troops, however, the SLR is a robust and dependable weapon with a maximum effective range of over 600m (656yds).

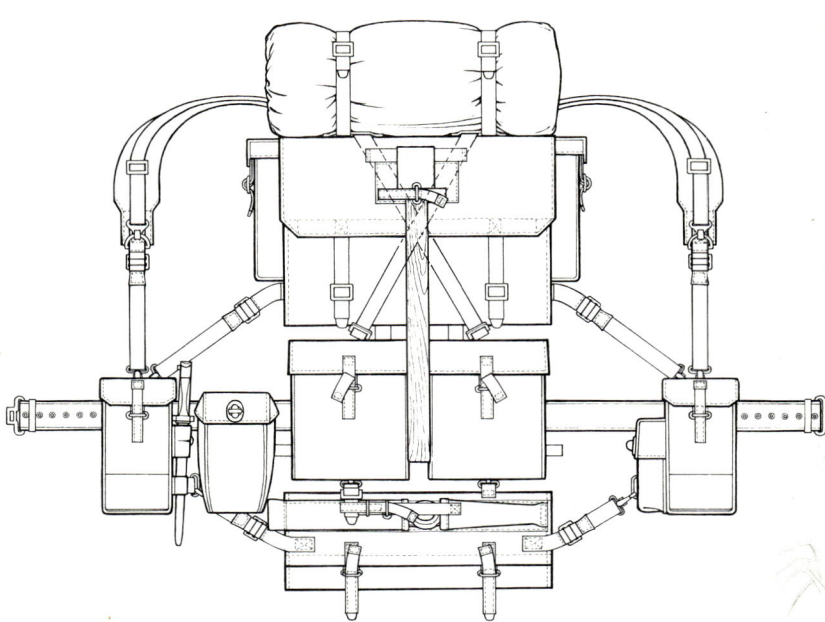

The British 1958-pattern webbing equipment is still worn by British soldiers, including those of the Parachute Regiment. On the belt itself, equipment comprises from the left, an SLR ammunition pouch with bayonet attached, a water bottle and, on the far right, a second ammunition pouch with side-pocket for a blank attachment for the SLR. Above the large pack (with pickaxe handle) is a rolled sleeping bag while below the pack are two 'kidney' pouches under which is slung a poncho roll.

BRITAIN AND THE COMMONWEALTH

The Royal Marines

Since 1945 the Royal Marines have seen action all over the globe, being involved in almost all of Britain's many small wars and peacekeeping operations. A small, flexible and highly mobile force, the Royal Marine Commandos have naturally been a first choice for dealing with trouble spots across the world.

One of the Marines' smaller but most noteworthy operations took place in Korea where 41 (Independent) Commando was attached to the US 1st Marine Division surrounded by Chinese forces at Chosin; during the epic fighting retreat 41 Commando lost 70 of their 200 men and earned a Presidential citation for their efforts. During the Suez adventure of 1956, 40, 42 and 45 Commando of 3 Brigade spearheaded the assault on Port Said.

More serious fighting was undertaken in Borneo where the Royal Marines were engaged in supporting the administration of the Sultan of Brunei against internal revolt and the attempts of the Indonesians to gain control of Brunei. In the thick jungles of Borneo the Marines honed their jungle-warfare skills to a fine edge out-fighting the Indonesian aggressors in a number of actions. In 1964 the Royal Marines were involved in Aden. For the next three years commando units fought it out with the rebel tribesmen in the scorched mountains of the Radfan, or acted as policemen in the notorious Crater district.

After Britain's withdrawal from the Far and Middle East, completed by 1971, the Royal Marines were redeployed to act as a crack assault force with a special role in defending Nato's northern flank.

The amphibious skills of the Royal Marines were put to the test during the Falklands conflict in 1982. The three commando battalions, 40, 42 and 45, were landed at San Carlos and 42 and 45 'yomped' across East Falkland to take part in the assaults on the Argentinian positions around Port Stanley.

In the early 1980s, the Royal Marines had a combined strength of 7750 men organised into a commando brigade (of three commando battalions), a commando artillery regiment, two engineer squadrons (from the army), a helicopter squadron, a logistic regiment and a number of specialist units including one Special Boat and two Raiding Squadrons.

Royal Marines of 42 Commando disembark from HMS Albion *onto a Westland SRN5 hovercraft near Indonesia in May 1965. Below: Weary but jubilant, Royal Marines pose with the Falklands flag after the successful recapture of the islands from Argentina. Armament here consists of a GPMG and FN SLRs, one of which is fitted with a sniper's telescopic sight.*

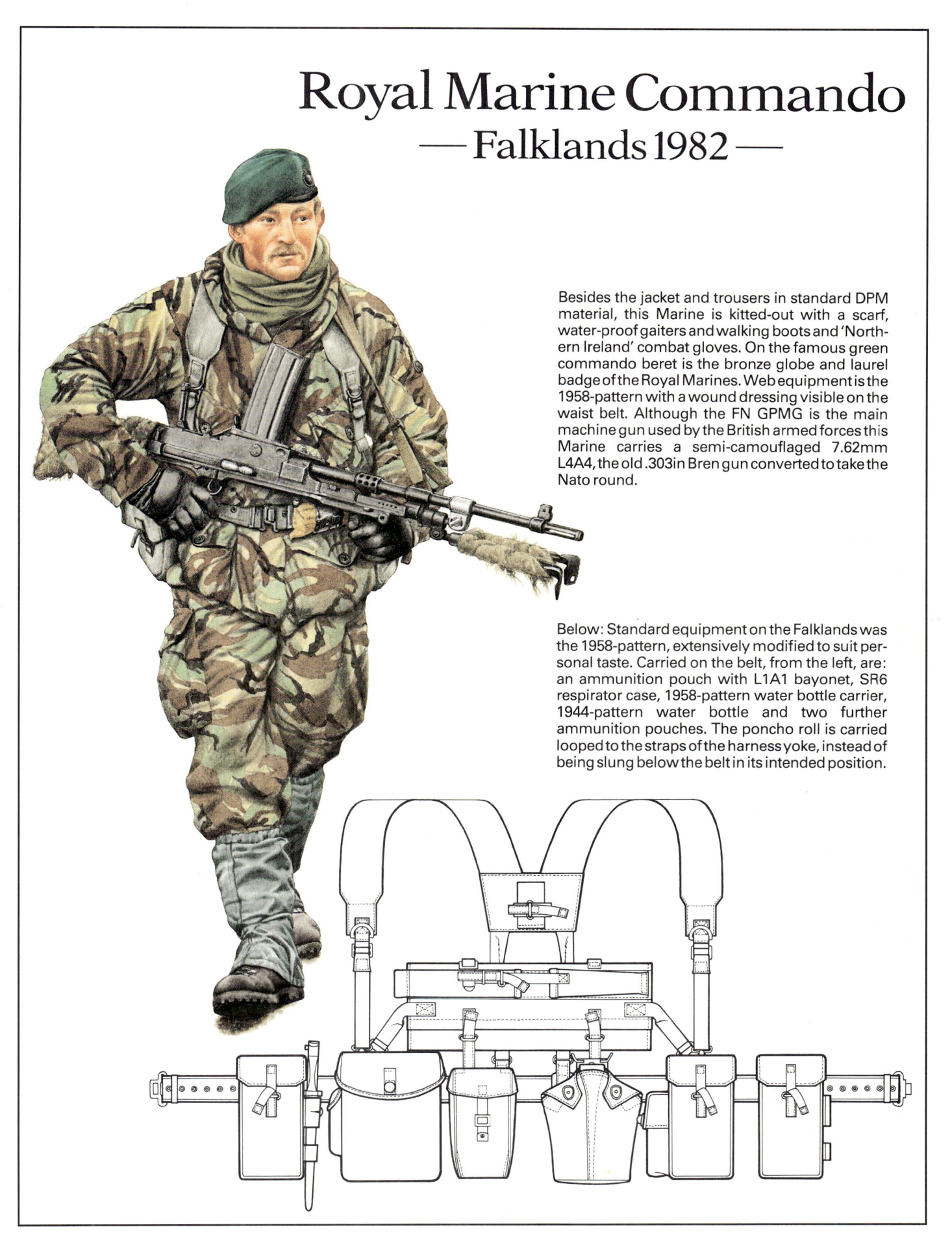

Royal Marine Commando
— Falklands 1982 —

Besides the jacket and trousers in standard DPM material, this Marine is kitted-out with a scarf, water-proof gaiters and walking boots and 'Northern Ireland' combat gloves. On the famous green commando beret is the bronze globe and laurel badge of the Royal Marines. Web equipment is the 1958-pattern with a wound dressing visible on the waist belt. Although the FN GPMG is the main machine gun used by the British armed forces this Marine carries a semi-camouflaged 7.62mm L4A4, the old .303in Bren gun converted to take the Nato round.

Below: Standard equipment on the Falklands was the 1958-pattern, extensively modified to suit personal taste. Carried on the belt, from the left, are: an ammunition pouch with L1A1 bayonet, SR6 respirator case, 1958-pattern water bottle carrier, 1944-pattern water bottle and two further ammunition pouches. The poncho roll is carried looped to the straps of the harness yoke, instead of being slung below the belt in its intended position.

BRITAIN AND THE COMMONWEALTH

The SAS in the Falklands

Above: An SAS trooper, armed with an M16 assault rifle, caught by the camera as he passes in front of a Westland Scout helicopter near Goat Ridge, East Falkland, 14 June 1982. The US-manufactured M16 is favoured by the SAS because it is light and capable of fully-automatic fire. The heavy personal load carried by the trooper is well illustrated.

The British Task Force sailed south towards the Falkland Islands in April 1982 and alongside the regular units of the British Army was D Squadron and part of G Squadron, 22 Special Air Service Regiment. Since its formation in the Western Desert in 1941, the SAS had built up a reputation as fighting soldiers that was second to none, and accordingly they were chosen to conduct the most dangerous and technically demanding missions.

The first task the SAS undertook was the deployment of D Squadron for the recapture of South Georgia alongside M Company of 42 Commando, Royal Marines. The British commander required information on enemy dispositions around Leith and D Squadron was allotted this responsibility. Getting ashore was a major problem: the extreme conditions proved too much for the helicopters and two crashed in a 'whiteout' while attempting to lift SAS troopers from a glacier during a blizzard on 22 April. Luckily there were no fatalities. The following day an amphibious operation got the men ashore, and once on land D Squadron and the Royal Marines had little difficulty rounding up the Argentinian garrison.

On 1 May surveillance patrols of G Squadron were landed by helicopter on East Falkland in conditions of utmost secrecy. For the next three weeks they crept around parts of the island, conducting close observation of Argentinian dispositions and troop movements and reporting back to base with vital information which enabled the Task Force commanders to decide on San Carlos as the main assault landing ground.

Meanwhile D Squadron had crossed over to the Falklands from South Georgia and as part of the preparations for the landing at San Carlos they were sent in to destroy the airfield on Pebble Island. On the night of 14/15 May canoes and helicopters made a secure landing on the island, some eight kilometres from the airstrip. Supported by naval gunfire and illuminating rounds the SAS troopers shot up the Pucara ground-attack aircraft with smallarms fire and rockets. An enemy patrol was encountered during their return journey only to be quickly silenced by automatic fire. Two men were wounded but all flew back to HMS *Hermes* having destroyed 11 aircraft as well as ammunition and explosives.

Soon after the Pebble Island success a Sea King helicopter crashed during a 'cross-decking' run between *Hermes* and *Intrepid* and 18 SAS troopers from both squadrons were drowned. For such a small unit this was an undeniable blow, but the fighting went on. D Squadron covered the main landings with a diversionary attack at Darwin and Goose Green on 21 May. This raid was a complete success; enemy reserves were drawn off from the San Carlos area, so much so that an intercepted Argentinian radio transmission talked of an attack of at least battalion strength. Once the main landings had taken place, D Squadron inserted a patrol on Mount Kent (subsequently reinforced). From Mount Kent they ambushed enemy patrols, carried out raids, continued with the process of information-gathering and lastly acted as a spearhead force for the Royal Marines who captured this key position on 31 May.

During the 1970s the role of the SAS had expanded to include civil/military counter-insurgency operations and accordingly they had developed their techniques into the realm of psychological warfare. On the Falklands they used this newly-gained experience to great effect. The CO of the SAS in the Falklands and Brigadier Julian Thompson, commanding 3 Commando Brigade, agreed on the need for some form of psychological operations, and as the British forces began to close on Stanley they set about exploiting the demoralised state of the Argentinian armed forces. The SAS role was to help set up the means to persuade the Argentinians that they had done all that honour demanded, that their situation was hopeless and that the surrender of their forces would avoid further pointless blood-letting.

At the beginning of June lines of communication had been established with Argentinian HQ, and on 6 June the SAS CO flew into Stanley to talk with the Argentinian commander, General Menendez. The British put their case and their appeal to honour proved particularly successful, so that on 14 June the Argentinians surrendered. At all levels, from the four-man teams operating deep behind enemy lines to the discussion of surrender terms, the SAS made a special contribution to overall British victory.

SAS Trooper
—Falklands 1982—

Britain's elite undercover force the SAS has always worn a diverse variety of equipment and dress as can be seen from this figure. The basic uniform consists of an SAS smock and Royal Marine issue DPM (disruptive pattern material) trousers. Besides the personalised belt kit, another unusual feature is the black wool balaclava helmet, widely used by the SAS for 'behind-the-lines' operations of the type encountered in the Falklands. This trooper is armed with a US-built 5.56mm Colt 'Commando' XM177, a cut down version of the M16 assault rifle; painted in camouflage colours, a spare magazine is taped onto the gun's 20-round magazine. Developed during the Vietnam War, the XM177 is a handier version of the M16, though its shorter barrel makes it considerably less accurate at long ranges.

The photograph above shows an SAS trooper laying an explosive charge; his FN SLR rifle is camouflaged with sacking – a common practice in the British Army.

Although this SAS trooper's kit conforms to the standard British '58 pattern, most soldiers evolve their own arrangement of kit; the one illustrated here would be typical of that worn during the Falklands conflict. From the left the items are a '58-pattern SLR pouch, compass case, '44-pattern water bottle, US M16 ammunition pouch (used as a small pack), British water bottle, US water bottle holder, and another '58-pattern SLR pouch.

47

BRITAIN AND THE COMMONWEALTH

The Blues and Royals

The Blues and Royals came into being as a regiment on 26 March 1969, a result of the amalgamation of the Royal Horse Guards (known as the Blues) with the First Royal Dragoons (the Royals). Both regiments trace their ancestry back to the middle of the 17th century and over the years they have acquired an impressive array of battle honours. The formation of the two regiments followed the restoration of Charles II to the British throne in 1660. During the next two decades Charles raised a number of regiments of horse and foot which became the historical basis for the British Army of today. The Earl of Oxford was appointed to command the Royal Regiment of Horse in 1661 and as a mark of respect to their colonel they wore coats of Oxford blue, in contrast to the red uniforms worn by other regiments. In 1687 the regiment adopted the title of Royal Horse Guards, although by this date it had acquired the nickname of 'the Blues'. The Royals' origins also went back to 1661 when a troop of horse was despatched to Tangiers to bolster up the garrison stationed there; on the troop's return to England it was reorganised and expanded in 1690 to become the Royal Regiment of Dragoons. While the Blues was an elite regiment of horse, relying on shock tactics through the combined power of the horse and sword, the dragoons were trained to act as mounted infantrymen, armed with light muskets as well as swords. During the 18th century, however, the Royals became a regular cavalry regiment like the Blues.

During the Napoleonic Wars the Blues were organised with the Life Guards to form the Household Brigade which fought alongside the Royals in the battles of the Peninsular War and at Waterloo in 1815. In the 19th century battle honours were won in the Crimea and in the various colonial wars that were fought to establish the Empire.

During World War I the Blues and the Royals played a part in the early battles of manoeuvre but once the trench deadlock set in at the end of 1914 the cavalry was either dismounted to take its turn manning the trenches or waited in frustration for the breakthrough that never came. Although World War II saw both regiments still on horseback they were subsequently transferred to armoured cars, the Blues distinguishing itself during the Allied advance into Europe in 1944-45.

After the war both regiments continued to be equipped with armoured cars, even if the Blues continued to ride horses when acting as ceremonial troops alongside the Life Guards. The ceremonial functions of the Blues were maintained after amalgamation with the Royals in 1969, although a major change for the 'new' regiment was the arrival of the Chieftain tank to replace the armoured cars. The Chieftains were not to last long, however, as the Blues and Royals adopted the new Scorpion light tank series in 1974.

Below: A Scorpion light tank crew of the Blues and Royals stops for a break during the arduous drive to Port Stanley, Falklands 1982. The regiment's nine vehicles (eight tanks and one recovery vehicle) comprised the only armoured element within Britain's Task Force, and coped extremely well with the difficulties of crossing boggy and rocky terrain. The tanks provided invaluable infantry support throughout the campaign and 3 Troop gave vital fire support on Wireless Ridge for 2 Para's assault.

Blues and Royals Tank Crewman
— Falklands 1982 —

Below: The victory parade for the Falklands Task Force, London, 12 October 1982. Two Scorpions and two Scimitars of the Blues and Royals drive past the saluting base.

Dressed in standard DPM (disruptive pattern material) combat jacket and trousers, and a woollen scarf and high leg boots to protect against the bitterly cold Falklands winds, this crewman is equipped with a plastic helmet fitted with a boom microphone. Normally the helmet would be worn only in the vehicle. The crewman has a pair of Avimo general purpose prismatic binoculars and is armed with a British 9mm Sterling L2A3 sub-machine gun. It is common practice to provide tank crews with a means of self-defence should they have to operate outside their vehicle.

Western Europe

The armies of Western Europe have enjoyed mixed fortunes since 1945. With the exception of those belonging to states which remained neutral during World War II – Sweden, Switzerland, Portugal, Spain, Ireland and Turkey – all emerged from that conflict tinged with the memory of recent defeat, either in 1940 or, in the case of the Axis powers, 1945. Some had made valuable contributions to Allied victory, but all had to accept that their liberation had been achieved principally through the actions of outside powers. Nor was there any time to relax in the postwar period, for the Soviet Union was now considered to be a major threat to Western security, necessitating the maintenance of powerful armed forces, preferably acting together. By 1955 the majority of West European states had joined the Nato alliance, and even those that remained outside it – Sweden, Switzerland, Ireland, Austria and (up to 1982) Spain – recognised the need for a military capability of some description. In some countries this has led to problems of military interference in the politics of the state: since 1945 elements of the French, Greek, Turkish and Portuguese armies have all attempted *coups d'état*, with varying success.

At the same time, the armies of Western Europe have, between them, experienced the full range of non-nuclear war. There have been mercifully few full-scale conventional campaigns – the Greek Army cut its postwar teeth in a bitter civil war against armed communist factions (1945–49), while the Turks fought in Korea (1950–53) and mounted a combined-force invasion of Cyprus (1974) – but nearly all West European states have devoted enormous resources to preparing for such an eventuality. The West Germans, for example, have avoided foreign involvement since the raising of the Bundeswehr in 1955, preferring to concentrate their military efforts on protecting the state against possible Warsaw Pact attack. This is reflected in their military organisation – they do not maintain an ocean-going navy or a large-scale airborne interventionary capability – and in the wide range of sophisticated weaponry they deploy, much of it domestically produced. Other states (with the notable exceptions of France, Sweden and Switzerland) make full use of US equipment, although there are indications that this causes some financial strain.

But conventional war is only one aspect of the West European experience, for three of the countries involved have fought costly counter-insurgency campaigns in their respective empires. As early as 1945, the Dutch were struggling to preserve their hold on what was to become Indonesia; a campaign that was terminated in 1949 as casualties mounted and the Netherlands, already weakened by five years of Nazi occupation (1940–45), proved neither willing nor able to sustain the struggle. A similar pattern emerged in the 1960s and early 1970s with the Portuguese, whose operations in Angola, Mozambique and Guinea-Bissau gradually alienated domestic opinion and led, in April 1974, to the overthrow of the Lisbon government by elements of a frustrated army. But the most traumatic defeat was suffered by the French in Indochina between 1946 and 1954, to be followed by a similar humiliation in Algeria between 1954 and 1962.

Since 1962 the French have shown a marked reluctance to become embroiled in counter-insurgency, but this has not prevented the use of certain elite elements of the army – notably the ubiquitous Foreign Legion – in the delicate process of intervention, often to save hostages or to protect Europeans trapped by the oscillations of Third World politics. The Belgians first demonstrated the possibilities in 1964, when they committed paracommandos to rescue hostages in Stanleyville, Zaire. The French, intent on maintaining influence in former colonial areas, followed suit in 1978 by sending a Foreign Legion parachute unit on a hostage-rescue mission in Kolwezi, also in Zaire, and since 1969 they have committed expeditionary forces to prevent a Libyan-backed takeover of Chad on three separate occasions. These forces have not enjoyed complete success – Chad is still riven by civil war – but they display a rapid deployment capability which provides the Paris government with a useful instrument of global foreign policy. Elite forces have also been used in many West European states as a response to domestic or international terrorism, and here the record of success is impressive. In Holland, for example, Dutch Marines (with army support) were used to break two train sieges (in 1975 and 1977) initiated by South Moluccan nationalists, while the West German GSG9 unit earned great respect for its brilliant rescue of hijacked air passengers at Mogadishu, Somalia, in October 1977. Most liberal democracies in Europe now maintain some sort of specially trained anti-terrorist force.

Finally, some West European states have also contributed to United Nations or Multi-National Force (MNF) peacekeeping operations. The Swedes, for example, are widely recognised as among the best UN troops available, partly because they represent a neutral state acceptable to most factions as impartial, but also because, with service in the Middle East (since 1956), the Congo (1960-64) and Cyprus (since 1964), they have gained valuable experience in a difficult military duty. Other states, notably France and Italy, have learned the same sort of lessons, although outside the UN framework. Their involvement in the MNF in Beirut (1982–84) was marred by a suicide bomb attack on the French barracks in October 1983 which killed 58, but it undoubtedly provided valuable military experience. The total fund of experience gained in a wide range of conflicts and commitments by the armies of Western Europe during what is ostensibly a period of peace is surprisingly large, and enables the various forces to maintain an impressive flexibility in the face of a whole range of security threats.

Right: French paras remain watchful while on patrol in Beirut during the early 1980s. The man on the right cradles an 89mm STRIM anti-tank rocket launcher, his comrade being armed with the new 5.6mm MAS automatic rifle. Alongside their American allies the French had little success in their 'peacemaking' role; they were perceived as acting in support of Amin Gemayel's regime (the French actually attacked the positions of the anti-Gemayel Druze militia) and were the subject of attacks from Shi'ite Muslim terrorists.

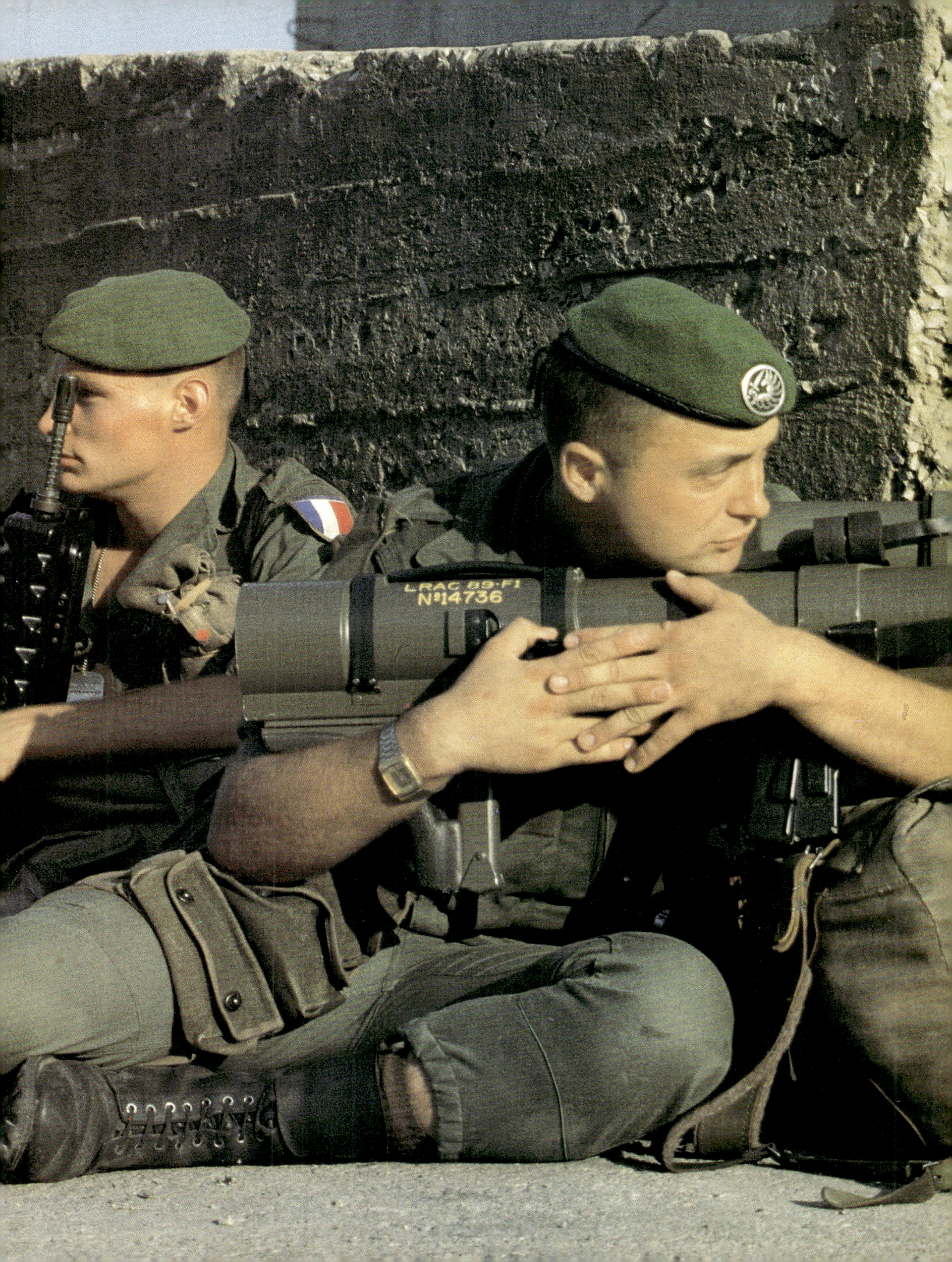
LRAC 89-F1
Nº14736

WESTERN EUROPE

The Dutch Army

The end of World War II did not bring peace to the Dutch Army; during the war the Dutch East Indies had been lost to the Japanese and when they surrendered in 1945 they handed over power to Indonesian nationalists who opposed any attempts by the Dutch to resume control over their former colony. The scene was set for conflict, and once suitable transport could be arranged contingents of the Dutch Army were sent to Indonesia under orders to suppress the nationalist rebellion.

The nationalist uprising was not easily put down and guerrilla war broke out. In order to safeguard European interests in the colonies reinforcements were sent out, and towards the end of the 1940s over 100,000 troops were engaged in security operations. The Dutch Army launched a number of anti-guerrilla sweeps – notably in July 1947 and in December 1948 – but while adding to the casualty toll on both sides they came to nothing. By the end of 1948 it was becoming obvious to the Dutch Army that the war could not be won and in the December of 1949 sovereignty of the colony was handed over to the nationalists.

Since the 1940s the Dutch Army has not been involved in war, but as a member of Nato it has met its small though important military obligation to the Western alliance. The Netherlands Nato contribution stands at a corps of two armoured brigades and four armoured infantry brigades organised into two divisions. Overall the army numbers about 67,000 men of whom 43,000 are conscripts.

The terms of military service are between 14 to 16 months in the army, after which the citizen is expected to attend refresher courses until the age of 35. A large short-leave reserve is maintained, which organised into armoured and mechanised brigades adds up to 145,000 men.

Despite some reservations as to the quality and commitment of a proportion of recruits, the Dutch Army is a well equipped one. The armoured forces are provided with Leopard 1 and 2 main battle tanks (MBTs) with a number of Centurion and AMX13 tanks in reserve. French, West German and US armoured personnel carriers (APCs) are in current use and a comprehensive range of towed and self-propelled artillery is deployed.

*Above right: Keeping their heads down, Dutch Marines work their way through an Indonesian village held by nationalist guerrillas.
Right: Wearing US M1 helmets and armed and equipped from US and British stocks Dutch troops negotiate rough country while on a counter-insurgency operation.*

Dutch Infantryman
—Indonesia 1946—

An interesting combination of uniform and equipment is worn by this soldier. Under a British steel helmet is a US Army olive-green fatigue cap. Also of US manufacture is the two-piece camouflage jungle suit, over which is worn British 1937-pattern web equipment. Armament consists of a British 9mm Lanchester sub-machine gun (with 1907-pattern bayonet) plus a 'long' holster, probably holding a .38 Smith and Wesson revolver.

Left: Dutch Marines crouch in a jungle clearing, after an Indonesian ambush during the first round of fighting in 1946.

WESTERN EUROPE

The Greek Democratic Army

The main resistance to the German occupation of Greece during World War II came from the Greek communists who, during the course of the struggle, built themselves up into a well-organised paramilitary force. At the end of hostilities the communists were thwarted in their plans to achieve power and instead began to conduct guerrilla operations against the government set up by the British and Americans.

Calling themselves the DSE (Dimokratikos Stratos Ellados – Greek Democratic Army) the communists started guerrilla operations in earnest in December 1946 and conducted an intense guerrilla campaign against the government until their final defeat in the Grammos Mountains in August 1949.

The DSE forces were never large; they took to the field with only 8000 fighters at the end of 1946 and grew to a strength of around 20,000 by November 1947, a level which remained more or less constant until the communist defeat in 1949. The active element of the DSE was only a part of the total communist opposition to the government. That the DSE was able to wage effective guerrilla war was largely a consequence of the poor quality of the government forces and the difficult mountain terrain of much of Greece.

Besides the terrain, the DSE was aided by the two adjacent communist states of Albania and (especially) Yugoslavia which provided the guerrillas with vital 'sanctuary' areas. Guerrilla bands could retire to the safety of these neighbouring countries to recoup their strength and new recruits could receive military and ideological training away from the battleground.

The organisation of the DSE changed during the course of the conflict. Initially it was based on loosely-organised bands of around 50 to 80 men operating semi-independently over a wide area. As guerrilla strength increased the bands developed into companies and battalions, and parallel with this development was a concerted effort by the Yugoslavia-based leadership to bring the guerrillas in the field more closely under their control. By 1948 the leadership was attempting to impose a regular army organisational structure onto the DSE so that by the end of the year there were eight 'divisions'.

As infantry the DSE was well-supplied with smallarms: rifles, sub-machine guns and machine guns were never in short supply; the weakness was the diversity of weapon types – Greek, Italian, German, British and American – which caused supply problems that the guerrillas' rudimentary logistical system was never able to overcome. More serious, however, was a dearth of support weapons. Although there were some mortars – highly useful in mountain warfare – artillery was scarce. The mine was a major guerrilla weapon. Having almost no motor transport of their own the DSE could place anti-tank mines at will and limit the mobility of the government forces.

Leadership in the DSE was of variable quality. The men who led the guerrilla bands in the mountains were often competent tacticians with much combat experi-

Above: Adopting a typically 'heroic' pose two members of the DSE gaze into the middle distance, armed with a British Bren light machine gun and a German MP40 sub-machine gun.

ence gained in the struggle against the Germans. At a higher level serious flaws were revealed. The overall strategy of the anti-government campaign varied according to which power group had come to prominence. As the war progressed, the largely civilian pro-Soviet Stalinists gained power, at the expense of the 'soldiers' who tended to be pro-Yugoslavian.

The Stalinists were impatient with the small-scale operations previously conducted by the DSE, and in 1948 they felt confident enough to dispense with guerrilla warfare and 'convert' to conventional warfare. This was to prove a fatal mistake, especially as the quality and numbers of the government forces had increased considerably during the course of the war, and generously supplied with US equipment – notably aircraft and artillery – they were able to outfight the DSE in a conventional war. The DSE, by waging a war of position, was exposed as the ill-balanced force that it was, and consequently was defeated. As a purely guerrilla army the DSE had been highly successful, outwitting the government troops, which outnumbered it by 10 to 1, for nearly four years.

Greek Democratic Army Guerrilla
—Greece 1947—

Although the Greek Democratic Army or DSE had no formal uniform, most guerrillas adopted some form of military dress, usually derived from a combination of Italian, German, Yugoslav or British sources. This female guerrilla is kitted out in British Army battledress trousers (dyed black) and British web anklets. Armament comprises a German 9mm MP40 sub-machine gun. The MP40 was a highly successful World War II design that featured a 32-round magazine and a metal stock which could be folded forwards — as shown here. The MP40 was the standard sub-machine gun of the communist forces during the Greek Civil War.

Above: DSE guerrillas were uniformed and equipped from a variety of sources, and these troops on parade are no exception, their uniforms and rifles coming from old Greek Army stocks.

WESTERN EUROPE

The Greek National Army

Following the withdrawal of German troops from Greece at the end of 1944 a fierce struggle developed between left and right-wing factions for control of the country. The communists and socialists had hoped to form a government but they were prevented from gaining power by British intervention which installed a right-wing government under Georgios Papandreou. Although the communists had been thwarted in their plans they were far from beaten and their opposition to the newly installed government broke out into full scale civil war in 1946.

The government forces – known as the Greek National Army (GNA) – were ill-prepared to face the communist threat and relied on the British and Americans for help. Although the British were unwilling to take to the field to suppress the communist threat they supplied the GNA with arms and instigated a training programme. British involvement decreased when the Americans began to take a strong interest in supporting anti-communist movements and from 1947 onwards the US was the major supplier of arms and equipment.

During the early battles with the guerrillas the GNA's weaknesses were revealed in plenty. As the old pre-war Greek Army had been destroyed in the German invasion and occupation of Greece the GNA was a new army without the traditions and continuity of development that are so important in building up an army into an effective fighting force. The officers did not have the confidence of the men, and many units were often unprepared to venture out into the mountains to take on the guerrillas, preferring to remain in their lowland bases.

Right: Mounted on horseback, government troops pursue guerrilla forces in the Pindus Mountains in central Greece. One of the main problems facing the GNA during the civil war was forcing the evasive guerrillas into a decisive action where superior firepower and weight of numbers could be brought to bear. Small mobile sections were thus often deployed to track the communist fighters through the mountains and engage them in small unit actions. Below: Armed with .45in Thompson sub-machine guns, GNA troops are briefed by an intelligence officer prior to a raid on a communist position.

In order to improve the quality of the Greek armed forces the Americans and the Greek High Command sacked unreliable or incompetent officers and toughened up the men through vigorous training exercises. To provide a mobile anti-guerrilla force capable of fighting in mountain terrain for long periods, battalions of commandos were formed.

As the regular army – spearheaded by commando units – began the process of attempting to clear the guerrillas from their mountain strongholds, a force was needed to provide a static defence for the towns and villages which the guerrillas relied upon for food and equipment. Their defence was assigned to a newly formed National Defence Corps which came under army control and acted as a link between the military and the police force.

American equipment and weapons increased steadily during 1947 and 1948 and American methods began to form the basis of GNA tactics. And if even by the end of 1948 the GNA remained a less than perfect fighting force its military conduct was considerably improved. When the new campaign began in the spring of 1949 the GNA was aided by two separate events, the squabbling between the DSE guerrillas which considerably reduced their effectiveness and the arrival of US Helldiver ground-attack planes. For the first time the GNA had real air support, and the Helldivers proved invaluable in blasting out the guerrillas from their mountain hideouts.

The final campaign in the Grammos Mountains conducted in August 1949 was a complete success for the GNA. A well-equipped and resolutely led GNA out-manoeuvred and out-fought the communists in a short but fierce series of engagements. By the end of September the guerrilla threat had been silenced and the GNA was finally triumphant.

Greek National Army Soldier
—Greece 1947—

This soldier reflects the British influence on the Greek government forces before the arrival of American equipment began to take effect. British battledress trousers (and web anklets) are worn, with, in addition, a British Army pullover and beret, the latter displaying the Greek Army's cap badge. Armament comprises the famous US .45in M1A1 Thompson sub-machine gun which was a common weapon with the GNA during the Greek Civil War.

Below: A GNA unit keeps a close watch for signs of guerrilla activity. Greece's sparse railway network was a prime target for guerrilla raids and sabotage operations during the civil war and all trains had to be provided with a substantial armed guard.

WESTERN EUROPE

French Foreign Legion Paras

Following the much publicised success of paratroop formations during World War II, the French Foreign Legion established a parachute instruction centre near Sidi-bel-Abbes in May 1948 which led to the formation of the 1st Foreign Legion Parachute Battalion (1 BEP) in July of that year. The newly-raised battalion was shipped out to Indochina in November 1948, and was soon followed by a second paratroop battalion. These two units were employed by the French as an elite mobile reserve, and casualties were correspondingly high; thus, for example, during the fighting withdrawal from the Cao Bang ridge in October 1950 the 1 BEP suffered 90 per cent casualties and as a result had to be temporarily disbanded.

In keeping with their role, both battalions found themselves a part of the heroic disaster of Dien Bien Phu. 1 BEP was para-dropped into the village in November 1953, and once the siege was joined in earnest early in the following year, 2 BEP parachuted into the beleaguered fortress in a vain attempt to hold off the Viet Minh attackers. In April 1954 the remnants of the two battalions amalgamated, but to no avail, for with the fall of Dien Bien Phu in May the two units were wiped out. After the debacle at Dien Bien Phu 1 and 2 BEP were re-formed, 2 BEP recruiting its men from 3 BEP – an Algerian-based depot battalion which had arrived in Haiphong in May 1954.

The Legion paratroopers were again in action during the short-lived Suez campaign when they were para-dropped into the port of Suez. The paras quickly secured their objectives and ruthlessly dealt with the uneven Egyptian opposition; however, the political defeat of the Anglo-French venture soon put an end to military operations and led to the evacuation of the paras from Egypt.

In 1955 1 and 2 BEP had been upgraded to regimental status and from their base in Algeria they began operations against the National Liberation Army

Above right: A French para leads a patrol through thick scrub just north of the French defences at Dien Bien Phu. During the 1950s the French Army was predominantly armed and equipped by its American ally, as is this para wearing a US M1 helmet complete with cigarette packet in the helmet band. Above left: Following an airborne drop these paras prepare to fire a mortar during the Kolwezi operation of 1978. The soldier in the right foreground is armed with an M1949 sub-machine gun.

(ALN), the military wing of the National Liberation Front. The next few years were to be the most controversial in the history of the Legion paratroops. While 2 REP was responsible for ensuring the success of the Morice Line strategy – denying the Algerian Nationalists a safe base in Tunisia – 1 REP's career was ultimately to be tarnished. During the initial stages of the conflict 1 REP was engaged in the out-country war with the guerrillas but in 1957 they were brought in to spearhead the offensive against the ALN in the capital itself – this was the beginning of the dirty and deadly struggle that achieved infamy as the battle of Algiers.

In this brutal and vicious fight – where torture was commonplace – the Legion paras destroyed the ALN's urban network, but as a consequence the nature of their war had changed from a simple military involvement to a political commitment to a French Algeria. Thus, when General de Gaulle instigated the process of France's disengagement from Algeria, 1 REP were in the forefront of the opposition to his policy. For 1 REP this took the form of a military coup, but when they found themselves virtually isolated in their attempt they reluctantly surrendered to the loyal French forces. As punishment the entire regiment was disbanded.

Since the heady days of Algeria the Legion paras have returned to their traditional role as servant of the French state. And despite ostensible peace they have seen plenty of action. Based in Corsica 2 REP has become France's 'rapid deployment force', ready to be flown out to trouble spots at an instant's notice – as was the case at Kolwezi in 1978 where they carried out a text-book rescue-service operation. Today's Legion paratroops act as an elite force – analogous to Britain's commandos and the Parachute Regiment – their function to safeguard French interests around the globe.

French Foreign Legion Para Captain
—Indochina 1952—

Even as late as 1952 soldiers of the Foreign Legion continued to be supplied with ex-World War II clothing from the Allied nations. This officer of 1 BEP wears a jacket of US Marine Corps camouflage material though retailored for Foreign Legion use; and likewise the trousers are retailored from British-issue windproof camouflage trousers. The helmet is also American – the unmistakable M1 pattern – as is the water bottle and the .30 M1A1 carbine with folding stock, manufactured especially for airborne troops. Rank is denoted by the three gold lines on a blue patch attached to the jacket front.

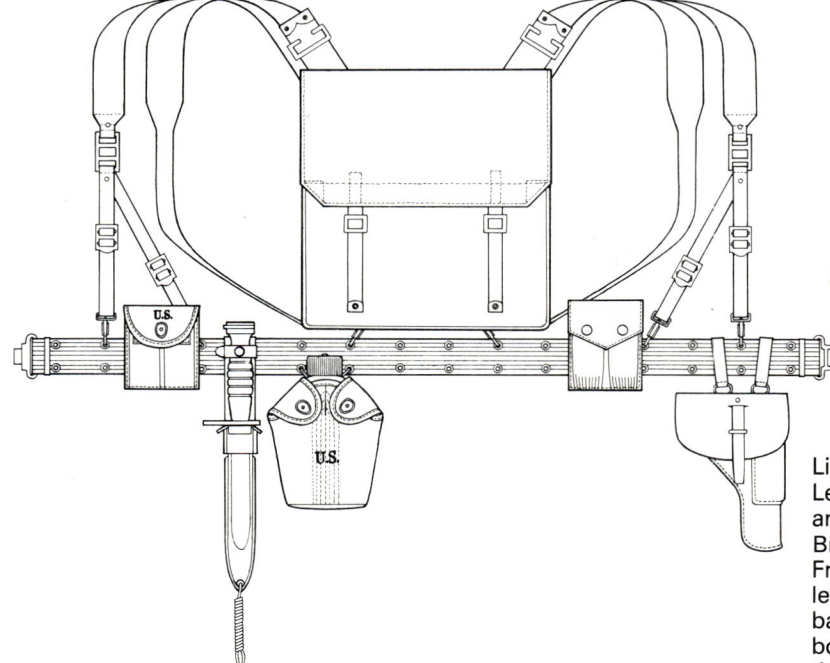

Like other French troops serving in Indochina, Legion paratroops wore a variety of US, British and French items of equipment. While the pack is British – the 1958-pattern model – the braces are French, and attached to the web belt are – from left to right – a US magazine pouch and M4 knife bayonet (both for the M1 carbine), US water bottle, US magazine pouch for pistol ammunition and a French leather pistol holster.

WESTERN EUROPE

The Swedish Army

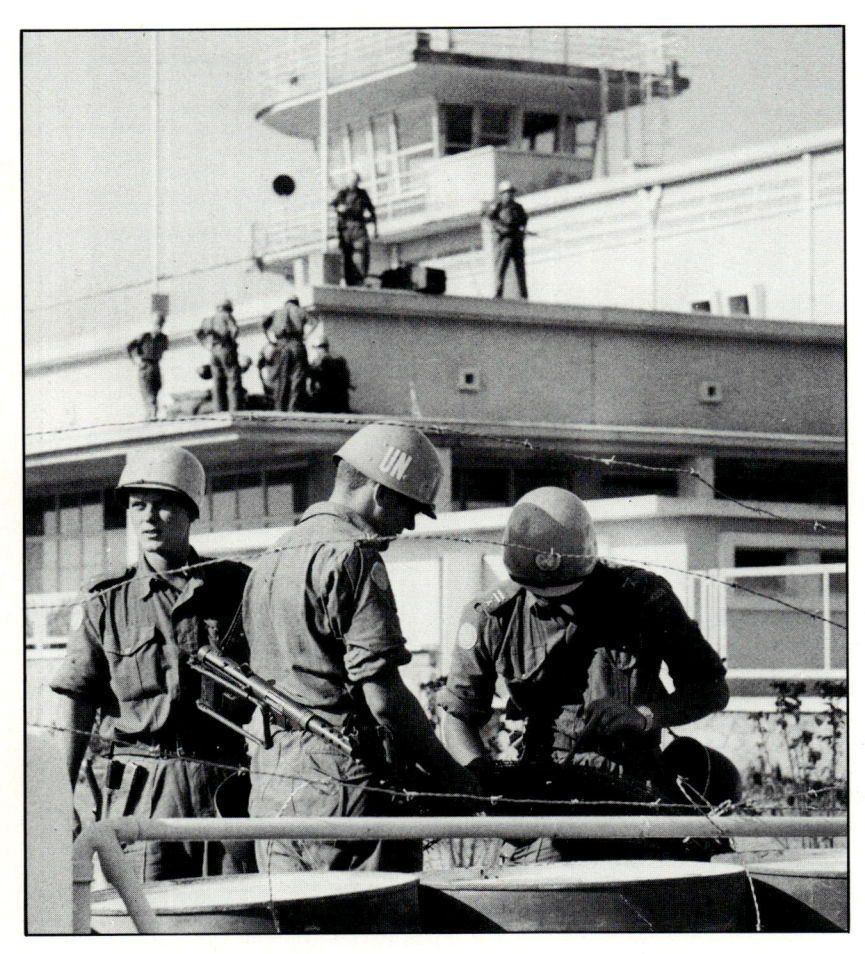

Sweden has maintained a strict neutrality for over a hundred years. Based upon her geo-strategic advantages she has remained aloof from the traumas of modern war, although has never felt secure enough to do without armed forces. In the event of invasion or threat, Sweden has for long been able to deploy large numbers of well-armed military units, drawn from a system of universal male conscription and reserve commitment which qualifies her as a 'nation in arms'.

The Swedish Army has at its core a regular cadre of professional officers and senior NCOs, about 10,000 strong, the main task of which is to train an annual intake of approximately 40,000 conscripts, most of whom are 18 years old. During their period of service (usually about 300 days), they are organised into field units raised in local areas and, when initial training is complete, these units are automatically transferred to the reserve as self-contained entities. Thereafter, by means of frequent mobilisation exercises and regular periods of refresher training, the reservists remain available until they reach the age of 47, after which many are absorbed into the 'Home Guard' on a voluntary basis. As this pattern of recruitment and training continues with each fresh batch of 18 year olds, the army is maintained at a very high level of potential strength; it is estimated that in the event of full mobilisation about 700,000 trained soldiers, backed by 100,000 Home Guard, could be made available in 72 hours. And when it is borne in mind that Sweden has a thriving domestic arms industry, producing equipment as sophisticated and innovative as the Stridsvagn STRV 103B S-tank, it may be appreciated that the army is by no means an insignificant force.

Above: Armed with Carl Gustav Model 45 sub-machine guns Swedish troops of the UN peacekeeping force secure the airport at Elisabethville in Katanga. Although troops from other nations were a part of the peacekeeping force it was the Swedish contingent that was the most important.

But the Swedes do lack operational experience – they have not fought a war since 1814 – and it is within this context that their involvement in United Nations peacekeeping, observer and truce supervision duties has assumed importance. As a neutral state, Sweden has always been a natural contributor to such duties, finding ready acceptance as a dispassionate member of the international community and, in accordance with her policy of non-alignment, she has always been a strong supporter of the UN. Thus as early as 1948 she sent observers to Palestine to help monitor the UN partition, and although this proved an abortive task in the face of Arab-Israeli hostilities it did mark the beginning of a long-term commitment to the Middle East which has included involvement in both UN Emergency Forces in Sinai and, since 1978, in southern Lebanon. Elsewhere, a Swedish medical unit saw service in Korea (1950-53) and, in 1960, Swedish infantry were among the first UN troops to enter the Congo. Indeed, the latter became a Swedish-controlled operation, with Sture Linner as Chief of Civilian Operations and Lieutenant-General Carl von Horn as military commander of ONUC (l'Organisation des Nations Unies au Congo), subject to the direction of a Swedish Secretary-General, Dag Hammarskjöld, and despite evidence that the soldiers were inadequately trained, finding it difficult to adapt to the climate, conditions and confusion of the Congo, they gradually gained invaluable experience.

This has not been wasted. Since 1964 the Swedes have maintained a battalion in Cyprus, contributing in no small measure to the difficult task of keeping Greek and Turk apart. Their courage was shown almost as soon as they arrived, when a small Swedish force entered the disputed village of Arsos and persuaded the fighting factions to surrender their arms, and two years later, in July 1966, a Swedish platoon, in a remarkable display of resolution, successfully prevented a Greek-Cypriot attack on the Turkish village of Melousha, to the east of Nicosia. These incidents indicated a growing confidence in Swedish military operations which has continued to be displayed not just in Cyprus but also in the equally difficult commitment to Lebanon. In neither case has the UN force prevented a resurgence of hostilities, but this should do nothing to detract from the achievements of the Swedish Army. It is now recognised as one of the most effective peacekeeping forces available to the UN and this, in turn, can only serve to enhance its domestic defence role.

Swedish Infantryman
—Congo 1960—

As befits a soldier serving in the climate and terrain of the Congo, a lightweight green drill uniform is worn along with green webbing. Although a 'Swedish' flash is worn on the upper left arm, this infantryman's UN insignia is more visible. Besides the UN badge – a hemisphere surrounded by laurel leaves in white on a blue background – worn on the right arm, he is distinguished by a blue helmet (US M1 pattern) with UN insignia painted in white. Arm of service – crossed rifles for the infantry – is indicated on slides worn on the shoulder straps. Sweden has a flourishing arms industry of her own and this soldier is accordingly armed with a 9mm Carl Gustav Model 45 sub-machine gun which features a folding metal stock and a 36-round magazine.

Below: Kitted out for winter warfare the crew of a light infantry mortar prepares to fire a round during exercises in northern Sweden. Below right: Swedish troops scramble aboard a carrier in Katanga during operations in the Congo, 1961.

WESTERN EUROPE
The French Army in Algeria

The war of Algerian independence was one of the most bitter of the many wars of colonial disengagement; it developed into a complex three-way struggle between the Algerian nationalist FLN (*Front de Libération Nationale*), the French government, and the European colonists. When the French Army began to arrive in strength in 1956, soon after its humiliating defeat at Dien Bien Phu in Indochina, its leaders were determined to try out the new theory about guerrilla warfare that they had developed to account for their failure. What the French officers failed to realise was that the communist revolution in Indochina was a war of an entirely different kind from the nationalist struggle in Algeria.

The military wing of the FLN, the ALN (*Armée de Libération Nationale*), had begun to escalate its terrorist bombing campaign in 1956 and by the end of the year the capital of Algiers was the main target. The French was to send in the crack 10th Parachute Division in January 1957 with a directive to restore law and order by whatever means necessary. The 3rd Colonial Parachute Regiment – under the ruthless leadership of Colonel Marcel Bigeard – was assigned responsibility for the Casbah, the centre of nationalist resistance. The paras developed a complex intelligence-gathering system, and, making full use of Muslim informers, began to build up a picture of FLN activities in the Casbah. So successful was this system that by October 1957 most of the leaders were in French hands and the FLN's power base in the Casbah was destroyed. This resounding military victory was to rebound on the French Army, however, when it became known that Bigeard's men had systematically tortured suspects and that an estimated 3000 Muslims had 'disappeared' under interrogation. Public opinion was outraged worldwide, and the FLN gained sympathy and material support from a growing number of international sources.

The war continued in the rural areas of Algeria, and the French Army was forced into the laborious process of tracking down the guerrillas in the mountains. As the war progressed, the French developed a system using pro-French Muslim units (*harkis*) to gather local information, while the crack Foreign Legion, paratroop and commando units acted as a fast-moving strike force, able to bring to battle and destroy the guerrillas once located.

As the neighbouring state of Tunisia was providing ALN units with arms and equipment and a safe haven from which to launch their attacks into Algeria, the French erected a barrier to prevent cross-border movement. Completed in September 1957, the Morice Line consisted of an electrified barbed-wire fence, patrolled day and night, adjoining a corridor of minefields. Attempts to cut through the fence triggered off alarms which brought down immediate artillery fire on the point of breakthrough, followed by motorised and helicopter units to round up the enemy. By April 1957 over 6000 guerrillas had been killed along the Morice Line.

The success of the Morice Line was followed up with a wave of counter-insurgency operations directed against the battered but still defiant ALN. At the beginning of 1959 the French Army was confident it had the guerrillas on the run, and the Challe Offensive was launched in February to finish them off. Moving eastwards from the mountains around Oran, a series of well-executed operations mopped up most of the remaining guerrillas.

Throughout the course of the war some members of the army had been disturbed by their government's lack of commitment to the maintenance of colonial rule in Algeria. Many senior officers sympathised with the European colonists (known as *colons* or *pieds noirs*) who were determined to preserve an *Algérie française*, and were outspoken in their criticism of state policy.

The appointment of General de Gaulle as president in June 1958 was enthusiastically greeted by the generals, but he had, in fact, little sympathy for the idea of an *Algérie française*. To the horror of the army and the colonists he instigated moves to come to a settlement with the FLN. An attempt by the colonists to seize power in Algeria in January 1960 was a failure, but revealed that sizeable elements of the army might throw in their lot with the *pieds noirs*. De Gaulle's purge of pro-colonist officers came to a head with the dismissal of General Challe, and in April 1961, Challe, with other senior officers, instigated an open revolt against the government.

Centring his rebellion on the 1st Regiment of Foreign Legion paratroops, Challe hoped to win over the other army units stationed in Algeria, but with a few exceptions they remained loyal to the central government. The revolt was a complete failure and signalled the end of the army's involvement in politics. De Gaulle pursued his policy of self-determination for Algeria, culminating in the Declaration of Independence in July 1962. The army's revolt had totally misjudged the feeling of the majority of Frenchmen, and against an opponent of de Gaulle's ability the dissident generals were unable to repeat their military success in the political arena.

Below: Men of the 3rd Colonial Parachute Regiment land in the Algerian desert south of Timimoun, 15 November 1957, as part of an operation designed to flush out and destroy an FLN guerrilla group. Within a fortnight, using the advantages of air-mobility and fighting skills, the paras achieved their aim.

French Army Para
— Algeria 1961 —

Left: Two French paratroop officers (of the Foreign Legion) discuss the course of events at a briefing during the Algerian War. Both wear camouflaged jackets and trousers. The officer in the foreground is kitted-out with parachute jump-boots.

The paratroop jacket (right) is in the standard French camouflage scheme (shown only on the left-hand side of the diagram) and has a number of features including a high button-up collar and bulky patch pockets; the wrists and jacket bottom are elasticated to ensure a snug fit during parachute drops and bad weather conditions.

French paratroop forces gained a notorious reputation during the savage fighting of the Algerian war of independence (1954-62), and this soldier is a typical paratroop foot-slogger of the later stages of the conflict. Both trousers and tunic are of the standard French camouflage pattern, while footwear consists of boots with leather gaiters for infantry action, in contrast to the high jump-boots worn by paratroops for airborne warfare. A distinctive feature of the uniform is the peaked cap which became the most common form of headgear for paratroops fighting in the deserts and mountains of Algeria. The webbing belt, by contrast, is standard French Army issue. Armament consists of the French 7.5mm M1952 (AAT Mle 52) general purpose machine gun, complete with 50-round ammunition belt. Allotted to the infantry section, the M1952 is capable of being used as a light machine gun (with bipod) or as a heavy machine gun when attached to the US-built M2 tripod. The gun can be re-bored to take the 7.62mm Nato round and M1952s manufactured for export are of this calibre.

63

WESTERN EUROPE

The Belgian Army in the Congo

Above: The Belgian Army found itself unexpectedly committed to operations in the Congo after the colony had been granted its independence in June 1960. These Belgian paracommandos and Congolese troops are organising roadblocks in Leopoldville. Although the Congolese troops are wearing American M1 steel helmets, the cut of the Belgian uniforms has a British appearance.

When the Belgian colony of the Congo (now Zaire) received its independence on 30 June 1960, the brief period of Belgian imperialism and overseas military commitment seemed to be at an end. Thereafter, it was presumed, the Belgian Army would be dedicated solely to the defence of Western Europe, within the framework of Nato.

To a large extent, this was the pattern that emerged. By the early 1980s the largely conscript army – comprising about 95,000 men, backed by 160,000 reserves and equipped with armour, armoured personnel carriers, artillery and air support – was clearly committed to Nato and prepared for conventional operations on the European mainland. Yet during the intervening 20 years (and particularly in the 1960s), Africa continued to attract Belgian attention. In the Congo, for example, a substantial body of Belgian officers and NCOs stayed behind after independence to command and train the local defence force and, when the new state collapsed into chaos later in July 1960, over 10,000 Belgian troops were flown in to protect commercial interests and personnel, especially in the southern province of Katanga (Shaba). They maintained a presence until June 1964, contributing to the confusion of Congolese affairs, but their withdrawal proved only temporary. Between August and November 1964 a fresh crisis threatened the Congolese government and led to renewed Belgian intervention, albeit on a smaller scale.

The trouble centred upon the eastern province of Kivu and came to a head on 5 August when rebel forces under General Nicholas Olenga (a supporter of Christophe Gbenya's Conseil National de Libération) seized the provincial capital of Stanleyville (Kisangani). In itself this was hardly a cause for international outcry, but in the process Olenga captured about 1500 foreign nationals – including 30 Americans and 600 Belgians – and held them hostage, hoping thereby to prevent outside support being given to the Congolese prime minister, Moise Tshombe. Amidst threats to the hostages' lives and rumours of massacre, both Washington and Brussels viewed the crisis with growing concern. At this period the Congo seemed to be in a state of near anarchy, with large areas of the country ungovernable, but the West was committed to supporting Tshombe in addition to any humanitarian concerns.

Facing escalation in Vietnam and an imminent presidential election, the Americans were loath to become directly involved in a rescue mission, however, and the onus of action fell to the Belgians. President Lyndon B. Johnson authorised the provision of US transport aircraft and a joint US-Belgian plan was formulated, but the projected paradrop on Stanleyville had to be a Belgian operation. Code-named 'Dragon Rouge', it envisaged a swift 'in-out' rescue mission, coordinated with a ground attack by a column of Tshombe's forces (including white mercenaries under Colonel Mike Hoare), commanded by the Belgian adviser Colonel Frederick Van de Waele.

The Belgians decided to use two battalions of their Paracommando Regiment for the assault on Stanleyville (the third battalion consisted of conscript recruits with less than a month's basic training), and despite problems of unfamiliarity with the American C-130s and a complete lack of accurate intelligence, 545 men, commanded by Colonel Charles Laurent, flew via Ascension Island to the Congo in late November. At 0600 hours on the 24th, 320 paras dropped onto the golf course at Stanleyville and, after slight delays, the 11th Paracommando Company moved into town to rescue the hostages. They were almost too late – 22 hostages were killed and 40 wounded as the rebels opened fire in panic – but by 1100 hours contact had been made with Van de Waele, Stanleyville had been secured and over 250 Europeans flown out. A similar operation – 'Dragon Noir' – two days later rescued a further 200 at Paulis (Isiro) to the northeast, and by the time of the Belgian withdrawal on 29 November, nearly 2000 hostages had been evacuated, all for the loss of only three paras killed. For an army with little combat experience (and virtually none in airborne operations) it was a remarkable achievement.

Such an interventionary capability is clearly a useful asset in any army – it was to be used again by the Belgians in May 1978 when the Paracommandos backed up French forces during the rescue of hostages in Shaba – but it should not overshadow the fact that the Belgian Army was, and still remains, a Nato force. With two brigades of 1st Belgian Corps stationed permanently in West Germany and a further two ready to move forward from Belgium in the event of a crisis, the defence of Western Europe clearly has top priority.

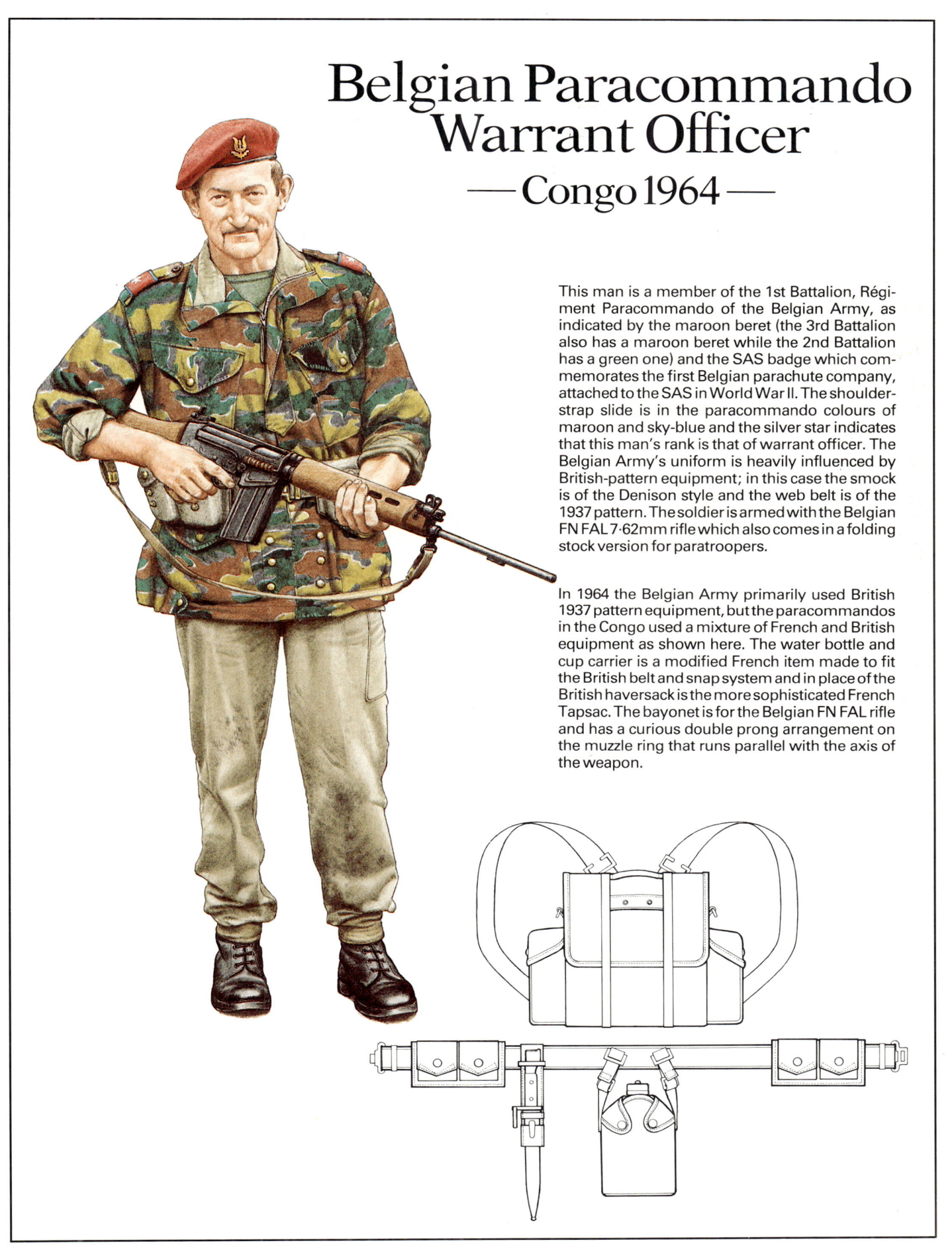

Belgian Paracommando Warrant Officer
—Congo 1964—

This man is a member of the 1st Battalion, Régiment Paracommando of the Belgian Army, as indicated by the maroon beret (the 3rd Battalion also has a maroon beret while the 2nd Battalion has a green one) and the SAS badge which commemorates the first Belgian parachute company, attached to the SAS in World War II. The shoulder-strap slide is in the paracommando colours of maroon and sky-blue and the silver star indicates that this man's rank is that of warrant officer. The Belgian Army's uniform is heavily influenced by British-pattern equipment; in this case the smock is of the Denison style and the web belt is of the 1937 pattern. The soldier is armed with the Belgian FN FAL 7·62mm rifle which also comes in a folding stock version for paratroopers.

In 1964 the Belgian Army primarily used British 1937 pattern equipment, but the paracommandos in the Congo used a mixture of French and British equipment as shown here. The water bottle and cup carrier is a modified French item made to fit the British belt and snap system and in place of the British haversack is the more sophisticated French Tapsac. The bayonet is for the Belgian FN FAL rifle and has a curious double prong arrangement on the muzzle ring that runs parallel with the axis of the weapon.

WESTERN EUROPE

The Portuguese Army in Africa

Left: Armed with West German G3 rifles a unit of Portuguese troops pauses in the bush while on patrol in Angola.

Although the Portuguese Army had been one of the few European armies not to be involved in World War II, it found itself embroiled in a long costly war in Africa during the 1960s and early 1970s. The three African territories of Guinea-Bissau, Angola and Mozambique were by far the most important possessions of the Portuguese Empire. In all three colonies nationalist revolts broke out in the early 1960s and developed into guerrilla wars of national liberation with the Portuguese Army forced to abandon its former role of colonial policeman and undertake a series of full-scale campaigns to suppress the guerrillas.

Limited troop levels and shortages of military resources led to a hesitant reaction by the Portuguese forces in the first stages of the war. The initiative lay with the guerrillas so that the army was forced on the defensive. This changed in 1968, however, when the Portuguese – having built up their forces – implemented all-out counter-insurgency warfare in their three African possessions.

The Portuguese were influenced by the Americans and besides having a reputed 2000 men trained in America in counter-insurgency warfare they adopted many methods and tactics then being employed in Vietnam. The two pillars upon which the Portuguese Army based its strategy were, firstly, a 'hearts and minds' campaign that concentrated upon a programme of civil improvements and, secondly, the comprehensive application of air power – utilising napalm and defoliants as well as conventional bombs – to interdict guerrilla supply routes and destroy their home bases. On the ground the brunt of the fighting was carried out by elite Portuguese units, namely paratroops, commandos and Marines. A large proportion of the colonial troops were drawn from the local black population, a ratio that was to increase as the war developed.

The Portuguese commitment grew steadily throughout the 1960s so that by the end of the decade an estimated 150,000 troops were stationed in Africa. While the Portuguese strategy was producing results in the field, the cost of the war to a relatively poor Western nation was taking its toll; increasingly the question being asked was whether the colonies were of real value to Portugal, especially as the human cost rose dramatically with some 11,000 dead and 30,000 wounded by 1974.

In the army itself this disillusionment found its fullest expression in the Armed Forces Movement, a group of radical officers whose dissatisfaction with the existing regime reached a peak in 1974 when they successfully carried out a military coup and established a provisional military government. The Armed Forces Movement regarded the colonial war as a fruitless anachronism; in Guinea-Bissau power was handed over to the nationalist organisation in 1974, and Angola and Mozambique followed in 1975.

By the 1980s the army had renounced its political role and returned to barracks. The war in Africa over, the size of the army was reduced to a realistic level in keeping with the requirements of national defence and Nato. In the early 1980s the army stood at 37,000 men (7000 regulars, the rest conscripts) divided into 15 infantry regiments and four armoured and three field-artillery regiments with engineer, signals and logistic support services.

Portuguese Para Corporal
—Mozambique 1970—

A French 1950-pattern camouflage uniform is worn by this soldier, as is a dark green paratroop beret; the cap badge is that of the air force, the arm of service which Portuguese paratroops came under. In addition, a paratroop brevet is worn above the right-breast pocket. Rank is indicated by the two light-blue chevrons on a slide attached to the shoulder straps. This soldier is armed with a West German 7.62mm HK21 general purpose machine gun.

Above: Black Portuguese troops in Angola stand to attention in ceremonial uniform during a parade.

WESTERN EUROPE

The Turkish Army in Cyprus

On 20 July 1974 elements of the Turkish Army, backed by air and naval units, invaded northern Cyprus. They were responding to a pro-Greek coup in Nicosia five days earlier which not only threatened the lives of the Turkish-Cypriot community but also opened up the prospect of the island being transformed into a Greek military base, only 64km (40 miles) from the Turkish mainland. As parachute forces landed in the Turkish-Cypriot village of Gönyeli, to the south of the St Hiralion Pass, and seaborne commandos carved out a beachhead to the west of Kyrenia, the chances of a swift and decisive campaign seemed high. The proximity of the island to Turkey ensured air and naval supremacy, the local Greek-Cypriot forces were weak, lacking manpower and heavy weapons, and surprise was total.

But the campaign was by no means an unqualified success. Heavy fighting in the St Hiralion Pass prevented an expansion of the beachhead and the road to Nicosia remained firmly closed. By 22 July the Turks had been forced to accept a ceasefire, and although they used the ensuing lull to build up their forces preparatory to a renewed offensive in mid-August, they could not achieve control of more than 40 per cent of the island, despite the deployment of an estimated 40,000 troops and 200 tanks. The Greeks, who did not intervene, were humiliated and the Greek-Cypriots could not stand before the sheer weight of Turkish numbers, but a combination of international pressure and domestic military shortcomings left the Turks in a less than ideal position. Since 1974 they have been forced to deploy a substantial garrison – currently 17,000 men, backed by 150 armoured fighting vehicles – on the island, their relations with the rest of Nato and particularly the United States have suffered and they must face the prospect of renewed conflict at all times. It is a classic case of the military option failing to achieve the desired political results – and the army is to blame.

It has always been a huge force – currently 470,000 men, organised into four armies and a host of support units – and, on paper at least, a relatively well equipped one, fielding an impressive array of tanks, artillery and even surface-to-surface missiles. But this is something of a facade, hiding a number of weaknesses which the 1974 campaign served to highlight. Because it depends to a large extent upon conscription, the army is unavoidably infantry-orientated and its soldiers, trained for only 20 months, lack the technical skills required for modern war. More importantly, the force has a tradition of deep involvement in the political processes of the Turkish state, organising full-scale coups in 1960 and 1980 – in the latter case producing a junta which has yet fully to relinquish power to civilian politicians. Such intervention dilutes the professionalism of the regular officer class, diverting its attention away from the acquisition of military skills, and this inevitably affects the army as a whole.

But there is more to it than that, for even without these problems the Turkish Army faces a dilemma which must undermine its capability to act decisively. Since the end of World War II it has been dedicated to the defence of the eastern Mediterranean area against the Soviet Union, contributing forces and base facilities to Western alliances such as Nato and Cento, protecting the vitally important Bosphorus Straits and permitting the deployment of American radars on the northern border with Russia. Yet since the 1960s a more immediate threat has gradually emerged which acts against these interests, for with the growth of conflict with Greece – a fellow-member of Nato – over both the Aegean islands and the future of Cyprus, the emphasis of defence priority has shifted. The 1974 campaign was a manifestation of this shift and one which disrupted the structure of Nato on its southern flank. The Greeks left the military framework of the alliance and the Americans imposed a crippling arms embargo on the Turks. Since then the situation has been improved, but as long as Turkish forces remain in Cyprus the army has to be prepared to divide its attention between two potentially conflicting defence priorities.

Above: The diverse origin of Turkish Army equipment is shown by these variously kitted men standing in front of war booty near Kyrenia. About 40,000 troops were deployed on Cyprus in 1974 but 10 years later the garrison had been reduced to 17,000.

Below: A Turkish machine-gun position in an olive grove manned by soldiers in leopard spot camouflage uniforms.

Turkish Soldier
— Cyprus 1974 —

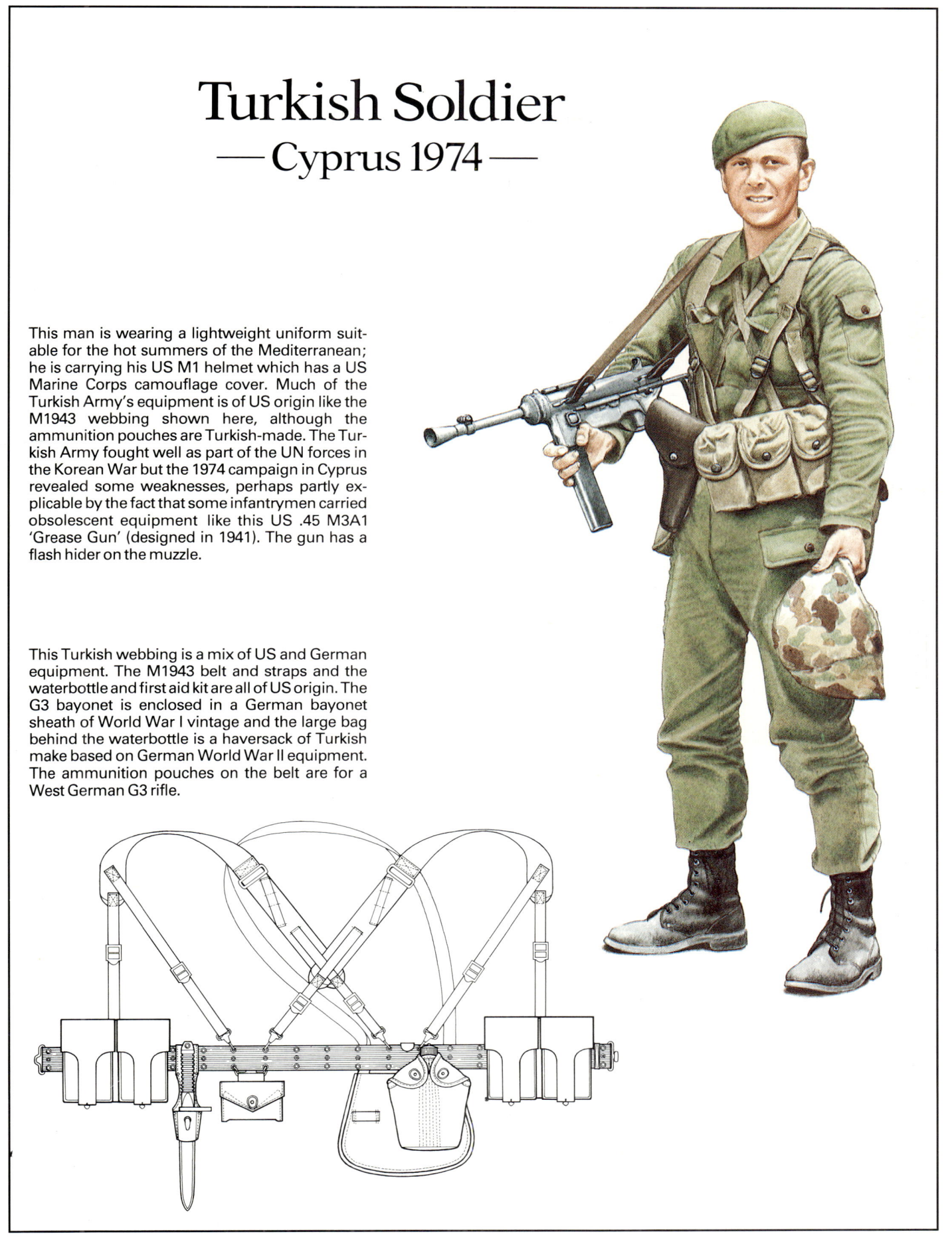

This man is wearing a lightweight uniform suitable for the hot summers of the Mediterranean; he is carrying his US M1 helmet which has a US Marine Corps camouflage cover. Much of the Turkish Army's equipment is of US origin like the M1943 webbing shown here, although the ammunition pouches are Turkish-made. The Turkish Army fought well as part of the UN forces in the Korean War but the 1974 campaign in Cyprus revealed some weaknesses, perhaps partly explicable by the fact that some infantrymen carried obsolescent equipment like this US .45 M3A1 'Grease Gun' (designed in 1941). The gun has a flash hider on the muzzle.

This Turkish webbing is a mix of US and German equipment. The M1943 belt and straps and the waterbottle and first aid kit are all of US origin. The G3 bayonet is enclosed in a German bayonet sheath of World War I vintage and the large bag behind the waterbottle is a haversack of Turkish make based on German World War II equipment. The ammunition pouches on the belt are for a West German G3 rifle.

WESTERN EUROPE

French Foreign Legion Paras in Kolwezi

Since 1945 there have been few full-scale airborne assaults and most armies have tended to use their parachute forces as elite infantry, committing them to battle by conventional means. But such forces retain the key advantages of flexibility and tough professionalism, and these can be exploited for small-scale airborne operations, particularly for rapid rescue missions. A combined mercenary and Belgian paratroop force showed the possibilities by rescuing over 2000 hostages held by Chinese-backed rebels in Stanleyville, Zaire, in 1964. The lesson was reinforced 14 years later, in the same country, by the French.

The crisis began on 11 May 1978, when 4000 members of the Congo National Liberation Front invaded the mineral-rich province of Shaba in southern Zaire. Within 48 hours they had seized the important mining town of Kolwezi – in itself a seemingly local affair, but one that assumed international proportions when reports began to filter through of a massacre of European mineworkers. Western powers were forced to take notice, and Britain, France, Belgium and the United States began to monitor the situation with growing concern. In the event, however, only the French were willing to act: on 17 May the 2nd Foreign Legion Parachute Regiment (2REP), stationed at Camp Raffali near Calvi on the island of Corsica, was ordered to stand by. Early the next morning the first troops boarded specially-chartered DC8 aircraft, and within 24 hours the entire regiment had moved out.

Such a rapid response reflected well on the capabilities of 2REP, but once in Zaire the problems began. As the situation in Kolwezi deteriorated, speed was of the essence, yet the Zaireans could provide no more than four C130s, capable of carrying less than half the regiment, and no time was available for reconnaissance of a suitable drop-zone (DZ). Displaying remarkable initiative, the commander of 2REP, Colonel Philippe Erulin, packed three companies onto the available aircraft and, with no knowledge of enemy strengths or dispositions, flew to Kolwezi. Arriving early on 19 May, the paras chose a DZ and literally jumped into the unknown.

Fortunately the rebels, intent on looting, were badly deployed, and the paras landed safely, moving swiftly into the town and setting up defensive positions. As they advanced, opposition hardened to produce some bitter house-to-house fighting, but by nightfall key buildings were in French hands and the first of the Europeans had been liberated. On 20 May a fourth company and the support sections of 2REP were landed without mishap, and by the 25th, for the loss of only five killed and 20 wounded, the paras had forced the rebels to withdraw towards Angola. Over 2000 Europeans were rescued in all.

The lessons were not lost on France's allies: over the next few years both Britain and the United States created rapid deployment airborne forces, capable of mounting similar operations. The paras had rediscovered a jumping role and for this they must thank the tough professionals of 2REP.

Above left: Colonel Philippe Erulin, commanding officer of the 2nd Foreign Legion Parachute Regiment at Kolwezi. A veteran of the Algerian War, Erulin was well suited to lead a difficult assignment. Above: Men of the 2nd Foreign Legion Parachute Regiment march towards Kolwezi from their dropping zone to the north of the town, 19 May 1978. The elephant grass provides good cover.

French Foreign Legion Para Corporal
— Kolwezi 1978 —

As a soldier in the 2nd Foreign Legion Parachute Regiment (2 REP) this corporal wears the French 'Satin 300' combat uniform, especially tailored for the Legion with short jacket and narrow trousers. Hanging from the webbing belt are a bayonet, a multi-pocketed bag for grenades and a leather pouch for holding weapon-cleaning equipment. French ranger boots – based on the US World War II model – are worn, while headgear consists of the green Legion beret with the regimental version of the French parachute badge. Other features include green rank chevrons fixed to the chest by a Velcro patch and a black scarf worn over the left shoulder – a field recognition sign for troops taking part in the Kolwezi operation.

Below: This webbing equipment is typical of that worn at Kolwezi and is based on US designs but with French modifications. Hanging from the belt are – from the left – a grenade carrier (with straps to tie onto the thigh), a pouch for spare MAT 49 magazines, a weapon cleaning-kit pouch, a water bottle and a second ammunition pouch. Attached to the shoulder straps is a First Aid pouch.

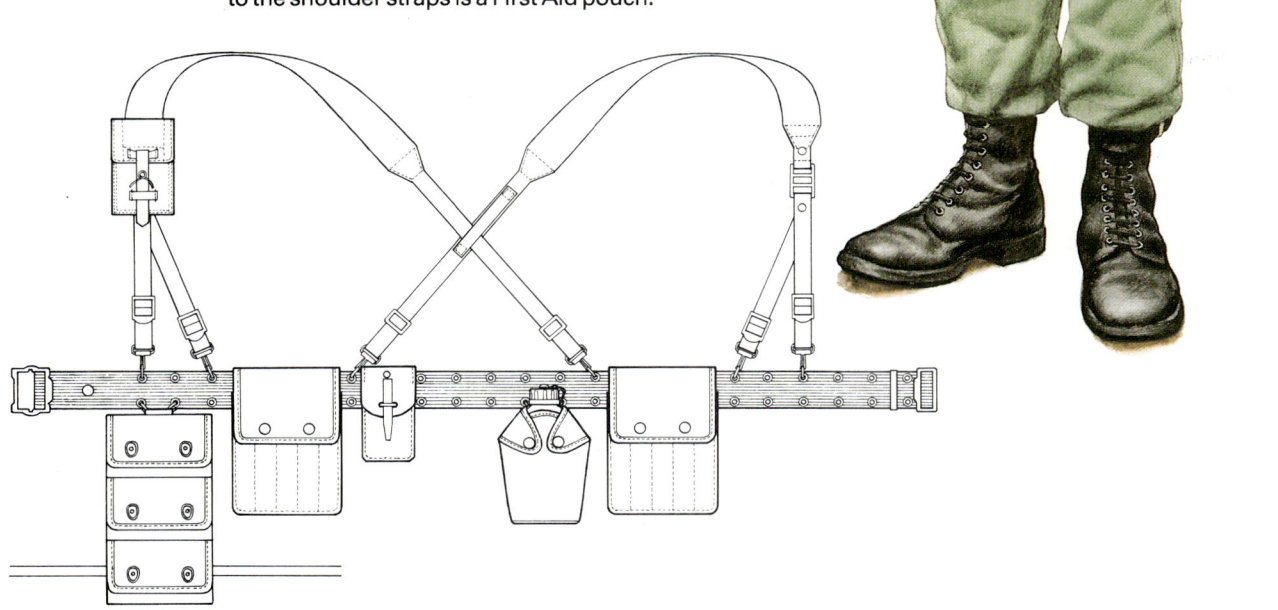

WESTERN EUROPE

The Italian Army in Lebanon

On 21 August 1982 the first elements of a special Multi-National Force (MNF), comprising troops from France, Italy and the United States, arrived in Beirut to supervise the evacuation of Palestinian and Syrian soldiers caught in the city by the Israeli invasion of the previous June (Operation Peace for Galilee). The commitment was not a lengthy one: by 30 August over 14,000 evacuees had been escorted on board ships bound for a variety of Arab states and on 10 September, as Lebanon enjoyed a period of relative calm, the MNF was withdrawn.

For the Italians, this was part of a policy of growing involvement in peacekeeping duties in the Middle East. Earlier in the year they had contributed a Coastal Patrol Unit of three minesweepers (90 men) to the Multi-National Force and Observers (MFO) in Sinai, deployed to guarantee the terms of the disengagement treaty between Israel and Egypt, and they had committed a token force of 40 men to the United Nations Interim Force in (southern) Lebanon (UNIFIL) that had been swept aside during Peace for Galilee. For a country dedicated to maintaining its defence exclusively within the framework of Nato, this was a significant departure, reflecting a new desire for influence within the Mediterranean area, and it was a policy that was soon to be repeated. As the Israelis renewed their assaults into West Beirut on 15 September 1982, in the aftermath of the assassination of the president-elect of Lebanon, Bashir Gemayel, the MNF was hastily reconstituted and redeployed. Each contributory power – at this stage still the United States, France and Italy – made a bilateral agreement with the Lebanese government, now under Gemayel's elder brother Amin, and was allocated a particular area in or around Beirut, where they were to create a buffer between the warring factions. The Israelis, under enormous domestic and international pressure as a result of the massacre by their Christian Lebanese allies of Palestinian refugees in the camps at Sabra and Chatila, pulled back to the south of Beirut as the MNF came ashore.

The Italian contingent was the largest of the three, comprising over 2000 men equipped with M113 armoured personnel carriers but few support weapons. The bulk of the force was made up of three battalions – one of Marines, one of paratroopers (the latter drawn from the elite *Paracadutisti* brigade Folgore) and one of mechanised infantry – backed by engineers, logistics personnel and a small headquarters staff. With the American 24th Marine Amphibious Unit dug in to their south around the international airport, and French Marines and Foreign Legionnaires to their north in the urban complex of Beirut itself, the Italians found themselves responsible for an area containing a host of potential problems. The relatively open nature of the ground in the south, on the perimeter of the airport, necessitated the construction of fortified posts in case of attack, while in the centre and north the sprawl of refugee camps, including Sabra and Chatila, needed constant patrolling and guarding. Furthermore, as the so-called 'Green Line', set up to separate the Muslim and Christian communities, bisected the Italian area, they had also to man crossing-points and monitor possible infiltration by the rival groups. The latter responsibility was made easier in February 1983 when a small contingent of British troops arrived to provide assistance.

Above: Italian paratroops, having just disembarked from their transports, form up before moving out into Beirut. The inhabitants of the city were reassured by the presence of the Italian contingent of the Multi-National Force, and it suffered fewer casualties than the US or French contingents.

The MNF remained in Beirut until February 1984, being withdrawn only when its position became untenable in the face of renewed inter-factional fighting. The Italians' low-key presence, reflecting a predilection for policing rather than aggressive support for the Gemayel regime, allowed them to escape the armed opposition that led both the Americans and the French to suffer substantial casualties; and the sight of Italian patrols, ostentatiously displaying their nationality on board uncamouflaged vehicles, was a reassuring one for the local population, particularly the Palestinian refugees. The withdrawal may have been an unsatisfactory end-result of the MNF experiment, but the commitment of the Italians was both impressive and, with the MFO and UNIFIL contingents still in place, a sign of future interest in the tortuous politics of the Middle East.

Italian Para Sergeant-Major
—Beirut 1982—

This sergeant-major of the Italian paratroops is dressed in camouflage jump overalls with knee-pads. Like many parachute units, that of the Italian Army has a maroon beret, shown here with the badge of the *Paracadutisti* branch of infantry. The silver star of Savoy on the collar points is a reminder of the Italian Army's origins in the army of the Kingdom of Sardinia-Piedmont. Rank is indicated by the chevrons on the left breast-pocket of the tunic, and there is a name-tag on the right breast-pocket. The belt is based on the British 1937 pattern webbing and the rifle is the BM59 Ital Para from Beretta, derived from the US Garand M1.

Below: Officers of the Multi-National Force meet on the Beirut docks; the man in the centre is an Italian paratrooper and two of his countrymen, members of the elite Bersaglieri, *are on the right. The Multi-National Force remained in Beirut from September 1982 to February 1984, when it pulled out at the renewal of Lebanese civil strife.*

Latin America

Until the Argentinian invasion of the Falkland Islands in April 1982, the armies of Latin America had appeared only rarely in the world headlines. With the exception of the 'Football War' between Honduras and El Salvador in July 1969 – a relatively minor affair, triggered by the result of a World Cup qualifying match, but indicative of a much deeper rivalry – there had been no conventional conflicts in the region since the Peruvian invasion of Ecuador in 1941. Although some Latin American armies had amassed a wealth of experience in internal security, they had also gained a well-deserved reputation for corruption, inefficiency and overt interference in the political processes of the state.

Several Latin American armies continue to occupy a central, controlling, place in the government of their states, based upon a tradition of military rule that in some cases dates back over 100 years. Once such a pattern exists, it is extremely difficult to break, as is evidenced by the fact that since 1945 there have been more than 70 successful (and over 50 failed) military coups in Latin America. The resultant juntas have varied considerably in popularity and effectiveness but most have been tempted to adopt repressive measures against their own people to prevent a counter-coup or popular revolution. Even so, many leaders have failed to ensure the survival of their governments, regardless of their ruthless approach to internal policing. For example, in July 1979 the Nicaraguan armed forces could not prevent a takeover of power by the Sandinista revolutionary movement, and in June 1982 General Galtieri's power in Argentina slipped dramatically through his fingers as his troops faced defeat in the Falklands. Other governments, turning a blind eye to the activities of quasi-official 'death squads', have surrendered their political credibility both at home and abroad. In extreme cases, such as in El Salvador in the early 1980s, this can lead to bitter and bloody civil war.

Attempts are often made to justify ruthless military behaviour in terms of the threat to Latin America from left-wing revolutionary groups, supported and supposedly orchestrated by Cuba and the Soviet Union. Fidel Castro's success in Cuba (1956–59), using revolutionaries and popular support to isolate, wear down and demoralise government armed forces preparatory to a seizure of political power, took most of Latin America (as well as the United States) by surprise; when Castro turned to the Soviets for aid in the early 1960s, the mainland governments acquired an acute fear of 'communist expansionism'. This fear was increased between 1962 and 1967, when revolutionaries based in Cuba tried to 'export' the model of their campaign to the countries of Latin America, aiming to create a belt of leftist governments that would isolate the United States. In the event, the attempt was a failure, culminating in the death of Che Guevara in Bolivia in 1967, but the effects on Latin American armies were dramatic. Taking full advantage of US offers of aid, many were trained specifically for counter-insurgency by CIA or 'Green Beret' advisers and received seemingly unlimited quantities of modern military equipment, including armoured personnel carriers, automatic smallarms and helicopters. Moreover, with the Cuban model available for analysis, military units were often deployed to remote rural areas, where the revolutionaries had hoped to initiate their campaigns.

In the 1970s and 1980s the fear of Soviet-backed Cuban expansionism did not abate. The commitment of Cuban troops to Angola in 1975, followed by similar moves into Ethiopia three years later, seemed to suggest a new global pattern of intervention, but the fall of the Somoza regime in Nicaragua in July 1979 brought the focus firmly back onto Central America, where trade and communications routes (particularly the Panama Canal) are vital to the US economy and strategic position. The success of the Sandinistas led to a new burst of US activity, manifested in aid to their opponents in Nicaragua as well as to those pro-American governments that remained in El Salvador, Guatemala and Honduras. Overt US intervention on the mainland was ruled out for fear of a 'second Vietnam', but this did not prevent an invasion of Grenada (October 1983) by US Rangers, Marines and paratroops, when Cuban involvement on the island seemed suddenly to increase and local politics took an extremist turn.

The combination of increased US aid and prolonged domestic experience of counter-insurgency undoubtedly boosted the confidence of many Latin American armies, and it is against this background that the Argentinian decision to defy a foreign power in the Falklands should be judged. On paper it was a tempting policy to adopt, for the Argentinians, apparently secure in their relations with the United States and desperate for international prestige, had the manpower and equipment to take the islands with overwhelming force. But it proved to be a miscalculation, not just because the British (backed by the United States) displayed unexpected resolve, but also because the Argentinian Army, after years of political involvement and concentration on internal policing, was not prepared for conventional war. Its conscripts were poorly trained, many of its officers were corrupt, and it lacked the technical expertise to exploit much of its Western-manufactured equipment to best advantage. Some Argentinian units – notably the Marines and Special Forces – displayed a degree of professionalism, but in the end the Argentinian Falklands garrison was overwhelmed by superior military skill. This is a problem that the Argentinian Army is likely to share with its counterparts elsewhere in Latin America: as political power-brokers and ruthless policemen, the armies have wide experience and, in most cases, proven ability, but on a modern battlefield, pitted against professional and well-trained soldiers, they are dangerously weak.

Right: A patrol of Eden Pastora's wing of ARDE, the Costa Rica-based Contra group, move warily through the Nicaraguan jungle, 1984. The patrol leader is armed with a US M79 grenade launcher, while his follower carries a Soviet AK-47 assault rifle: a typical 'mix' of weapons which does nothing to simplify logistics.

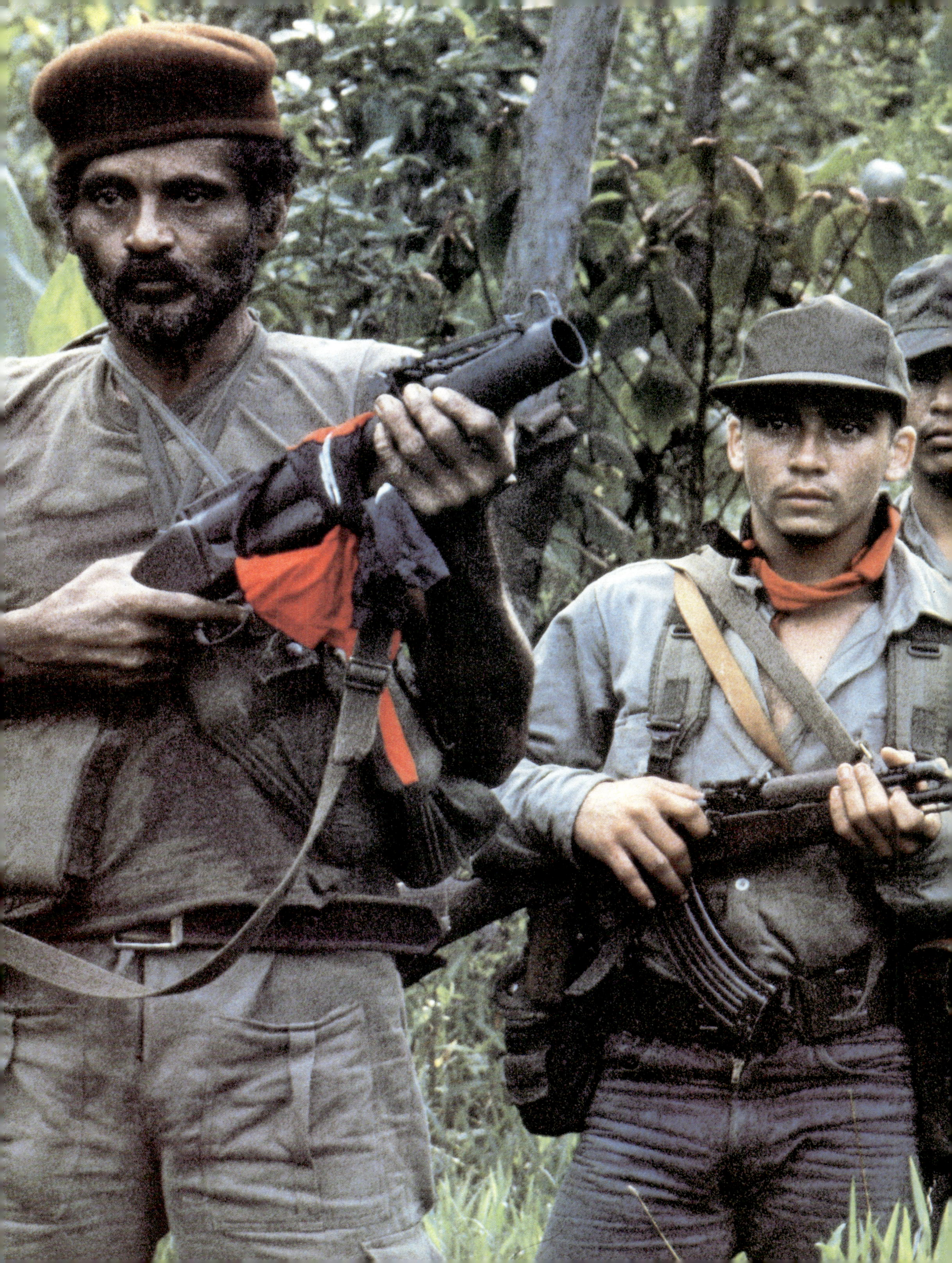

The Cuban Revolutionary Army

On 2 January 1959 revolutionary fighters of Fidel Castro's 26 July Movement entered Havana, the capital of Cuba. The incumbent president, Fulgencio Batista, had already fled and, despite continued opposition from small groups of police and army personnel, the revolutionaries were soon able to seize control. It was a remarkable achievement, coming only two years after Castro's initial landing in the eastern province of Oriente, and it seemed to mark a new era in the history of revolutionary guerrilla warfare. The protracted nature of such conflicts, emphasised and practised by Mao Tse-tung in China between 1927 and 1949, was apparently out of date; instead, as Castro had shown, small groups of dedicated fighters could now undermine and defeat the security forces of a state in a much shorter time, delayed only by the need to establish rudimentary bases and some measure of popular support.

But in reality the Cuban revolution was much more complex. Opposition to Batista – a corrupt and inefficient dictator who came to depend more and more on repression to survive – took many different forms, of which Castro's campaign was only one. Castro himself had come to prominence in Cuba by leading an abortive assault on the army barracks at Moncada on 26 July 1953 – an incident that bore more resemblance to traditional Latin American methods of direct action than to the lengthy process of Chinese-style revolution – and his subsequent

Above: Three members of Fidel Castro's forces just after entering the town of Santa Clara. Dressed in fatigues, they are armed with (from left to right) a US 0.3in M1903 Springfield, a US 0.3in M1 Carbine and a US 0.3in M1 Garand.

success in the remote mountains of Oriente Province (the Sierra Maestra) could not have been achieved without firm support from elsewhere. The urban wing of the 26 July Movement, led initially by Frank País, was in fact more strongly established in Oriente than the *fidelistas* (Castro's personal followers) in the mid-1950s, and its campaign of unrest in the towns undoubtedly prepared the way for the development of a rural guerrilla movement, diverting security forces away from the mountain bases at key times. The urban activists also set up an infrastructure of support, capable of channelling food, weapons, recruits and intelligence to Castro's men, while other groups – notably the radical Directorio Revolucionario and the communist Partido Socialista Popular – mounted separate attacks on Batista. Castro's main contribution was to act as a focus, attracting and absorbing the disparate opposition groups preparatory to an armed assault on the centre of power which could only be carried out by the experienced guerrillas under his command. The fact that they succeeded gave Castro eventual victory, but it did not mean that they alone created the revolution.

In fact, for much of their two-year campaign, the *fidelistas* were remarkably weak, suffering all the disadvantages of operating in a remote, inhospitable region, isolated from their support networks and unsure of the attitude of local peasants. Within four days of the initial landing in Oriente, nearly three-quarters of Castro's fighters had been killed or captured in an army ambush, leaving the remainder to wander rather aimlessly through difficult terrain, short of food, armaments and information. Castro's qualities as a guerrilla leader were certainly tested during this period, as a small but viable fighting force was gradually created, capable of taking on and defeating isolated army outposts, but he was perhaps fortunate that Batista proved unable to engender support for his regime as the various opposition factions developed. By early 1958 Castro could still field less than 100 armed guerrillas, and although he had begun to carve out a 'safe base' in the Sierra Maestra, it was a slow business, fraught with the dangers of betrayal and sudden defeat. This makes the expansion of the guerrillas during that year – initially to a new base in northern Oriente and then to link up with other groups in the central provinces of Cuba – all the more remarkable, although it is interesting to note that even as late as December Castro could command no more than 1500 fighting men. Without the collapse of Batista under a myriad of other pressures, it is difficult to see how the revolutionaries could have prevailed.

Nevertheless, the success of the *fidelistas* implied that Castro had evolved a new and effective theory of revolutionary war and this led other, similar, groups to emulate his example. The fact that they all failed in the Latin America of the 1960s reinforces the point that Cuba was a unique experience, skilfully exploited by Castro but not entirely of his making.

Cuban Revolutionary Soldier
—Cuba 1959—

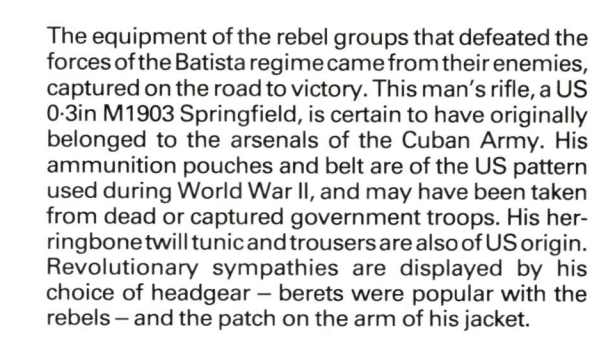

The equipment of the rebel groups that defeated the forces of the Batista regime came from their enemies, captured on the road to victory. This man's rifle, a US 0·3in M1903 Springfield, is certain to have originally belonged to the arsenals of the Cuban Army. His ammunition pouches and belt are of the US pattern used during World War II, and may have been taken from dead or captured government troops. His herringbone twill tunic and trousers are also of US origin. Revolutionary sympathies are displayed by his choice of headgear — berets were popular with the rebels — and the patch on the arm of his jacket.

Below: Cuban revolutionaries guard Castro as he enters the newly-captured town of Santa Clara, in January 1959. These battle-hardened veterans of the campaigns in the Sierra Maestra mountains of southeastern Cuba are well equipped with arms either smuggled to them by their compatriots in the towns or captured from the soldiers of the Batista regime.

LATIN AMERICA

The Cuban Army in Angola

The southern African state of Angola was destined to receive its independence from Portugal on 11 November 1975. Despite attempts by the outgoing colonial rulers to create a viable successor government, rival nationalist factions, supported by a variety of outside powers, fought an increasingly bitter civil war as that date approached. Best placed to seize control was Dr Agostinho Neto's Movimento Popular de Libertação de Angola (MPLA), but its hold on the central provinces of the state, including the capital Luanda, was seriously threatened from two directions. In the north, units of Holden Roberto's Frente Nacional de Libertação de Angola (FNLA), aided by regular troops from Zaire, were moving perilously close to Luanda, while in the south a combined assault by Jonas Savimbi's União Nacional para a Independência Total de Angola (UNITA) and elements of the South African Defence Force had taken vast tracts of territory. As the FNLA and UNITA were also receiving financial aid and weapons, via the CIA, from the United States, the chances of Neto even surviving until independence seemed slim.

He was saved by the timely arrival of a substantial expeditionary force from Cuba. Committed in response to urgent requests from both Luanda and Moscow, the Cubans were no strangers to Angola or to the MPLA. A small group of 'advisers' had been attached to Neto's command since the early 1960s, and their enthusiasm for social, agricultural and military projects had ensured their popularity. To the Soviets, aware that the deployment of their own troops would lead inevitably to superpower confrontation, the Cubans constituted an ideal 'proxy' force, although there is evidence to suggest that Fidel Castro, the Cuban leader, would have answered Neto's call for increased aid even without pressure from Moscow. This is implied by the fact that 480 'instructors' – carried across the Atlantic in three ships (*Vietnam Heroico*, *Coral Island* and *La Plata*) – arrived in Luanda in early October 1975, before the South African invasion.

Despatched into the central provinces to set up training camps for the MPLA, these instructors caught the full force of the South African/UNITA attack and, in the words of a Cuban spokesman, they were forced 'to break off their classes to lead their apprentice soldiers against the invaders, teaching them during lulls in battle'. It was a tough baptism of fire, made worse by the lack of heavy weapons available, and the inevitable defeat of these men triggered a larger Cuban commitment. The decision seems to have been taken in Havana on 5 November, although the fact that a battalion of 650 'well trained and politically educated' soldiers could be deployed within 48 hours suggests the existence of a contingency plan. Even so, the movement across the Atlantic on board aged Bristol Britannia transport cannot have been pleasant, particularly as the soldiers had to carry arms and ammunition with them. As soon as they landed, they were sent north to defend Luanda but, once again, their shortage of heavy weapons left them vulnerable to FNLA/Zairean attack.

It was at this point that the Soviets made a crucial contribution for, as more Cubans flew in, they provided tanks, rocket-launchers and artillery to the expeditionary force. This strengthened the forces to the north of Luanda to a decisive extent; on 12 November, 24 hours after independence had been granted, they caught an FNLA/Zairean spearhead in the open and, after blasting it into panic-stricken retreat with Katyusha rockets, opened the way for an MPLA advance. The Cubans then turned to blunt the South African/UNITA assault and, as more reinforcements arrived by both sea and air, the balance of power in Angola tilted towards Neto. By January 1976, with an estimated 11,000 Cubans deployed, the opposition had wilted. The US Congress had cut off all aid to Angola for fear of another Vietnam, the Zaireans had retreated in some disarray and the South Africans had pulled back into Namibia. The fighting was by no means over – the subsequent resurgence of UNITA activity has forced the Cubans to maintain an expeditionary force of 19,000 men in Angola – but a pattern of Cuban intervention had been established. It was to be repeated over the next few years, notably in Ethiopia. The Cubans had proved an extremely effective interventionary force; their cohesion and discipline and their Soviet-supplied weaponry had been the deciding factors in the Angolan Civil War.

Above: A Cuban soldier has his boots polished while off-duty in Luanda, the capital of Angola. In his hip holster he carries a PM-63 9mm Polish machine pistol.

Cuban Soldier
—Angola 1976—

This man's equipment, as would be expected, is dominated by Soviet items. The steel helmet is of Soviet design, as is the ammunition pouch. The survival knife is an interesting piece of equipment, with an insulated scabbard and hilt enabling it to be used as a wirecutter; he carries it in place of a bayonet for his 7·62mm AKM assault rifle. The green fatigues and web belt have a faintly American character, but are probably of Cuban make.

Below: Cuban and Angolan troops on a training exercise in the Angolan bush; they are armed with a combination of Soviet AKMs and West German Heckler and Koch G3s (probably handed over by Portuguese troops). Cuban troops played an important role in defeating the South African intervention in Angola in 1975-76, and remained in Angola after the end of the civil war to continue defending the MPLA regime.

LATIN AMERICA

The Salvadorean Army

led El Salvador to invade Honduras on 14 July. Advancing in three columns the Salvadorean forces were immediately successful and only an OAS ceasefire prevented the total destruction of the Honduran Army.

Since 1969 the army of El Salvador has mainly been involved in counter-insurgency operations. During the early 1970s left-wing opposition to the regime broke out into active guerrilla warfare and by the end of the decade the country was engaged in a full-scale civil war. The accession to power of Roberto d'Aubisson in 1982 was a major victory for the political right and since then the army has found itself allied alongside right-wing death squads in the fight against the guerrillas. In 1979 the leftist guerrilla movements were united in the FMNLF (Farabundo Martí National Liberation Front) and since then they have had considerable success amongst the rural population of El Salvador. And despite vast quantities of US aid – in terms of arms, equipment and advisers – the army has been unable to put down the guerrilla movement. Casualties have been high: 40,000 killed (mainly civilians), and yet despite the ferocity of the struggle neither side seems capable of outright victory.

Unlike its other Central American neighbours El Salvador has a strong military tradition based upon a professional officer corps, one relatively unaffected by the massive corruption so typical of the region. Chile was a major influence, its Prussian-derived military thinking shaping the style of the army in El Salvador. Chilean advisers were responsible for the direction of the War College from its foundation in 1941 until 1957, and although the United States has now become the major outside influence the Chilean traditions of old-fashioned élan are still unmistakably in evidence.

The 'football war' of 1969 against Honduras revealed the Salvadorean Army as an effective military instrument. Border clashes combined with an incident against a visiting Honduran football team

Above: Armed with West German G3 rifles, a fully equipped unit of El Salvadorean infantry patrols the countryside. Right: A young El Salvadorean relaxes after government troops have retaken a town. Armed with a G3, he also carries an American M67 'Baseball' fragmentation grenade.

Salvadorean Infantryman
— El Salvador 1980 —

Over an olive green uniform, US M1943 web equipment is worn, although the belt is the M56 model. America also supplies the M1 steel helmet and the nylon and black leather tropical boots. While the US M16 rifle is a common form of armament in the El Salvadorean Army, this soldier carries a West German 7.62mm G3A3 rifle.

Below: This equipment is based on the US 'ALICE' (All-purpose Lightweight Individual Carrying Equipment) model. The twin ammunition pouches are for the 7.62mm calibre of the G3 rifle, rather than the US 5.56mm M16 type. The water bottle is carried in an insulated carrier (with pockets for water purification tablets) while a folding entrenching tool is attached to the belt in a plastic carrier.

LATIN AMERICA

The Argentinian Army

The Argentinian armed forces were at a remarkably low point in public esteem when they agreed to hand over power to a democratically-elected government in 1983. In part this was due to their failure to deal with the nation's economic crisis and the brutality with which they had enforced internal security at the end of the 1970s, but its chief cause was their humiliating defeat at British hands in the 1982 Falklands conflict. Much of the blame for failure to match British troops in battle is ascribed to the Argentinian conscription system. Although Argentinian officers and NCOs are professional soldiers, the average infantryman is a conscript who serves a single year in the army; out of an army of 100,000 men some 80,000 are conscripts. There is no iron law which says that conscripts will not fight as well as volunteers but the one-year term of conscription is too short for Argentinian soldiers to complete training and gain much familiarity with their business. This deficiency was highlighted because their British opponents were so intensively trained and, particularly in the case of British paratroops, had undergone a savage and gruelling selection procedure before being allowed to join their regiments. Of course, the Argentinian insistence upon short-term, mass conscription is designed so that the army will act as a 'school of the nation' and foster national consciousness among recruits. This has its own value but it is at the expense of military efficiency.

British observers were reluctant to blame the Argentinian conscripts for their national debacle. They pointed out that the campaign was obviously desperately badly handled by the regular officers and NCOs. On the most basic level it transpired that supply was chaotically handled although the Argentinians had weeks to take up their positions and move up stores. Indeed it seemed that the Argentinian Army had no idea of a modern ration system and there were disturbing implications of the quality of their leadership in the more generous scale of officers' provisions. But, aside from the inability to manage the supply of a field force, Argentinian officers also showed an apparent ignorance of the principles of tactics and the conduct of war; during a long approach march the British were never counter-attacked and the discovery that the Argentinians had laid unmarked minefields is notorious.

Above: A forlorn-looking Argentinian conscript stands guard by a rudimentary bivouac line, armed with a somewhat obsolete US-made M3A1 sub-machine gun.
Below: A section of Argentinian Marines prepares for action against the British on the Falkland Islands. In contrast to the poorly-trained and badly-led conscripts who made up the bulk of the Argentinian armed forces the Marines were quality troops.

Criticism of the officer corps is all the more surprising in that Argentina has the national means for very thorough officer training. Cadets are schooled at the Colegio Militar which was founded in the nineteenth century and there is a long-established Staff College in the Escuela Superior de Guerra. For the highest military education there is the Centro de Altos Estudios. In addition to this Argentinian officers often go to the USA for training so there is no lack of academic teaching behind them. In the light of this it seems probable that the muddles in organisation and command owe quite a lot to the fact that many Argentinian officers have been sidetracked from military matters into politics and government and, most importantly, Argentina had not been at war since 1870; sheer lack of practice left the officer corps at a disadvantage.

Bearing these problems in mind the Argentinian Army's performance is not so discreditable as it seems. It is never a matter of pride to be turned out of strong prepared positions by a numerically inferior enemy or to have incompetence in the administration of a field force so publicly displayed. Although their reputation is lower now, the Argentinian armed forces were considered the best on the South American continent before the Falklands conflict and there is no doubt that, if they drew the lessons from their defeat, their performance would be much improved. Unfortunately from their point of view they are unlikely to see this practical benefit. Quarrelling between responsible officers and secrecy over the course of events leading to defeat make disinterested inquiry difficult.

Argentinian Marine Corporal
— Falklands 1982 —

Well equipped to deal with the cold of the Falklands winter, this Marine wears a quilted anorak over his standard green uniform. Underneath the US M1 helmet (with camouflage cover and tinted goggles) is a peaked cap with its ear flaps down. Attached to the chest is the insignia of rank (two red chevrons) and nationality (blue/white/blue patch) and carried over the shoulders are bandoliers for smallarms ammunition, while around the waist is a US web belt with canvas ammunition pouches. Like their British opponents the Argentinian ground forces were armed with the 7.62mm FN FAL rifle, fitted in this instance with a folding stock.

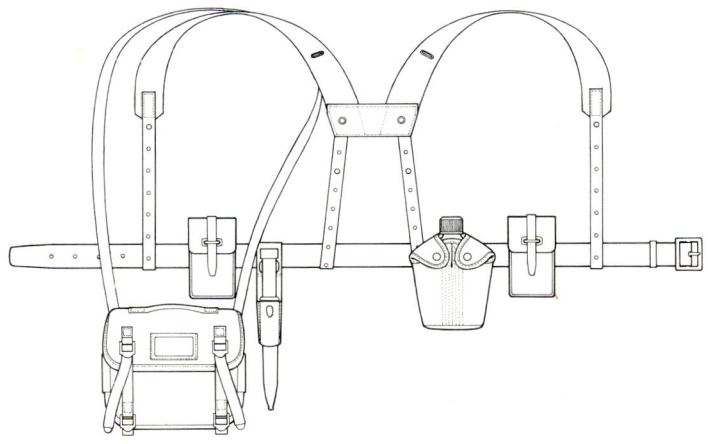

Above: Marines were, as a rule, better kitted-out than other Argentinian troops and this typical set of equipment includes ammunition pouches, bayonet frog, belt and shoulder straps in grey-green leather with a water bottle and side-pack in canvas.

Argentinian Special Forces

Special forces exist to carry out high-risk military operations that demand a greater degree of expertise and professionalism than is likely to be found in ordinary units. By their very nature, such forces invariably enjoy the benefits of the most modern weapons and equipment available, together with intensive training in their allotted tasks, often in cooperation with similar units of allied states. In 1982, at the time of the Falklands War, Argentinian special forces, represented by two companies of Marine Commandos (*Buzo Táctico*), were no exception. Trained to carry out clandestine operations, they were encountered by the British both in the initial Argentinian invasion of the islands and in the subsequent campaign of liberation.

Of the two companies in question, one – numbered 601 – appears to have been the more permanent, with its sister-unit (602) being raised specifically for the war from among commando-trained personnel elsewhere in the Argentinian Marines. As with so many special-force units, much of the organisational detail of these companies is shrouded in secrecy, but it has been reported that 601 – and, by implication, 602 – contained men who, in more peaceful times, had received specialised training from the US Rangers and even the British Special Air Service Regiment. What is known for sure is that neither company contained conscripts and that both, unlike the bulk of the Falklands occupation force, maintained their morale and military cohesion throughout the war.

As might be expected, 601 Company was heavily involved in the initial invasion on 2 April 1982. The first Argentinians ashore were frogmen of the company, sent in before dawn to capture Cape Pembroke lighthouse at the entrance to Port Stanley harbour, and they were followed at 0430 hours by up to 150 commandos (probably the full complement of the company), who were landed by helicopter at Mullett Creek, a small inlet some 5km (3 miles) to the southwest of the town. Once ashore, they divided into two groups, the larger of which headed north towards the Royal Marine barracks at Moody Brook. The intention was to neutralise the small British garrison preparatory to the main invasion – a typical special-force task – and although the move had been pre-empted and the commandos attacked an empty building, the speed and violence of their assault showed the level of their training in such operations. Beginning at 0615 hours, they surrounded the barracks, kicked open the doors and systematically destroyed each room with fragmentation and phosphorus grenades as well as sustained smallarms fire. If the Royal Marines had been in residence, few would have survived.

The fact remains, however, that this was largely wasted effort, implying a failure to appreciate the military skill of the opponent, and subsequent events reinforce the view that the men of the *Buzo Táctico* were not as efficient as might have been expected. As soon as it was realised that the Moody Brook assault had not succeeded, the commandos hurried to join the rest of the company, which had the task of snatching the Governor of the Falklands, Rex Hunt. But, once again, the move had been foreseen, and although the battle for Government House was one-sided, with the British troops outnumbered and outgunned, the Argentinian commandos failed to seize their victim and suffered casualties in the process. At least three men were hit, including an officer (killed as he tried to enter Government House), and three others temporarily captured. Photographs of Royal Marines surrendering to *Buzo Táctico* personnel, distinctive in their olive-drab uniforms and dark-blue knitted hats, suggested a military potential that, in reality, was not being fully realised.

This was made more apparent on 26 May, when 16 members of 602 Company tried to set up an observation post at Top Malo House to monitor the actions of the British liberation force. Attacked by elements of the Royal Marines Mountain and Arctic Warfare Cadre, they put up strong resistance, eventually succumbing to superior firepower, but they had clearly failed to carry out a task – covert surveillance – for which they had been specifically trained. As a fighting unit, the *Buzo Táctico* may have enjoyed advantages of morale, but in the end it did little to justify its claim to be a 'special force'.

Above: Argentinian special-force personnel – members of 601 Company of the Buzo Tactico – search a captured British serviceman (probably a member of the Falklands Defence Force) in the gardens of Government House, Port Stanley, 2 April 1982.

Buzo Tactico Commando
—Falklands 1982—

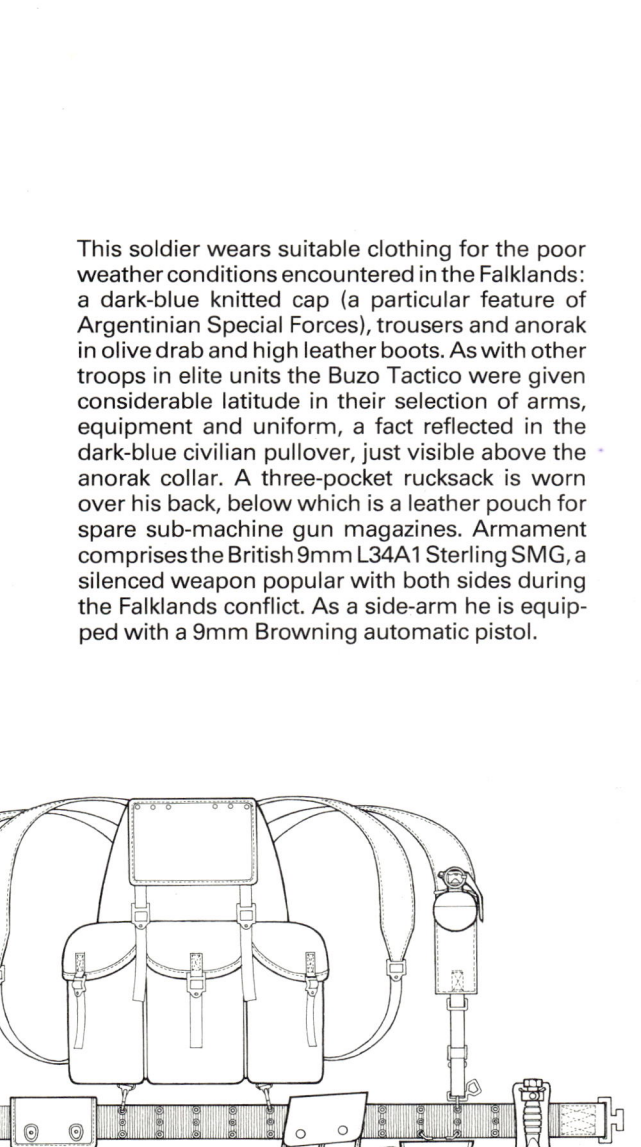

This soldier wears suitable clothing for the poor weather conditions encountered in the Falklands: a dark-blue knitted cap (a particular feature of Argentinian Special Forces), trousers and anorak in olive drab and high leather boots. As with other troops in elite units the Buzo Tactico were given considerable latitude in their selection of arms, equipment and uniform, a fact reflected in the dark-blue civilian pullover, just visible above the anorak collar. A three-pocket rucksack is worn over his back, below which is a leather pouch for spare sub-machine gun magazines. Armament comprises the British 9mm L34A1 Sterling SMG, a silenced weapon popular with both sides during the Falklands conflict. As a side-arm he is equipped with a 9mm Browning automatic pistol.

Above right: Underneath the rucksack is a US web belt with a selection of arms and equipment representing the variety of weapons carried by Argentina's Special Forces. From the left: an Argentinian ammunition pouch for holding FN rifle magazines; an old knife bayonet; a web magazine pouch for the Israeli-produced Uzi sub-machine gun; a brown leather pouch for soldiers armed with the Sterling SMG; a Browning pistol in a black leather holster; and a survival knife in its sheath. Attached to the webbing shoulder straps are two grenades.

Africa

The history of Africa since 1945 has been dominated by a process of decolonisation. When World War II ended, almost the entire continent was ruled by European powers intent on retaining control; 20 years later, independence had been granted to the majority of African states. In some cases, the transition was relatively smooth, but elsewhere, as the colonial powers resisted a rising tide of nationalism, the process was violent, leaving a legacy of bitterness and political confusion. Many of the new states emerged within borders imposed by the Europeans for strategic or economic convenience and immediately faced problems as central authorities were opposed by ethnic, tribal or religious minorities. Often civil war developed – in the Congo/Zaire (1960–64), Chad (since 1960), Nigeria (1967–70), and Angola (1975–76) – further weakening the state and leaving it vulnerable to outside interference and internal chaos.

In such circumstances armies proliferate, and quite often they become the key to state survival. In theory, they exist to protect the state against external attack, but with certain notable exceptions – the Somali assault on Ethiopia (1977) and the Tanzanian invasion of Uganda (1979) – such inter-state conflict has been rare. Yet many African countries insist on maintaining large armed forces, partly to enhance national prestige and provide a central body loyal to the government, but also because they are needed to carry out internal policing duties. This can be dangerous: deployed to oppose dissident (often tribal) groups with whom the soldiers may well feel sympathy, the army can become frustrated and resentful of its association with an unpopular central authority. Some armies (particularly those with a strong pre-independence tradition) accept their anomalous position and carry on to do their job dispassionately, but a significant proportion do not. Since 1960, when the first wave of declarations of independence swept Africa, there have been more than 50 successful (and over 70 abortive) military coups, producing regimes that range from the popular to the overtly tyrannical. Examples of the latter include the rule of Idi Amin in Uganda and that of the Emperor Bokassa I in the Central African Empire (now the Central African Republic). Whatever the outcome, the army is weakened by such experiences, which channel its energies into the pursuit and exercise of political power instead of into the acquisition of professional skills.

This is reflected in the record of those African armies that have been called upon to fight, for few have been able to mount decisive campaigns, despite being supplied with modern weapons and equipment from outside sources. During the Nigerian Civil War of 1967–70, for example, both the Federal and secessionist Biafran authorities raised large armies, but neither possessed the organisation, efficiency or tactical skill needed for easy victory. In this case, the Nigerian officer class (which contributed to both armies) had been weakened by its involvement in the coup and counter-coup of 1966 – but there were also other factors. Recruits, raised on a tribal basis, proved difficult to train, particularly in the art of cooperation with other tribal groups, and few were technically skilled enough to make the best use of modern equipment. In the end, Federal victory was achieved by superior numbers and fairly indiscriminate firepower; a horde of troops made more lethal by their access to European-supplied armoured cars, automatic weapons and aircraft, but incapable of mounting any subtle manoeuvres. Similar trends may be discerned in the armies of Chad, Zaire, Somalia and Ethiopia, as they found themselves involved in unexpected, full-scale conflicts.

But it would be wrong to dismiss the fighting abilities of African soldiers too lightly, for regardless of the experiences mentioned so far, the fact remains that many African states owe their independence in part to the activities of guerrilla forces, some of which enjoyed a significant success. A proportion of such forces fared badly against armies adept in the art of counter-insurgency: in Algeria the ALN had been contained by the French by the early 1960s, and in Namibia/South West Africa, SWAPO was still finding it difficult in 1985 to make much headway against the South Africans. However, most did achieve a degree of tactical initiative that undoubtedly contributed to European decisions to pull out. In Angola, for example, the various nationalist factions (the MPLA, FNLA and UNITA) managed to put enough pressure on the Portuguese to prepare the way for political change, and a similar contribution was made by FRELIMO in Mozambique and by the PAIGC in Guinea-Bissau. Such a tradition can be important in that it boosts national confidence and prestige, although it is worth pointing out that in most cases the army that emerged out of these guerrilla forces after independence immediately presumed a right to participate in government thus reinforcing the African trend towards military rule.

Africa's armies, like the states they serve or control, therefore face enormous problems. In the Congo/Zaire in the early 1960s it was only the deployment of UN troops to reverse the attempted secession of Moise Tshombe's Katanga (Shaba) province (itself dependent for its security on European mercenaries) that prevented a break-up of the state. This was to be repeated in 1964, when Belgian paracommandos intervened, and again in 1978, when it was the turn of the French Foreign Legion. Elsewhere, it was the deployment of Cuban forces, backed by Soviet weapons, that gave the MPLA victory in Angola (1975–76) and enabled the Ethiopians not only to mount a counter-attack against the Somalis (1978) but also to move against the Eritrean nationalists in the north. Such a dependence is indicative of Africa's political and military problems, and as long as they persist the level of violence in the continent is unlikely to diminish.

Right: Black troops, loyal to Portugal, parade for the camera, Mozambique, 1974. They are all dressed in Portuguese Army uniforms and carry West German 7.62mm Gewehr-3 (G3) assault rifles, manufactured under licence by Fábrica Militar de Braço de Prata (FBP) in Portugal. By 1974 over 60 per cent of Portuguese forces in Mozambique were black.

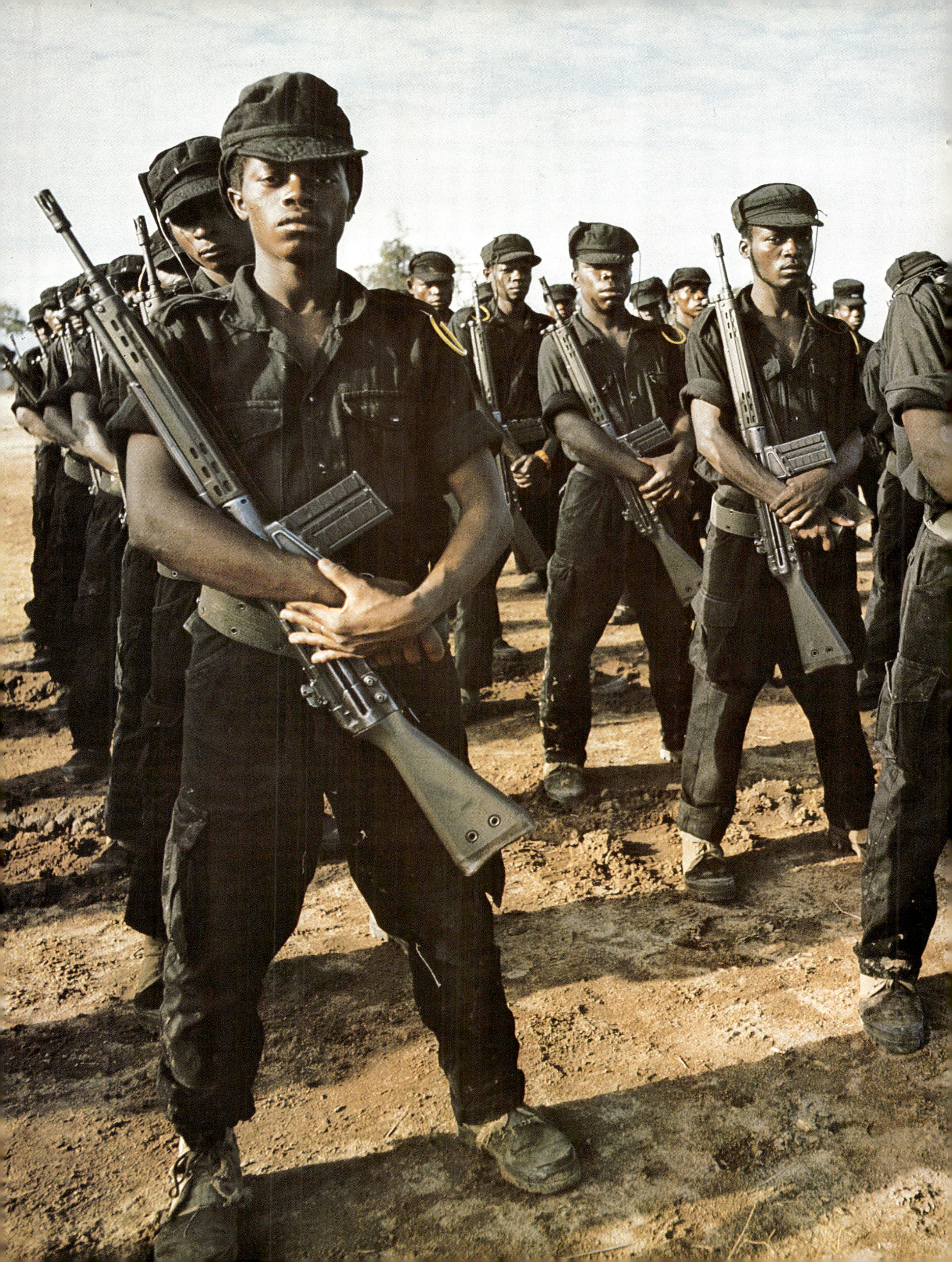

The Algerian National Liberation Army

The wave of guerrilla attacks on 1 November 1954 that marked the beginning of the Algerian struggle for independence was poorly coordinated and easily contained by the French authorities. Although substantial elements of the nationalist opposition had recently come together politically under the banner of the Front de Libération Nationale (FLN), they had been unable to field more than 400 active fighters, loosely organised into units serving six Wilayas or combat zones, covering the whole of Algeria. A violent reaction by the European settler population, backed by the army, quickly forced the guerrilla groups to disperse.

Nevertheless, the attacks acted as a powerful symbol of resistance and new recruits flocked to join the FLN. At first they swamped the delicate infrastructure of the Wilayas and it was not until mid-1956 that surviving FLN leaders, meeting together in the Soummam Valley in Kabylia, created a more rigid military framework, centralising the guerrillas under the control of the Armée de Libération Nationale (ALN). Battalions, companies and sections were set up in each of the Wilayas, new leaders (many of them former members of the French Army with combat experience in Indochina) were appointed and a 'passive' organisation of some 30,000 Muslim supporters was established. Unfortunately, arms and equipment were in short supply and, as French counter-measures increased in effectiveness, the impact of the new force was slight. In 1957 the urban network of the ALN in Algiers was destroyed by General Jacques Massu's 10th Parachute Division and the rural groups began to feel the effects of army *ratissages* (offensive sweeps) through the Wilayas.

Above: An ALN soldier, armed with a Lee Enfield Mark III*, stands watch at an outpost near the Tunisian border.

A sanctuary was set up in neighbouring Tunisia, but the construction of a sophisticated border barrier – the Morice Line – in 1957 prevented its exploitation. As morale collapsed and the rate of desertion climbed steadily, the ALN was effectively split in two, with the 'internal' guerrilla groups isolated from their 'external' supporters across the border.

The FLN strategy at this stage was to forge links between the two ALN wings, using the Tunisian-based units as reinforcement to the dwindling guerrilla bands, but the Morice Line, with its electrified fence, minefields and army patrols proved a difficult barrier to breach. Attempts to storm the Line led to heavy casualties – in April 1958, for example, over 600 ALN members out of a force of 820 were pursued and killed by French troops around Souk Ahras – and it soon began to seem as if the revolution was doomed, particularly when, in early 1959, the French initiated a series of offensive sweeps into the Ouarsenis mountains (the Challe Offensive) which enjoyed immediate success. The onus for revolutionary action passed to the political leaders of the FLN (themselves split between 'internal' and 'external' groups), with only scattered guerrilla attacks occurring. The nationalists now had to decide how to maintain the impetus of their revolt when the military initiative seemed to have passed to the counter-insurgency forces of the French government.

It was in these inauspicious circumstances that Colonel Houari Boumedienne was appointed chief of staff to the ALN in Tripoli in December 1959. He immediately set about improving the military potential of the revolution, imposing strict codes of discipline on units frustrated by their inability to enter Algeria, and introducing a large measure of political indoctrination. New and heavier weapons, chiefly of Soviet origin channelled through Egypt, were received and the strategy of the ALN – by now comprising some 20,000 soldiers – was radically altered. Full-scale attacks on the Morice Line were stopped, and although guerrilla raids were still carried out, backed whenever possible by cross-border artillery strikes, the main aim was to preserve the 'external' ALN as a conventional army, capable of seizing political power for the FLN leaders once the French had been forced to withdraw. The 'internal' guerrilla leaders, tainted with failure, were to be denied the fruits of the revolution, which were to be enjoyed by those 'externals' who were now exploiting the French political desire to terminate a costly colonial war. As the French Army in Algeria suffered the trauma of the Generals' Coup (April 1961), President de Gaulle actively pursued negotiations which were to lead to independence in March 1962. As soon as that occurred, the ALN carried out its new role, marching in to claim victory and the right to rule, initially for Ahmed Ben Bella but then, in June 1965, for its architect and commander, Boumedienne. The transformation from guerrilla force to political power-broker was complete.

Algerian National Liberation Army Soldier
— Algeria 1960 —

In the early stages of the Algerian Revolution the Armée de Libération Nationale (ALN) relied almost entirely on captured equipment from the French security forces. As an organisational infrastructure developed outside Algeria, the ALN began to acquire supplies from nations sympathetic to its cause, especially the countries of the Arab world. Naturally, because the French Army ended World War II equipped primarily with US weapons, there was a preference for American-made arms to complement those captured already. This man carries a 0.3in M2 carbine, although his ammunition pouches are for the earlier M1. He is wearing a US Army M1943 combat jacket and French Army trousers, a combination common to the ALN. The high standard of equipment suggests that this man is a member of an 'external' ALN unit, as the 'internal' ALN forces had great difficulty in maintaining a reasonable level of armament.

Above: Soldiers of the ALN (Armée de Libération Nationale) on parade during a rally in one of their camps in Tunisia. They are armed with a variety of weapons including M2 carbines and at least one German MP44 assault rifle.

AFRICA

Mercenaries in the Congo

Between July 1960 and November 1967 the ex-Belgian colony of the Congo (Zaire) was in turmoil; political and tribal rivalries, left unchecked by the departing Belgians and fuelled by outside interference, led to rebellions, attempted secessions and virtually continuous civil war. Initially, between July 1960 and January 1963, the violence centred upon the southern, mineral-rich province of Katanga (Shaba), where Moise Tshombe's declaration of secession had to be countered by troops of the central government's Armée Nationale Congolaise (ANC) and the United Nations (UN). Although Tshombe was defeated, he was subsequently recalled from exile to become prime minister of the Congo (June 1964), only to face a widespread rebellion in the east, known as the Simba War, which lasted until his overthrow by General Joseph Mobutu in November 1965. There then followed a period of pro-Tshombe plots against Mobutu which lasted until November 1967, despite Tshombe's abduction and imprisonment in Algeria five months earlier.

It was against this confused background of events that white mercenaries played their part. The first such men were recruited by Tshombe in Katanga soon after the secession at a time when he had little armed force available, and they helped to defend the embryonic state against the poorly coordinated ANC in 1961 before succumbing to the overwhelming numbers and weapons of the UN a year later. Tshombe clearly valued their services, however, for he called upon them again to fight the Simbas, building up such a rapport that they remained loyal to him even after Mobutu's coup and were responsible for many of the plots and rebellions of the later period. Men such as Robert Faulques, Bob Denard, Mike Hoare, John Peters, Jean Schramme, Siegfried Mueller and Rolf Steiner led a motley collection of Belgians, Frenchmen, Britons, Germans and South Africans in a series of operations which soon caught the public imagination. Although small in number – there were rarely more than 300 active fighters – the mercenaries had an impact out of all proportion to their strength. This, in turn, created a mystique of invincibility which did not, however, stand up to close analysis.

Above: Wounded during fighting in the Congo, this mercenary wears a French airborne camouflage smock and bush hat with American webbing. He is carrying a Sterling SMG with butt extended.

The motives of the mercenaries were mixed. Not all fought for money – the usual contract for £100-180 a month was generous by 1960s standards but payment could never be guaranteed – nor for the loot they might collect, although these were obviously contributory factors. The majority, at least in the early stages, were former professional soldiers who knew no other occupation: misfits from the British Army, ex-Legionnaires or paras from a French Army suffering the traumas of the Algerian War, ex-Wehrmacht or SS men with nowhere else to go, and other ex-members of World War II elite units to whom peacetime was tediously mundane. Some were undoubtedly idealists, convinced that they were defending the West against a rising tide of communism; others, known as *les affreux* ('the horrors'), were psychopaths to whom killing was a pleasure. Perhaps the only common denominator was a pursuit of danger and excitement: for which the Congo provided an ideal environment.

At first the mercenaries enjoyed some success, based upon their relative military expertise and experience in the tactics and weapons of the West. They operated in small groups, using jeeps armed with machine guns to advance rapidly and ruthlessly through enemy lines. This worked well against the ill-organised and poorly-led ANC in the early months of Katangan secession, and was equally effective against the Simba tribesmen of 1964-65, but as soon as the mercenaries encountered the UN, with its armoured cars and air power, and then the improved ANC of Mobutu's time, inherent weaknesses began to show.

Discipline among such a disparate group of basically self-interested men was always a problem, and although some units – notably Mike Hoare's 5 Commando – fought as coherent formations, others found it difficult to survive. Officers were convinced that they knew best, often disobeying the orders of their superiors and black paymasters and displaying all the signs of complacency and racism which inevitably undermined efficiency. By 1967, when Schramme and Denard mounted an invasion of southern Katanga in an effort to overthrow Mobutu, things had degenerated so far that the operation was little short of a fiasco. The mercenaries were forced to retreat into Angola and Rwanda, leaving behind a powerful memory which ensured the continuation of the mercenary mystique but did little to affect the future development of Zaire.

Mercenary Soldier
—Congo 1964—

Top: Mercenary leader Bob Denard with two other officers armed with .45in Colt automatics. Above: An officer of 5 Commando rescuing some nuns. The mercenaries tended to adopt rank badges similar to those in use in the Belgian Army. Belgian influences were strongly felt in its former colony of the Congo, even extending to the mercenary forces.

A member of 5 Commando, this soldier is wearing a Belgian armoured battalion badge on his commando beret. His webbing and smock, although of Belgian origin, are based on British patterns. The smock was designed from the Denison model used by British paratroopers, while the webbing is based on the British 1937 pattern. The holster is for a Browning or Colt automatic pistol, and the bayonet is for an FN FAL rifle. Mercenaries tend to have no definitive uniform, so this figure must be taken as typical rather than standard.

AFRICA

The Biafran Army

On 30 May 1967 Lieutenant-Colonel Chukwuemeka Ojukwu declared the independence of the predominantly Ibo Eastern Region of the Federation of Nigeria, creating the Republic of Biafra. It failed to attract widespread international recognition or support and, from the start, faced a Federal government under General Yakubu Gowon that was determined to reunite Nigeria whatever the cost. By January 1970, surrounded by three Federal divisions, which mustered over 60,000 men equipped with armoured cars, artillery, aircraft and virtually unlimited supplies, Biafra was forced to surrender. In retrospect, its demise seems to have been inevitable.

Yet the fact remains that Biafra did survive against apparently insuperable odds for nearly three years, fighting a bitter and destructive war which was not always one-sided. To a certain extent this was a result of Federal weaknesses – the Federal Army was often poorly led, tactically inept and too easily demoralised – but there was more to it than that, for there can be no doubt that Biafra defended itself remarkably well. At first glance this may seem surprising, for the Biafran Army was never large – barely more than 40,000 men at its height – and was poorly equipped, lacking heavy weapons, ammunition stockpiles and a modern air element. Moreover, for much of its existence it had to survive on inadequate supplies, receiving little from outside sources and depending to a significant extent on what it could capture from the enemy. On closer analysis, however, it is apparent that the Biafrans enjoyed certain hidden advantages which, although insufficient to ensure final victory, did prolong the war.

The first of these was the fact that the Ibo tribe contained within it a hard core of military expertise and experience which could be exploited. It has been estimated that over 50 per cent of the pre-1966 Nigerian Army officer corps was Ibo, and although a significant number of these men failed to survive the coups and massacres of 1966-67, enough remained to form the solid backbone of the new Biafran Army. They were supported, moreover, by most of the Biafran population, who were willing to bear enormous sacrifices to defend their state. This could never act as a substitute for outside support, but it did mean that the army was never short of manpower and its morale remained high even under the most severe conditions of blockade and defeat. In addition, the energy and resourcefulness of the Ibo people was devoted to the war effort, producing rudimentary military equipment and home-made weapons which sustained the frontline forces when all else failed. In this they were aided by some very capable white mercenaries, notably 'Colonel' Rolf Steiner, who raised the Fourth Biafran Commando Brigade in 1968, and Count Carl Gustav von Rosen, who flew Swedish-built Minicon light aircraft against Federal targets with demoralising effect in 1969. Finally, as the Federal forces closed in, the Ibos began to operate

Top: Biafran soldiers who are manning an outpost along the Niger River; they are armed with a variety of small arms. The skull belongs to a northern Nigerian. Above: Biafran soldiers near Owerri form up for inspection of their machine guns. Both of these groups of soldiers are exceptionally well-equipped for the Biafran Army, which found it difficult to acquire sufficient munitions.

on their own territory and this enabled them to move swiftly across terrain which their enemy, who were tied to the roads and tracks by heavy dependence on modern weapons, often regarded as impassable.

Taken together, these advantages read like a recipe for guerrilla warfare, and it was perhaps one of the weaknesses of Biafran strategic thinking that such operations were not carried out on a more regular basis. To begin with, Ojukwu wasted valuable manpower and resources on conventional military operations such as the invasion of the Mid-Western Region of Nigeria in August 1967, and it was only after these had failed completely in 1968-69, defeated by the growing numerical strength of the Federal forces, that he took the advice of Steiner and adopted guerrilla tactics. By then it was already too late to save Biafra, but the fact that the Federal Army, suffering the effects of constant ambush and hit-and-run attacks, took another year to defeat its enemy, shows what could have been achieved. Biafra was, in the final analysis, unsuited to conventional warfare; to stand any chance at all of long-term survival, the army should have exploited its natural advantages of popular support, high motivation and extensive local knowledge.

Biafran Soldier
— Nigeria 1968 —

The Biafran forces faced great difficulties in getting equipment. Virtually any sort of quasi-military tunic or trousers would be worn, either light khaki like this man's tunic, olive green like his trousers, jungle-pattern camouflage or even civilian clothes. Headgear could be berets, tropical hats or bush hats: this man is wearing a light khaki cap with earflaps which he has tucked up inside the crown. He has unconventional footwear – wellington boots – and is armed with a Czech 7·62mm Vz58 assault rifle together with the appropriate bayonet and ammunition pouches.

Below: Newly trained troops soon to go into action are encouraged by their NCO. The Ibo soldiers had good morale throughout the war and enthusiastically supported the Biafran Republic.

AFRICA

The Nigerian Federal Army

The Nigerian Civil War (1967-70), fought between the Federal government and the secessionist Eastern Region (Biafra), has been described as the first of Africa's modern wars, fought by armies theoretically organised, commanded and equipped along contemporary lines. In practice, however, this modern ideal was hard to achieve. The Nigerian Federal Army's efforts were plagued by inexperience and chaotic disorganisation. In fact the Nigerian government's problems were similar to those experienced by many black African governments in countries where the traditions of civil/military relations have little binding force and where loyalty to government institutions or to a constitution can easily be eroded by tribal, religious or personal allegiances.

When the war began the Federal Army was little more than a policing force, mustering less than 9000 men organised and equipped in the British style and although it contained a central core of well-trained, professional officers, their ranks had been thinned dramatically by the political events of 1966. The two coups of that year, in January and July, probably liquidated up to half the officer class, and this loss was made worse for the Federal side in early 1967 when the majority of Ibo officers withdrew to the Eastern Region to raise the Biafran Army. What remained was a very small rump of professionalism which was soon spread thinly to cope with the huge expansion of Federal forces in response to the war, and its influence was further diluted by the need to commission large numbers of new officers, many of whom were ill-educated and only partially trained. At the same time, as the Federal Army mushroomed in size – by early 1970 it contained over 200,000 men – the standard of recruits inevitably declined and the pre-war logistic infrastructure cracked under the strain. This meant that, despite Federal access to relatively sophisticated equipment – ranging from mortars and machine guns to armoured cars and heavy artillery – the soldiers and many of their officers had no idea how to use it to best advantage. The Federal Army soon became an unwieldy instrument of war, capable of little more than bludgeoning attacks using overwhelming numbers and firepower, and there can be little doubt that this prolonged the war.

Below: The Nigerian Federal Army could count on a better flow of equipment than its Biafran opponents. Their men went into battle well-supplied and backed by Saladin armoured cars.

Such weaknesses were further exacerbated by the poor organisational and command structures of the army. By 1968-69, the Federal authorities were fielding three divisions, each comprising more than 30,000 men, poised to crush the Biafrans in a multi-pronged assault, but each was a separate army, commanded by officers of widely differing capabilities who were jealous of their positions and did little to ensure a coordinated approach to the war. The 1st Division, under Colonel Mohammed Shuwa, was the most professional of the three, probably because it contained a hard core of the pre-war army in its ranks, but there were times when it seemed more concerned with internal discipline and organisation than actual fighting; that tended to be left to the 3rd Commando Division under the aggressive and charismatic Colonel Benjamin ('Black Scorpion') Adekunle, but even it was slow-moving when the opposition seemed strong. The 2nd Division, commanded initially by the rather ill-organised Colonel Murtala Mohammed and then by the easy-going Colonel Ibrahim Haruna, achieved little throughout the war, earning itself the dubious nickname of the 'Tortoise Division' among the civilians and military hierarchy back in Lagos. By 1968-69 the higher command had precious little control over events at a front line many miles away over difficult terrain, and the three divisional commanders found themselves enjoying a remarkable degree of autonomy. The fact that they used this to enhance their individual positions, even to the extent of poaching recruits and supplies earmarked for their 'rivals', was a recipe for chaos.

Yet the fact remains that the Federal Army did win the war, chiefly by means of its sheer size and firepower. Tactics were crude and command arrangements poor, but a military leviathan capable of defeating its enemy in the end was created. As it was a mass of semi-trained, vaguely organised troops made more devastating by their access to modern equipment, it may be seen as typical of the new armies of the Third World that have emerged since 1945.

Nigerian Federal Army Soldier
— Nigeria 1968 —

The rapid expansion of the Nigerian Federal Army during the civil war produced an increased demand for military supplies which was filled haphazardly. This man, however, has attained a high standard of equipment with the provision of all the accoutrements demanded by a soldier. Most of these are of British design, but the helmet is the M1 model from the United States, often seen with mottoes written on. His boots are those worn by the British Army in jungle operations and are made of canvas and rubber. The webbing is the British 1958 pattern and the water bottle is also British, of the 1944 pattern. He is armed with a 9mm Sten Mk II sub-machine gun.

Below: Two men of the Nigerian Federal Army break down the door of a television transmitter room in Enugu, the capital of Biafra. Armed with FN FAL rifles, they show the reasonable standard of equipment that the Nigerian Federal government was able to maintain during the Biafran War.

AFRICA

The Chadian Army

The central African state of Chad covers a huge area – some 1,284,000 square km (386,209 square miles) – and has substantial uranium deposits, but its population is small (about 4,850,000), poor and divided by politics and religion. When the French granted independence in August 1960, they handed over power in the capital Fort Lamy (now N'Djamena) to François Tombalbaye, a black African Christian from the south. His policies, aimed specifically against the Arabic-speaking Muslims of the north, helped to trigger a civil war which is still being fought today.

But the war has not remained a simple case of south against north. This may have been the case in the 1960s and early 1970s as Tombalbaye's rivals, organised into the Front de Libération Nationale de Tchad (FROLINAT), conducted a guerrilla campaign, but the situation became more complex in April 1975 when Tombalbaye was killed in a military coup instigated by the chief of staff of the Armée Nationale de Tchad (ANT), General Malloum. The guerrilla war continued despite substantial French military and economic aid, and after a period of confusing intrigue the 11 factions fighting for control of Chad formed the Gouvernement d'Union Nationale de Transition (GUNT) in November 1979. The new leaders soon proved incapable of working together: President Goukouni Oueddei, the FROLINAT leader, dismissed Defence Minister Hissène Habré, who subsequently formed the Forces Armées du Nord (FAN), in March 1980. Habré withdrew to the mountains of the north and reopened the civil war. In June 1982 he attacked N'Djamena, overthrowing Goukouni, who followed tradition by moving north with elements of the GUNT army. Habré hastily formed the Forces Armées Nationales Tchadiennes (FANT) by grafting his FAN units onto those of the ANT which remained, only to be counter-attacked and defeated at Faya Largeau in the central provinces. A French expeditionary force – the third since 1969 – rushed to Habré's aid and prevented the collapse of the government forces. Indeed France's policies have added to the problems of the historian in describing events in Chad, in spite of the fact that successive French governments have generally tried to act in the interests of political stability in the country.

It is thus exceptionally difficult to describe, let alone assess the value of the Chadian Army, for the force which fights for Habré today is clearly different to that which operated under Tombalbaye 20 years ago. On paper, there is a degree of continuity – the 4000-man pro-government army continues to contain a mix of infantry, motorised infantry, light artillery, parachute and reconnaissance companies, backed by a 6000-strong gendarmerie – but the effects of constant political turmoil must be widespread. As Goukouni recovered from Habré's attack remarkably quickly in 1982, his GUNT force must still contain members of the original ANT, just as Habré's FANT force must owe something to previous pro-government formations. Whatever the case, however, it seems safe to say that to be a Chadian soldier must be an extremely confusing profession.

Even so, certain common factors do exist. Regardless of the man in power or the military acronym in use, pro-government forces are undeniably French-dominated. The Chadian Army, whether ANT, GUNT or FANT, tends to have been trained by French 'technical advisers' and to deploy weapons of French origin – currently Panhard AML-60 and AML-90 armoured cars, 90mm and 122mm artillery pieces, 81mm and 120mm mortars, and 68mm and 89mm recoilless anti-tank guns. There are exceptions – the small Chadian parachute contingent, which seems to have remained loyal to N'Djamena, was trained by the Israelis, and some American equipment is now beginning to appear – but to a large extent the future of Chad lies in French hands. In exchange for valuable mineral rights and airlanding facilities, the French provide not only forces on the ground but also up to 50 per cent of the defence budget, and without them no government could survive, particularly as the opposition – again, regardless of its political or ethnic bases – is supported by Colonel Gaddafi of Libya, intent on exerting control over the northern mineral-rich Aouzou Strip. Habré's army is too small, lightly armed and politically confused to stand alone: what is needed is a strong, ethnically-mixed army, capable of establishing and maintaining the rule of an effective central government. It is unlikely to emerge in a multi-racial, multi-religious state such as Chad, subject to constant outside interference and internal dissension. The future is not bright for Chad's divided army.

Below: Men of Hissène Habré's FAN who have chosen to wear a cross-section of modern military fashion, wearing olive drab and jungle or leopard spot camouflage; the only military hat is cut like a French paratrooper's combat hat. The machine gun is a Chinese Type 54 12·7mm heavy machine gun, a copy of the Soviet DShKM.

Chadian National Army Soldier
— Chad 1970 —

This man is part of the crew of a Panhard armoured car; he is wearing French AFV crewman's headphones over his green fatigue hat. The tunic appears to be a variant of a French paratrooper's and the trousers and boots are also of French origin. He is lightly equipped — a bayonet from a Type 56 assault rifle (the Chinese version of the AK-47) hangs from the roof-rack 'octopus' around his waist. The forces fighting for control of Chad are equipped from a variety of sources and standardisation is difficult to achieve.

Below: Infantrymen of Hissène Habré's Forces Armées du Nord in N'Djamena, March 1980. These men are wearing a variety of headgear, ranging from a beret to a shemagh. The man in the foreground carries a French MAT 49 sub-machine gun; the others are armed with Belgian FN FAL rifles.

The Angolan National Liberation Front

The struggle against Portuguese rule in Angola was complicated by the number of differing resistance movements operating at variance with each other. While the main fight was sustained by the left-wing MPLA there were two other important groups, the FNLA and UNITA. Under the leadership of Holden Roberto, the FNLA (Frente Nacional de Libertação de Angola) was in essence a tribal organisation which had come into being as a focus for the grievances of the rural Bakongo peoples of northern Angola.

The FNLA was helped from the outset in receiving aid from Zaire, whose border with Angola stretched over 2100km (1300 miles) and provided a frontier region of mountains, swamps, jungle and elephant grass which could be easily penetrated by FNLA guerrillas. The connection with Zaire was strengthened when Joseph Mobutu – Holden Roberto's brother-in-law – became president. Not only did Zaire provide help to the FNLA it also acted against the rival MPLA whose Marxist aspirations were seen as a threat to the Mobutu regime.

Guerrilla activities were conducted against Portuguese installations in northern Angola throughout the 1960s, and by the end of the decade the FNLA had built up a force of up to 8000 guerrillas although it was unlikely that more than 1000 men would be inside Angola at any one time. FNLA weapons and equipment came from a number of sources: besides direct help from Zaire the guerrillas managed to acquire smallarms from both the Portuguese and from the other guerrilla groups.

The FNLA as an ostensible movement of national liberation was fatally flawed by two critical weaknesses. In the first instance, its revolt was tribally inspired and so was never able to mobilise the whole country to make the war against the Portuguese an Angolan struggle, and secondly, the FNLA ignored the political dimension of guerrilla struggle in favour of military adventurism which was easily contained by the Portuguese Army, which always proved to be more than a match for the guerrillas on a purely battlefield level.

By the early 1970s the brunt of the guerrilla war was being borne by the MPLA and it was becoming obvious that they would take over when the Portuguese left. Accordingly the FNLA began to see the MPLA as the main threat to its power and began to mount operations against its former ally. And as an anti-Marxist organisation the FNLA began to receive help from America and South Africa, both concerned to prevent a left-wing regime gaining power in Angola. When Portugal left Angola in 1975, outright civil war broke out. The FNLA sent a column southward to try to take the Angolan capital, Luanda. Aided by their Cuban allies the MPLA engaged the FNLA in battle, decisively beat them and chased them back to Zaire.

During the late 1970s a tough Angolan attitude towards Zaire – which included a number of incursions into border territory – encouraged the Zairean president to respect Angolan sovereignty and reduce his support for the FNLA. Since then the FNLA has been reduced to being a minor irritant to the MPLA regime in Angola.

Below: FNLA leader Holden Roberto (patterned shirt) parades triumphantly through the streets of Huambo (Nova Lisboa) during the FNLA drive to overthrow the MPLA, December 1975. By 1975 considerable numbers of white mercenaries were in FNLA employ, including these shown here acting as a presidential bodyguard.

FNLA Mercenary Guerrilla
—Angola 1975—

During the civil war in Angola the FNLA recruited a large number of white mercenaries to stiffen their armed forces, and this soldier is a fairly typical example. A simple olive-green drab uniform is worn and the rifle is the Soviet 7.62mm AKM. Although both America and South Africa helped the FNLA in 1975, a considerable amount of their weaponry was derived from communist-bloc sources.

Below right: Well-equipped by FNLA standards, a group of soldiers stand guard at an airport.
Below: A more typical picture of FNLA troops, taken deep in the bush of Angola. Ragged patterned trousers were a feature of the FNLA, but despite their appearance these men are armed with the highly effective AK assault rifle.

AFRICA

The Rhodesian African Rifles

Above: Armed with 7.62mm self-loading rifles, a mixed patrol of Rhodesian African Rifles moves cautiously through thick bush in the heart of the war zone in Rhodesia.

The Rhodesian African Rifles (RAR) was one of the main forces of the Rhodesian Army engaged in tracking and destroying the guerrilla units of ZAPU and ZANU, which operated both from across the Rhodesian border and from within Rhodesia itself, trying to establish the state of Zimbabwe. Physical training had long been a characteristic of the RAR and it was renowned for its ability to cover huge distances on foot at speed. The experience in counter-insurgency that the regiment had gained from its service in Malaya during the late 1950s proved extremely useful against guerrilla forces during the late 1970s, and the RAR had an enviable record in this period, fighting to preserve an essentially colonial Rhodesian society. It is, therefore, somewhat ironic that when the creation of the Rhodesian African Rifles was first mooted in the late 1930s there were loud cries of protest from the members of the white settler community.

The Rhodesian Native Regiment had fought with distinction against the Germans in East Africa during World War I, though immediately after the war the regiment had been disbanded and absorbed into the British South Africa Police, and so the creation of a regular black African unit with white officers was not without precedent. By the late 1930s, however, it seemed that the white population had conveniently forgotten the great exploits of the Rhodesian Native Regiment and opposition to the raising of a new African unit was fierce. But on 3 September 1939 war was declared in Europe, and within a very short while it became clear to the Rhodesian administration that, with almost 70 per cent of the available white manpower serving outside the colony, the country's internal security was itself at risk. Consequently, during May and June 1940, the Rhodesian African Rifles was finally formed.

From the early stages, the RAR placed a high emphasis on athletic training programmes and physical fitness. Training programmes were characterised by two 80km (50 mile) route marches per week. At first, recruitment was mainly among the Shona tribe, but by 1941 the Ndebele too were joining in numbers. Yet despite the intensity of the training and the gradual emergence of the regiment as an effective fighting unit, it was not until 1943 that the RAR finally received official recognition of its military value, when it was notified of its intended inclusion in Allied operations.

After a period of jungle training to the south of Nairobi from November 1943 to March 1944, during which the regiment was finally properly equipped, the RAR embarked from Mombasa for Ceylon on 5 September 1944. After further training in Ceylon, the regiment re-embarked for Burma on 2 December 1944 – though at this point the RAR had no knowledge of its new destination.

Although the RAR arrived in Burma at about the time the campaign was drawing to an end, the operations in which these men were involved in the Arakan mountain range saw them display an enthusiastic fighting spirit. On returning to Salisbury after the war it seemed likely that the regiment would be disbanded (as had the Rhodesian Native Regiment), but high-level protest prevented this, although for some years it existed in only a secondary capacity.

The period of inactivity ended when the RAR was posted to the Suez Canal zone (where it soon gained a reputation for efficiency), whence it was moved to Malaya in 1956. During the period of two years that it served in Malaya, the RAR gained a wealth of experience in counter-insurgency techniques at a period when British forces were proving very effective against the communist guerrillas.

After the unilateral declaration of independence by Ian Smith's white-run Rhodesia in 1965, the guerrilla groups of ZAPU and ZANU gradually began to step up their pressure on the security forces. At first, the RAR was deployed in the north of the country, along the Zambezi. The formation of the elite Selous Scouts in 1973 was resisted by many of the officers in the RAR, who feared that their best men would be lured away; but in the event the RAR carried on in an effective counter-insurgency role until the end of the war, with over 2000 men, in three battalions, engaged for most of the period.

After the election of a new government and the proclamation of the state of Zimbabwe in 1980, the RAR continued in service and was engaged in the fighting that took place inside the country in 1981 to maintain order. Now, however, the RAR was under the command of one of its erstwhile foes, Robert Mugabe, who had led the ZANU forces in the long guerrilla war.

Rhodesian African Rifleman
—Rhodesia 1976—

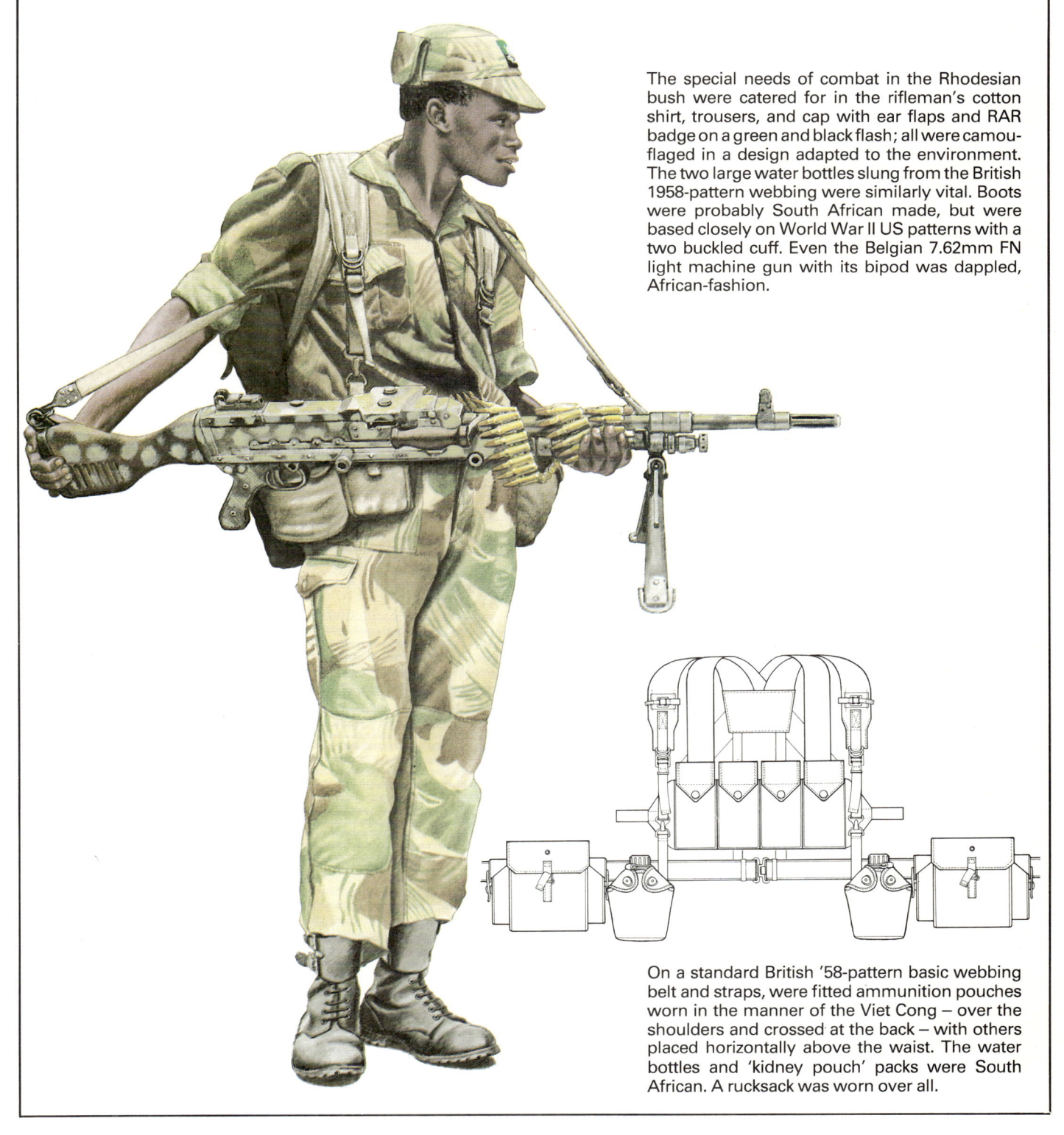

The special needs of combat in the Rhodesian bush were catered for in the rifleman's cotton shirt, trousers, and cap with ear flaps and RAR badge on a green and black flash; all were camouflaged in a design adapted to the environment. The two large water bottles slung from the British 1958-pattern webbing were similarly vital. Boots were probably South African made, but were based closely on World War II US patterns with a two buckled cuff. Even the Belgian 7.62mm FN light machine gun with its bipod was dappled, African-fashion.

On a standard British '58-pattern basic webbing belt and straps, were fitted ammunition pouches worn in the manner of the Viet Cong — over the shoulders and crossed at the back — with others placed horizontally above the waist. The water bottles and 'kidney pouch' packs were South African. A rucksack was worn over all.

AFRICA

The Selous Scouts

Formed in December 1973 and disbanded less than seven years later in March 1980, the Selous Scouts had a short operational history; but during their existence they gained a reputation as the best bush soldiers on the African continent. The Selous Scout Regiment was named after the Victorian explorer Frederick Courtney Selous who had played a leading role in the exploration and conquest of Rhodesia.

Under the leadership of Lieutenant-Colonel Ron Reid Daly the Selous Scouts were organised as a combat reconnaissance force, their chief function being to locate the elusive nationalist guerrillas in the bush and relay information back to the main body of the Rhodesian security forces. The Scouts were a strictly volunteer force and, of the many who signed up to join, only 15 per cent emerged from the training programme to be allowed the right to wear the brown beret of the Selous Scouts.

Although the vast majority of the officers and most of the senior NCOs were white, the numbers of black troops within the unit increased steadily so that, at one point some 80 per cent of the Scouts were black. Besides the Rhodesians a few American and British soldiers volunteered.

The success of the Selous Scouts in carrying out their mission can be gauged from a statement issued by Combined Operations, Rhodesia, which officially credited them with being responsible for the death of 68 per cent of all nationalist guerrillas killed in Rhodesia during the course of the war. By comparison, only 40 Scouts were killed in action.

The Selous Scouts attained a maximum strength of over 1500 men. Their basic tactical formation was the troop, each made up of three sections of eight men. Once in the bush, however, the section was usually divided into two 'sticks', groups small enough to remain undetected by enemy eyes and yet sufficient to be operationally effective.

Besides their ostensible function as intelligence gatherers, the Selous Scouts had a second, clandestine, role to play. Selected black Scouts would infiltrate the nationalist areas, both in and outside Rhodesia, to gain a true picture of guerrilla activities and intentions. A basic Selous Scout strategy was the elimination of the nationalist leaders, either by capturing them, so that they would be useful for interrogation purposes, or as often happened by simply assassinating them. Most of these undercover operations were small-scale affairs but occasionally full-scale cross-border raids would be launched. The most successful was the audacious attack against the ZANLA Nyadzonya camp in Mozambique on 9 August 1976. Disguised as Frelimo troops from Mozambique, fewer than 100 Selous Scouts surrounded the camp, some 5000 strong, and in a whirlwind attack completely destroyed it, accounting for more than 600 of the enemy, the majority of them guerrillas.

That such a small force could cause such destruction was clear proof of the tactical superiority of the Scouts over the nationalists. But in the end this was not enough; the wind of change was blowing against the whites in Rhodesia, and the triumph of Robert Mugabe in the supervised elections of 1980 signalled the demise of the Selous Scouts.

Above left: Armed with the 7.62mm FN FAL rifle and carrying only ammo pouches and the US-type plastic water bottle, two Selous Scouts move cautiously through arid countryside in search of signs of guerrilla movement. Above: Two Selous Scouts put their fieldcraft to good use as they take a break from patrol and light a small fire on which to brew up. Extremely dry kindling would be used in order to provide a smokeless fire. During a night operation such a fire would be made in a hole in the ground some 300mm (12 inches) deep as even the tiny light of a cigarette can be spotted at a range of up to 800m (½ mile) in the dark.

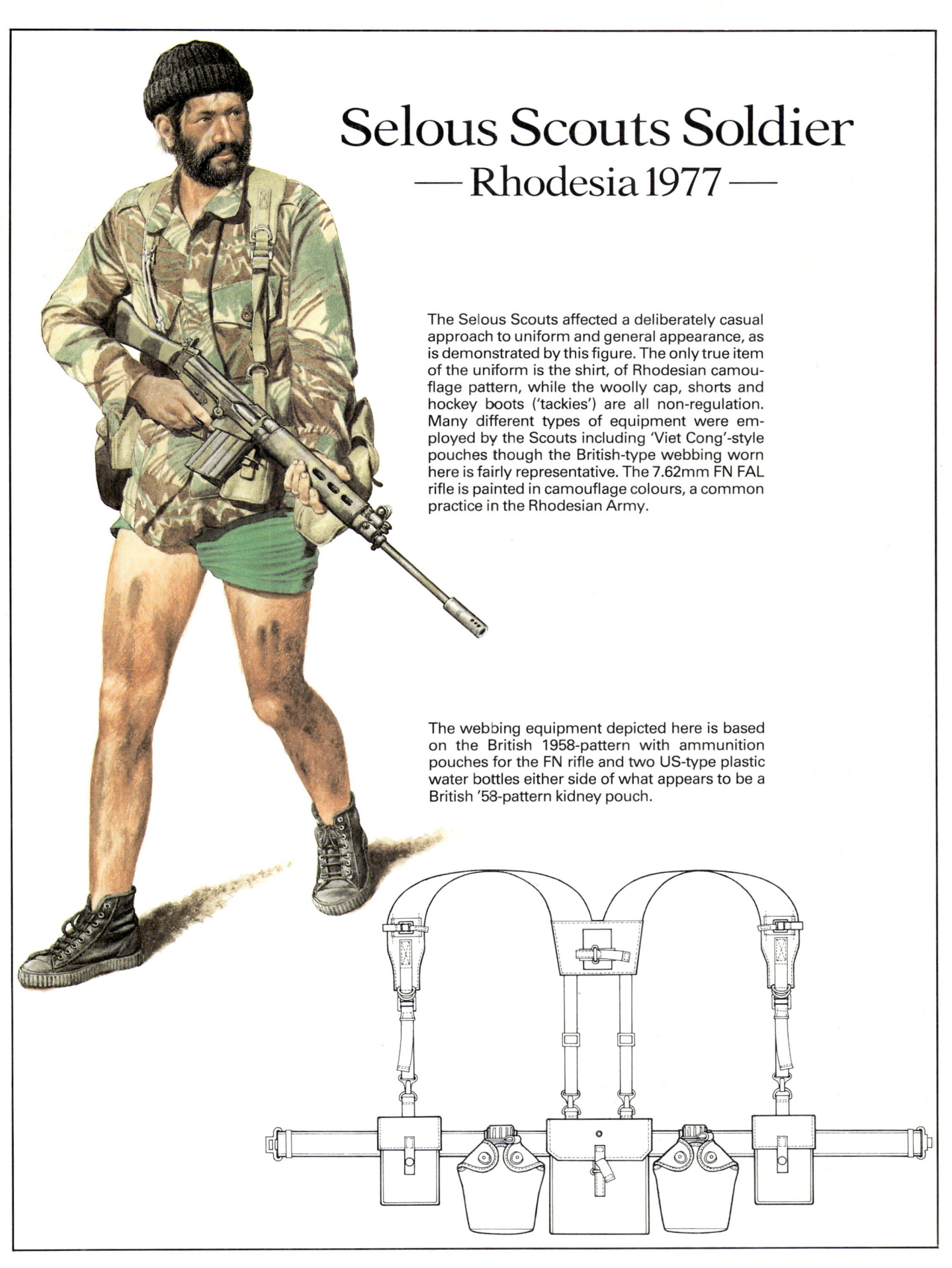

Selous Scouts Soldier
— Rhodesia 1977 —

The Selous Scouts affected a deliberately casual approach to uniform and general appearance, as is demonstrated by this figure. The only true item of the uniform is the shirt, of Rhodesian camouflage pattern, while the woolly cap, shorts and hockey boots ('tackies') are all non-regulation. Many different types of equipment were employed by the Scouts including 'Viet Cong'-style pouches though the British-type webbing worn here is fairly representative. The 7.62mm FN FAL rifle is painted in camouflage colours, a common practice in the Rhodesian Army.

The webbing equipment depicted here is based on the British 1958-pattern with ammunition pouches for the FN rifle and two US-type plastic water bottles either side of what appears to be a British '58-pattern kidney pouch.

AFRICA

The Patriotic Front

Opposition to white rule in Rhodesia could be traced back to the 1940s but it was only in the early 1960s that this opposition was raised to the level of violent conflict. The aspiring black nationalist leaders – Joshua Nkomo, the Reverend Ndabaningi Sithole and Robert Mugabe – had begun to organise their supporters into political parties but their efforts were met by severe repression from the ruling white political party, the Rhodesian Front, under Ian Smith. The two main black political groups – Sithole and Mugabe's ZANU (Zimbabwe African National Union) and Nkomo's ZAPU (Zimbabwe African People's Union) – were banned in Rhodesia, and with Ian Smith's declaration of unilateral independence in 1965 the nationalist struggle moved underground.

Despite fierce differences between ZANU and ZAPU (which were to continue into the 1980s) the nationalists were agreed upon the aim of black majority rule. Both organisations had moved their headquarters to Zambia in 1964 and from there they began to organise a campaign of guerrilla resistance. Inexperienced in the craft of guerrilla warfare, they looked to outside help: ZAPU guerrillas received training from the Soviet Union, China and North Korea while ZANU men were trained by Ghana and Tanzania.

During the 1960s, their general strategy was to infiltrate bands of guerrillas into Rhodesia to carry out sabotage missions with the intention of wearing down their opponents' will to resist. In this policy the guerrillas were uniformly unsuccessful, however. Although reasonably well-armed and with some rudimentary military training, the guerrillas were no match for the elite forces – both black and white – that were fielded by the Rhodesian Army, who with superior local intelligence were able to destroy the infiltration groups with little difficulty.

The essential flaw in the ZAPU/ZANU strategy was in assuming that their guerrillas would automatically receive the support of the black population in Rhodesia, and that military action would increase the people's political awareness. Although broadly sympathetic to the nationalist cause, the black population was politically ignorant, knew little of either ZAPU or ZANU and, under the control of the whites, was unable or unprepared to assist the guerrillas in the bush.

This state of affairs was to change in the 1970s, however, as political resistance to the Smith government began to develop amongst the blacks within Rhodesia. The increase in white military activity combined with a growing black political consciousness led to the beginnings of widespread support for the guerrillas.

Their position was further strengthened when the former Portuguese colony of Mozambique became independent in 1975. Mozambique's long border with Rhodesia greatly facilitated guerrilla crossings into the country. Aid to the guerrillas increased considerably during the 1970s, and large numbers of Soviet, East German and Cuban military instructors were sent to Zambia and Mozambique. Better armed, equipped and trained, the guerrillas began to have more military effect. A favoured tactic was the use of the land mine which the guerrillas found a handy weapon in obstructing the movement of Rhodesia's fast-moving security forces.

In 1976 ZAPU and ZANU partially buried their differences under the banner of a combined Patriotic Front. The Patriotic Front's military leadership was never of the highest quality and the victory of the black nationalist forces was a political and not a military triumph. Isolated and under pressure from the US and Great Britain, Rhodesia was forced to the conference table and there its fate was decided in favour of a black-ruled Zimbabwe. The Patriotic Front guerrillas played their part in this success to the extent that by refusing to give up fighting – over a period of nearly two decades – they maintained international interest in the struggle. It was their staying power which forced both white Rhodesia and the rest of the world to accept the fact that black nationalist aspirations would eventually have to be met.

Armed with Soviet 7.62mm SKS carbines two ZAPU guerrillas rest in a training camp near the Rhodesian border. Although adequately equipped with smallarms the Patriotic Front guerrillas lacked the expertise in handling the advanced weaponry that could have posed a serious challenge to the Rhodesian security forces.

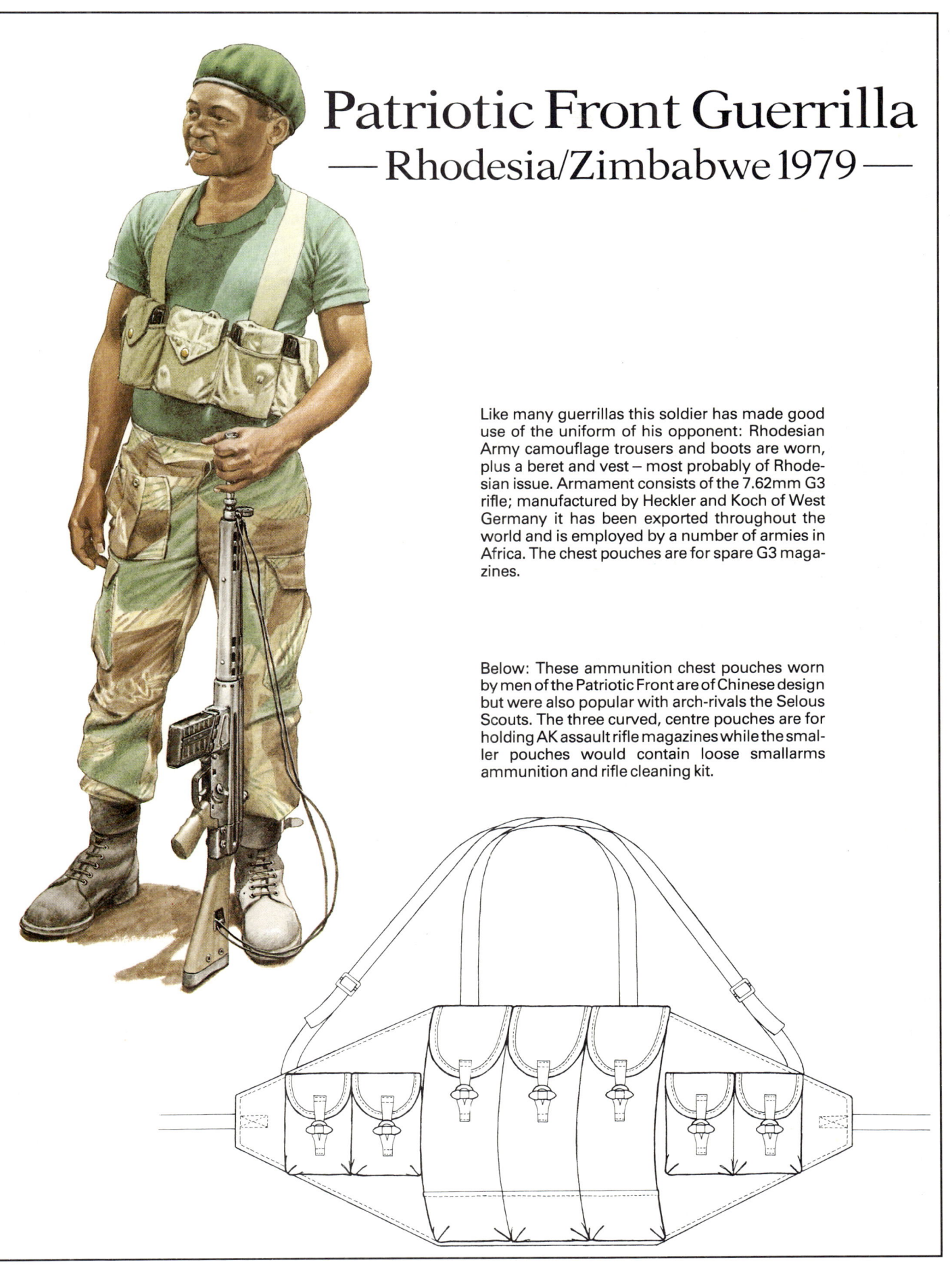

Patriotic Front Guerrilla
— Rhodesia/Zimbabwe 1979 —

Like many guerrillas this soldier has made good use of the uniform of his opponent: Rhodesian Army camouflage trousers and boots are worn, plus a beret and vest – most probably of Rhodesian issue. Armament consists of the 7.62mm G3 rifle; manufactured by Heckler and Koch of West Germany it has been exported throughout the world and is employed by a number of armies in Africa. The chest pouches are for spare G3 magazines.

Below: These ammunition chest pouches worn by men of the Patriotic Front are of Chinese design but were also popular with arch-rivals the Selous Scouts. The three curved, centre pouches are for holding AK assault rifle magazines while the smaller pouches would contain loose smallarms ammunition and rifle cleaning kit.

AFRICA
The Eritrean Liberation Movement

Above: Jubilant supporters of the EPLF take a ride on an M41 light tank, recently captured from regular Ethiopian forces. Left: Eritrean guerrillas prepare to fire a mortar.

When Britain relinquished its caretaker rule of Eritrea in 1952 the United Nations agreed that the territory should become part of Ethiopia, but as a federated state with a large degree of local autonomy. However, given Eritrea's strategic importance on the Red Sea and Ethiopia's own imperial ambitions, Eritrea's semi-independence was not to last, and in November 1962 Ethiopia annexed the province and established its own administration.

Resistance to Ethiopian rule was widespread, and solidified behind an Eritrean liberation movement which was to become the Eritrean Liberation Front (ELF). Despite the general popularity of resistance to Ethiopia, the Eritrean nationalists were bedevilled by a factionalism which has always prevented them from presenting a united front. Within the ELF controversy as to the movement's political objectives came to a head in the early 1960s and brought about the formation of a breakaway group, the Eritrean People's Liberation Forces (EPLF). Marxist-inspired, the EPLF emerged as a highly disciplined guerrilla movement, their cause championed by radical Arab governments including Syria, Iraq and Libya. A third group emerged in the 1970s, the ELF Popular Liberation Forces (ELF-PLF) which again adopted a policy of resistance to Ethiopia, but carried on its own separate guerrilla struggle.

The inevitable decline of Haile Selassie's Ethiopian empire during the early 1970s allowed the Eritreans to make substantial gains, so that only a few beleaguered outposts remained in government hands. The revolution in Addis Ababa and the rise of the Soviet-backed Mengistu Haile Mariam regime in Ethiopia was a serious blow to the guerrillas. Well-supplied with Soviet weapons and equipment, the Ethiopians launched a major offensive at the end of 1977 which forced the guerrillas back into the mountains. But as the Eritreans could field an estimated 40,000 battle-hardened men, the guerrillas were far from beaten and indeed continued to inflict a series of bloody set-backs on the Ethiopian regulars. Armed with Soviet weapons provided by friendly Arab nations the Eritreans were well able to hold their mountain strongholds, even though the Ethiopians made life difficult for the guerrillas with their newly-supplied MiG fighter-bombers.

In 1982 Mengistu fielded a reported 120,000 men in an effort to destroy the Eritrean stronghold of Nafka, but the desperately-fought defence of the guerrillas proved too much to overcome and the much-vaunted Ethiopian attack ground to a halt with heavy losses. Since the war broke out in 1962 a minimum of 100,000 casualties have been suffered by both sides and at least 300,000 refugees have been forced to flee from the fighting. The ability of the Eritrean guerrillas to hold the Ethiopians, despite the latter's Soviet backing, will almost certainly ensure a continuance of the war unless a diplomatic solution can be arrived at, and given the intransigence of both sides this seems an unlikely event.

Eritrean Liberation Front Guerrilla
— Eritrea 1979 —

This guerrilla's outfit is of unidentified origin except for the British 1937-pattern webbing and ammunition pouch containing spare magazines. Armament is not one of the AK series but a Czech 7.62mm Vz58 assault rifle. Similar in appearance to the AK, the Vz58 utilises a different firing mechanism although the AK-47's 7.62 × 39mm cartridge is used.

Below: Armed with cut-down AK assault rifles Eritrean guerrillas are drilled in the rudiments of parade ground discipline. Observers rate the Eritreans as amongst the toughest of guerrilla forces.

The South African Army

Above: South African troops are briefed by an officer before setting out on a patrol near the South African border. Right: Armed with FN FAL rifles troops of the South African Army march past at the double.

After contributing to the Allied cause in World War II the South African Army has for the most part developed in isolation from her former Western partners. Although South Africa has not been involved in any proper war since 1945 the potential threat from her neighbouring black states and from her own black population has necessitated the maintenance of a strong army which by 1983 had become the force described below.

The nucleus of the South African Army is constituted by a force of around 15,500 regulars whose main responsibility is to train the conscripts who will make up the army in the event of hostilities. At any one time up to 50,000 white conscripts will be undergoing training by the regulars. Each conscript serves 24 months with the colours, after which he is transferred to the Active Reserve for 12 years, during which time he serves a total of 720 days. Following this, he then serves for five years in the Citizen Force Reserve and then may be called upon to serve with the Commando Force (a 12-day a year military commitment) until the age of 55.

The South African Army is organised into two divisional HQs which are responsible for an armoured brigade (two tank and two MICV-borne infantry battalions) and a mechanised brigade (one tank and three MICV-borne battalions) as well as four motorised brigades (each of one armoured car battalion and three infantry battalions), a special reconnaissance regiment and an artillery contingent of nine field, four medium and seven light anti-aircraft regiments.

The artillery units are armed with 75 5.5in field guns, 65 25pdr gun howitzers and 40 155mm G-5 towed guns, and a number of self-propelled guns including 25pdr Sexton SPGs as well as more modern G-6 SP howitzers. The anti-tank element is provided by 6pdr, 17pdr and 90mm guns, while infantry support weapons include 81mm and 120mm mortars. A missile-equipped anti-aircraft regiment deploys three batteries of Crotale and three batteries of Tigercat missiles. Support services include 15 field engineer squadrons and three regiments of signals.

The armoured edge of the South African Army is provided by 250 Olifant tanks (updated Centurions) supported by 1200 Rafel MICVs (mechanised infantry combat vehicles), 500 light APCs (armoured personnel carriers) and 1400 Eland armoured cars. A particular feature of the South African armed forces has been the development of an indigenous arms industry since the 1967 arms embargo by the United Nations. Most weapons are based around existing models and then utilised for South African needs, a notable example being the 5.56mm G-4 rifle based on the Israeli Galil.

South Africa is a strong believer in forward defence and has committed large numbers of troops to Namibia to suppress the SWAPO guerrilla movement and to launch raids into Angola. Given that South Africa continues with her apartheid policies then it seems inevitable that the hostility of the black nations to the north will ensure that the South African armed forces have to remain on the alert.

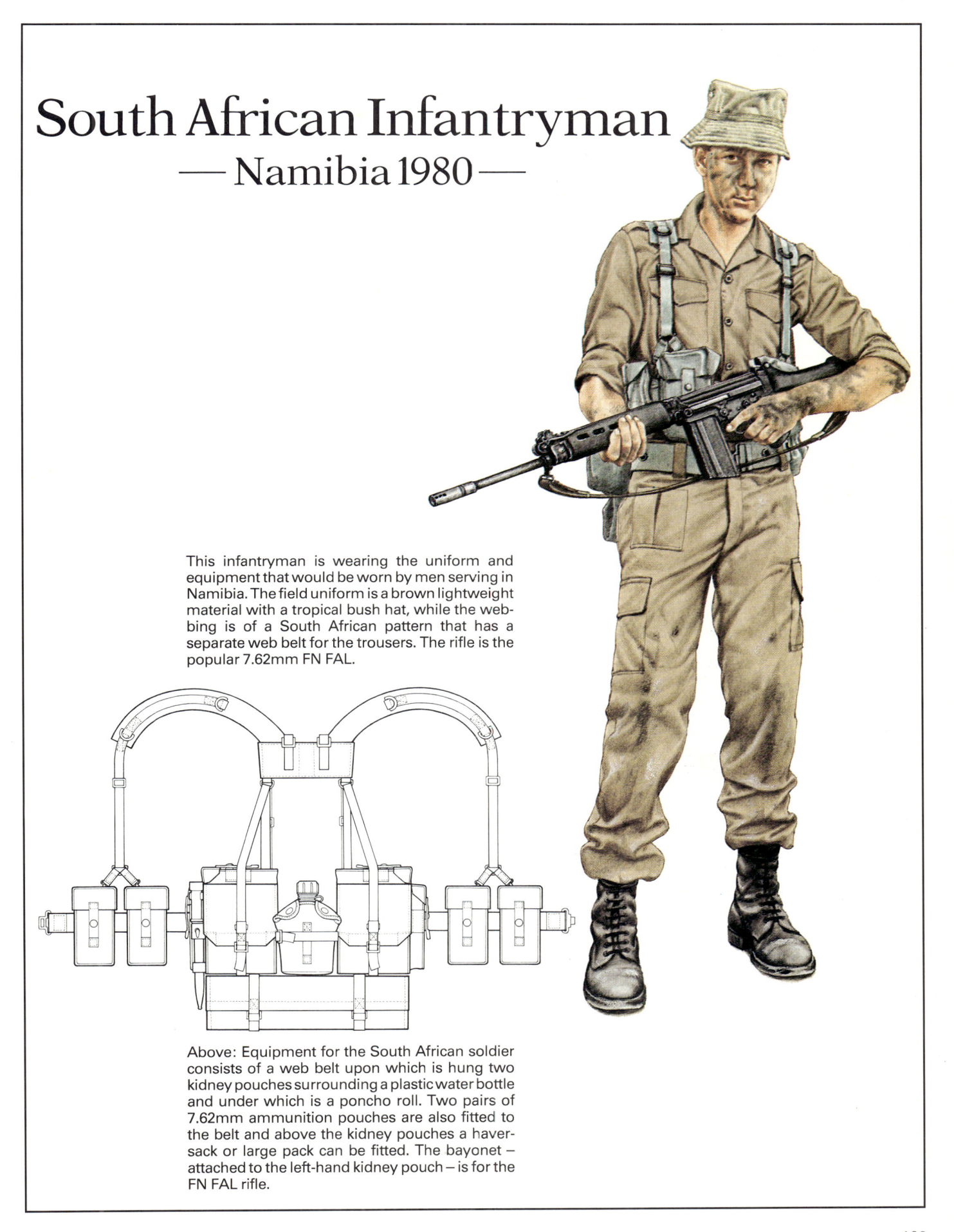

South African Infantryman
— Namibia 1980 —

This infantryman is wearing the uniform and equipment that would be worn by men serving in Namibia. The field uniform is a brown lightweight material with a tropical bush hat, while the webbing is of a South African pattern that has a separate web belt for the trousers. The rifle is the popular 7.62mm FN FAL.

Above: Equipment for the South African soldier consists of a web belt upon which is hung two kidney pouches surrounding a plastic water bottle and under which is a poncho roll. Two pairs of 7.62mm ammunition pouches are also fitted to the belt and above the kidney pouches a haversack or large pack can be fitted. The bayonet — attached to the left-hand kidney pouch — is for the FN FAL rifle.

The Middle East

The Arab-Israeli confrontation is now well into its fourth decade, and has six major conventional conflicts to its credit. In 1948 the newly-created Israeli Defence Forces (IDF) were weak and poorly structured, drawing their expertise from a number of uncoordinated guerrilla groups which were desperately short of conventional weapons. Smallarms, armoured cars, a few tanks and artillery pieces and a wide variety of World War II combat aircraft were hastily gathered together as a total of five Arab armies, numerically strong and comparatively well equipped, invaded the Jewish-held areas. Yet the IDF succeeded in defending the territory of the new state of Israel and even assumed the offensive, defeating each of its enemies in turn.

This pattern was soon to be repeated as the IDF refined its organisation to create a unique 'nation-in-arms', based on the mobilisation of substantial reserves in the event of a crisis, and further developed its tactical skill with the benefit of more modern equipment. By the early 1950s a distinctive Israeli strategy had emerged, emphasising the need for short decisive attacks on any Arab force that constituted a threat to the state's survival. In October 1956 this was put into effect in Sinai, when IDF units, spearheaded by paratroops, defeated a numerically superior Egyptian army, well-equipped from Soviet sources and occupying prepared defensive positions. The swiftness of the IDF advance was an indication that a new and extremely effective force was in the making. This became obvious 11 years later when, in a six-day blitzkrieg (5–10 June 1967), the IDF, now reliant on a combination of swift-moving armour and devastatingly effective airpower, defeated the armies of Egypt, Jordan and Syria.

But there were weaknesses in this strategy, analysed and exploited by the Egyptians and Syrians immediately after the Six-Day War. Unsupported armour could be stopped using the Soviet-supplied Sagger anti-tank missiles, aircraft could be prevented from providing close support by air-defence weapons from the same source (SAM-2, -3, -6 and -7, plus ZSU-23/4 cannon), and the element of surprise could catch the Israelis unprepared and unmobilised. By the Yom Kippur War of October 1973 these lessons had been absorbed by Arab armies that were better trained and commanded than before, and the IDF had to fall back on courage, initiative and superior equipment to survive. But survive it did, forging new tactical skills in the heat of battle and deploying all the latest US-supplied technology to achieve a remarkable victory. By June 1982, when the IDF invaded southern Lebanon in an effort to root out the Palestinian guerrillas, the strategy of blitzkrieg, using all-arms combat teams and virtually unassailable airpower, had been refined to a new level of effectiveness. For the first time, Israeli-produced equipment was on show, and although much of the fighting was done with Western-supplied and Israeli-modified weapons like the Centurion main battle tank (MBT) and F-15 jet fighter, both the Merkava MBT and Kfir jet were combat-tested, apparently with impressive results. The campaign may not have achieved all its political aims, but militarily the IDF had proved that it was still the leading exponent of conventional war.

By that time, however, the Arab-Israeli conflict was not the only one affecting the Middle East, for in September 1980 Iraqi forces invaded Iran. Despite Iraqi access to Soviet equipment (supplemented by selected Western items) and Iran's possession of sophisticated American weapons originally purchased by the Shah before his overthrow in 1979, both armies failed to display the tactical flair required for victory. Iranian Revolutionary Guards were sacrificed in wave after wave of frontal attacks on prepared Iraqi fire positions, and the war seemed set to continue its attritional stalemate for some time.

The implication is that it is not weapons that win wars, but the men who deploy, fire and maintain them. This theory is reinforced when the guerrilla forces of the Middle East are examined, for their record of success is poor, despite their access to sophisticated weapons, predominantly Soviet in origin. Even the Palestine Liberation Organisation, with its widespread political support and previous reputation for terrorism on an international scale, is now virtually a spent force militarily, having been defeated by the Israelis in southern Lebanon and forced to withdraw from Beirut. Similar problems were experienced in the mid-1970s both by the Kurds, overwhelmed by Iraqi forces, and the Dhofari rebels, defeated in a British-led counter-insurgency campaign. Although in all cases it is possible that the guerrillas will re-emerge in the future, they will still find victory elusive if they have not in the meantime absorbed the need for training, command, leadership and tactical skills.

Below: Iraqi commandos, distinctive in their camouflaged uniforms and helmets, show their enthusiasm during a training run in desert conditions. Armed with Soviet-supplied weapons, men such as these have faced heavy fighting in the war with Iran since September 1980.

Palmach Infantryman
—Palestine 1948—

As with other irregular armies, the members of the Israeli Palmach were armed and equipped from a variety of sources. This infantryman is no exception in that he wears British khaki drill trousers, a drill shirt of American origin, a civilian woollen cap and a red-and-white shemagh worn as a neck scarf. Equipment comprises a US Army cartridge belt (of World War I vintage) and a US World War II canteen and cover. During the 1940s the Israelis procured a considerable amount of their weapons from Czechoslovakia and this soldier is armed with a Model 24 rifle, the Czech version of the German 7.92mm Kar 98k carbine. By the late 1940s the Model 24 was clearly obsolete but, chronically short of armament, the Israelis were glad of whatever weapons they could pick up on the international arms market. The bayonet is for the Model 24 although the bayonet frog is of a British pattern.

Left: Members of the Jewish Palmach – shock companies of the Haganah defence force – use the cover of a ruined house during a firefight with hostile Arabs, 1948. Equipped almost entirely from ex-British stocks, the men are using a .303in Lee Enfield service rifle (left) and a 9mm Sten sub-machine gun.

THE MIDDLE EAST

The Egyptian Army in the 1948 War

Above: Student NCOs at the Egyptian Infantry School in Cairo. They are armed with 7·92mm FN self-loading rifles; the shorts indicate a summer uniform.

On 14 May 1948 the Egyptian 3rd Division, which comprised five infantry battalions supported by armour, artillery and substantial air elements, invaded the southern region of the newly-declared state of Israel. Commanded by Major General Ahmed Ali el Mawawi, the force was divided into two brigade groups, each responsible for a specific axis of advance. On the left, the bulk of the division (about 5000 men) pushed along the coast towards Gaza and Tel Aviv, aiming to link up with Iraqi and Jordanian troops advancing out of Samaria; on the right, another 2000 men, reinforced by the Egyptian-officered Muslim Brotherhood, penetrated the Negev Desert in the direction of Beersheba, hoping eventually to make contact with the Jordanian Arab Legion around Jerusalem. The Israelis, desperately short of trained manpower and heavy equipment, were faced with apparently insuperable odds and their defeat seemed inevitable.

Yet it was the Arabs who lost the war, suffering a series of humiliating set-backs on all fronts in a campaign conducted in fits and starts throughout the remainder of 1948. By early 1949 the Egyptians had been forced to negotiate an armistice—the first in a series of similar arrangements between Israel and the other Arab powers—and although a variety of factors contributed to this defeat, ranging from a lack of Arab coordination to the military expertise of the nascent Israeli Defence Forces (IDF), in the final analysis it was due to the failure of the Arab armies in the field. The Egyptian Army was no exception, displaying many of the tactical and command weaknesses that were to bedevil Arab attempts to defeat the Israelis over the next 35 years.

Problems were apparent from the start of the 1948 campaign. When the Egyptians began their advance, they did so in a mood of confidence which disguised the existence of fundamental military weaknesses. The two attacking columns, tied to existing roads or tracks by their dependence upon wheeled transport, were unwieldy and slow-moving, enabling the Israelis to prepare for their arrival at predictable points, and there was little command coordination or mutual support. Moreover, once committed to battle, the 3rd Division proved to be dangerously inflexible, adhering strictly to a text-book approach that took no account of terrain or the nature of the opposition. As early as 15 May, in an assault on the coastal-route village of Kfar Darom, defended by only 30 Jewish settlers, the full scale of the problems became apparent as the infantry and armour failed to cooperate and the artillery succeeded merely in hitting elements of its own attacking force. Nor was this an isolated incident: by the time of the first UN ceasefire in June, both Egyptian columns had been halted far short of their objectives. A similar pattern was repeated as the fighting resumed in July, and although the Egyptians were able by sheer weight of reinforcements to push closer to both Tel Aviv and Jerusalem, they failed to defeat the rapidly consolidating forces of the IDF. Indeed, when the second ceasefire ended in October, IDF units were well-placed to mount counter-attacks which split the Egyptian brigades into isolated pockets and forced them to begin withdrawing. By February 1949 the armistice was the only option short of complete surrender.

The campaign inevitably affected the Egyptian Army, although in ways which did little to improve its immediate military potential. Many of the younger, more nationalistic officers – men such as Gamal Abdel Nasser and Anwar al Sadat – felt a deep sense of humiliation and shame, and placed the blame squarely at the feet of the corrupt and ineffectual King Farouk. The Free Officers Movement was founded in 1949 in the immediate aftermath of the armistice and it was this group which overthrew the monarchy in 1952. In their concentration on political aspects of Egyptian affairs, they ignored the tactical lessons of 1948, neglecting to recognise the deep social divisions between officers and men, the poor training and inflexible tactics which made the Egyptian Army a slow-moving, predictable force, easily defeated by the considerably more adaptable and agile IDF. It was to take two more campaigns and two more defeats – in 1956 and 1967 – for these lessons to be comprehensively absorbed and for the modernisation of the Egyptian Army to get under way.

Egyptian Soldier
— Palestine 1948 —

Although the British were instrumental in laying the foundations of the modern Egyptian Army, the uniform has only a vague resemblance to British battledress. The standard outfit for combat and fatigues was a light khaki denim one-piece overall, fly-fronted; there is one pocket over the left breast. The beret was khaki except for artillerymen (black), military police (red), and cavalry (green); no cap-badge was worn by enlisted men. The boot-and-gaiter arrangement is identical to British practice. This man is armed with a Short Magazine Lee Enfield Mk III* with a 1907 pattern bayonet.

Below: Egyptian troops celebrate the capture of Deir Suneid settlement in the Gaza Strip on 24 May 1948. The 'tin hats' are of British make.

THE MIDDLE EAST

The Arab Legion

In October 1920, Captain F.G. Peake, a British officer serving with the Palestine Police, established a small military force whose task it was to maintain the internal security of the British mandated territory east of Palestine which was to become known as Transjordan. Initially this force, entitled Al Jaysh al Arabi (the Arab Army) but generally known as the Arab Legion, consisted of five officers, 75 mounted riflemen and 25 mounted machine gunners. A year later, however, Peake was ordered to increase the Legion's complement to some 750 men, organised into two infantry companies, two cavalry squadrons, an artillery troop and a signals section. Throughout the 1920s, under British command and with British finance, the Arab Legion continued to expand and, in 1931, a further unit, the camel-mounted Desert Patrol, was raised by Major J.B. Glubb to put an end to the raiding activities of nomadic desert tribesmen against Arab villages in the area.

By the outbreak of World War II, Glubb had assumed command of the Legion and, faced with the increasing threat of German influence in Syria and Iraq, the Desert Mechanised Force was enlarged to form the Mechanised Regiment. The Arab Legion saw action in both the Iraqi and Syrian campaigns of 1941 and 1942 in which it fought well and by 1945 had increased in number to some 800 men. In 1946, Transjordan became fully independent but the Legion remained under British command with a great many British officers staying on under contract. As a consequence the Legion had a distinctly British outlook for a Middle-Eastern formation, with uniforms, equipment, weapons, training and tactics being of British origin.

The first real and prolonged test of the Arab Legion's capability came a few years later, in 1948, with the withdrawal of British forces from Palestine and the formation of the state of Israel. On 15 May 1948, the Arab Legion crossed the River Jordan, safeguarding the Nablus and Ramallah areas against Israeli intervention, and on 19 May Glubb ordered an assault to secure the Old City of Jerusalem. After nine days of heavy fighting, constantly hampered by lack of reserves, ammunition and supplies, the Legion held the Old City and by the time peace was restored in April 1949, they had retained control of the whole of the West Bank. On the signing of the Rhodes Armistice, the West Bank became part of the Kingdom of Jordan.

The 1948 Arab-Israeli War saw a rapid expansion of the Arab Legion to some 10,000 men and the Jordanians continued this policy of enlargement bringing the force up to 25,000 by 1956. During this period the Legion diversified extensively. Nine infantry battalions were grouped into three brigades, forming the basis of a division, while a 10th battalion, known as the Hashemite Regiment, was raised in reserve. In 1952, the infantry-attached armoured car units, equipped with Marmon-Herrington Mark IV vehicles, were reorganised into the 1st and 2nd Armoured Car Regiments and in 1954, following the shipment to Jordan of a number of British Archers (17-pounder self-propelled guns), the Arab Legion Armoured Corps was formed. A year later, with the receipt of British Charioteer tanks (upgunned Cromwells), the 3rd Tank Regiment became operational.

A similar development programme was effected in the Arab Legion Royal Artillery. During the 1948 War the Legion's artillery inventory consisted of a mere eight gun-howitzers, but by 1954 three field-artillery regiments had been formed, equipped with British 25-pounders as well as a light anti-aircraft regiment armed with 40mm Bofors guns and an anti-tank regiment fielding 17-pounder anti-tank guns.

The increase in the Legion's size and importance within Jordan was paralleled by a growing Arab nationalism opposed to the British element within the Legion. The crisis over Egyptian control of the Suez Canal was coming to a head and anti-British feeling was high in the Arab world. Thus on 1 March 1956, King Hussein, under pressure from a group of Jordanian officers, dismissed Glubb Pasha, the Legion's commander-in-chief, and his departure was followed immediately by remaining British officers serving with the Legion. The Legion's name was changed to the Jordan Arab Army and from then on remained a solely Arab force.

Above: Photographed on the occasion of the Arab Legion Day parade in 1955, an officer of the Legion sits proudly aboard his camel. Camel-mounted troops were first introduced into the Legion with the creation of the Badieh or Desert Patrol by Glubb Pasha in 1931. Recruited mainly from among the Bedouin tribes, the Desert Patrol was renowned for its valour and high morale.

Arab Legion Sergeant
—Jordan 1953—

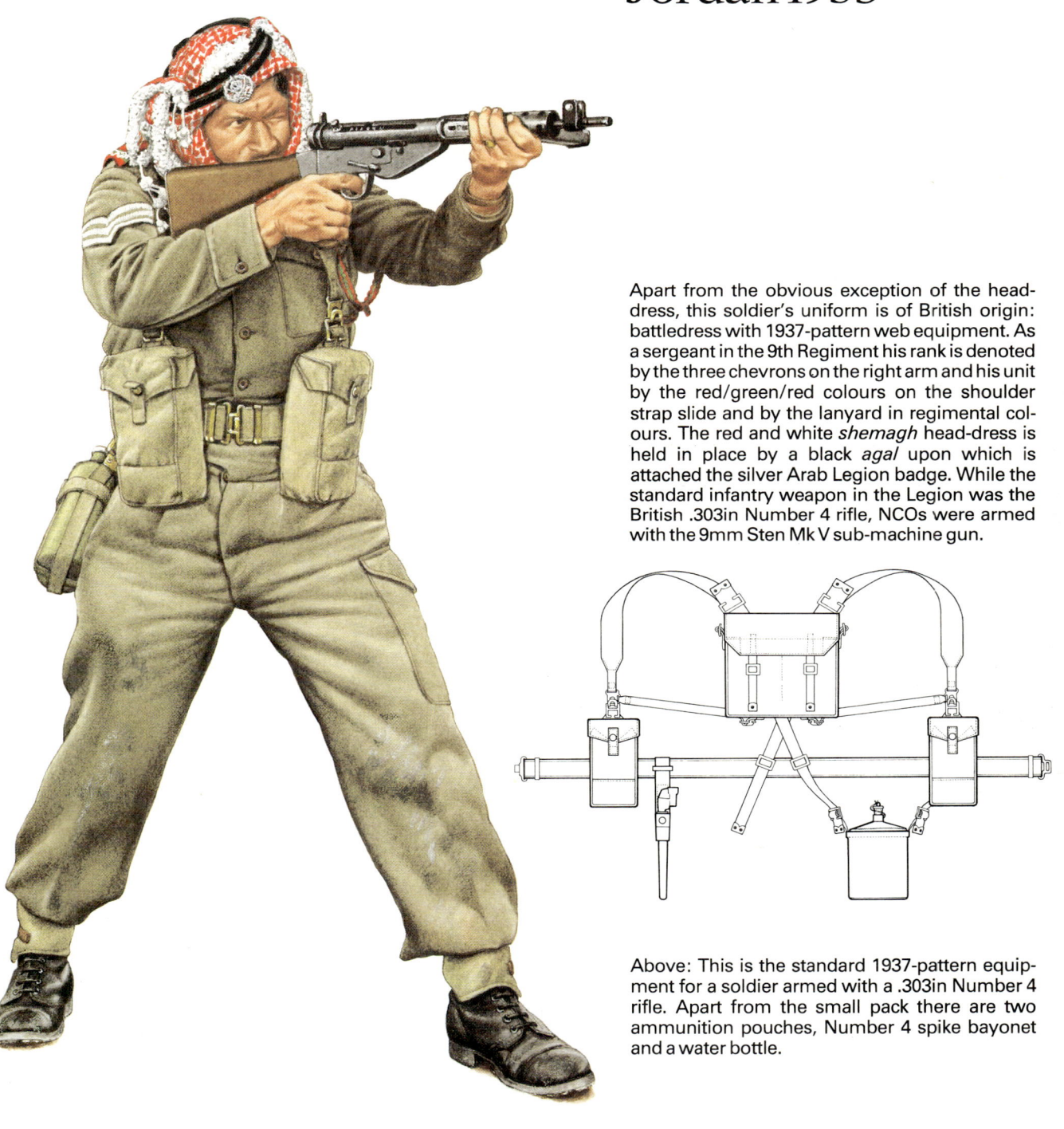

Apart from the obvious exception of the head-dress, this soldier's uniform is of British origin: battledress with 1937-pattern web equipment. As a sergeant in the 9th Regiment his rank is denoted by the three chevrons on the right arm and his unit by the red/green/red colours on the shoulder strap slide and by the lanyard in regimental colours. The red and white *shemagh* head-dress is held in place by a black *agal* upon which is attached the silver Arab Legion badge. While the standard infantry weapon in the Legion was the British .303in Number 4 rifle, NCOs were armed with the 9mm Sten Mk V sub-machine gun.

Above: This is the standard 1937-pattern equipment for a soldier armed with a .303in Number 4 rifle. Apart from the small pack there are two ammunition pouches, Number 4 spike bayonet and a water bottle.

THE MIDDLE EAST

The Israeli Army

By 1967 the organisation of the Israeli Defence Forces (IDF) reflected the strategic problems of the Jewish state. Despite military success in the 1956 Sinai campaign, when IDF units had routed a numerically-superior Egyptian army, the Israelis had been forced by international pressure to pull back to the unsatisfactory borders of 1949. With Syrian artillery on the Golan Heights overlooking northern Galilee, Jordanian troops threatening the thin coastal strip and the tenuous link with Jerusalem, and the Egyptians still capable of fielding large forces in Sinai, Israel was dangerously vulnerable to the nightmare of a concerted Arab attack.

The Israeli answer was to continue the concept of a 'nation-in-arms', whereby all fit citizens received military training before transferring to a reserve which, by 1967, was capable of producing an IDF of over 260,000 service personnel on full mobilisation. But if this became necessary, it was inevitable that the economy of the state would suffer through the sudden loss of manpower, so it was recognised that any campaign had to be kept as short as possible. Equally, as the superpowers had already shown in 1956 that they would step in to stop the fighting after only a few days for fear of uncontrolled escalation, it was essential for the IDF to achieve immediate success, destroying enemy forces and seizing territory that could be occupied or 'traded off' for future security. What resulted was the concept of a rapid, decisive, blitzkrieg-style assault, using airpower to clear the skies and fast-moving armour to penetrate Arab defences, demoralise their ground forces and occupy vital territory. Infantry would be committed to make the initial breakthroughs and to mop up by-passed enemy positions, but by the mid-1960s it was obvious that the Air Force and Armoured Corps were enjoying top priority, particularly in terms of re-equipment and supply.

To many observers, both inside and outside Israel, the Six-Day War of June 1967 confirmed the correctness of this chosen strategy. The Air Force gained immediate supremacy by making pre-emptive strikes on Arab airfields, and the armour swept forward on three fronts to destroy potentially overwhelming enemy ground forces. By 10 June, in a stunning display of military skill, the IDF had defeated the Egyptians, Jordanians and Syrians, leaving Israel in possession of all Sinai, Samaria, Judea and Jerusalem, and the Golan Heights. The contribution of the infantry, however, had been largely ignored. Despite hard fighting in Sinai, particularly around Rafah and Umm Katef, a predominantly infantry assault on Jerusalem (carried out by paras in the infantry role) and an initial breakthrough on the Golan by the Golani Infantry Brigade, it was the armour that took the bulk of the credit for victory. This led to an unfortunate concentration on the tank within the IDF that was to prove fatal in the early days of the Yom Kippur War of October 1973. It was to take the heavy losses of that war to reassert the need for 'all-arms' combat teams, in which infantry units, by now fully mechanised, played a crucial part. It was a lesson well worth learning.

Below: A patrol of Israeli paras in wooded country, somewhere on the West Bank (Judea-Samaria), June 1967. As the man on the left reports in by field radio, his colleagues, armed with FN-FAL rifles and a shoulder-launched anti-tank weapon, search for signs of the enemy.

Israeli Infantryman
— Six-Day War 1967 —

Israeli troops march to the front line during the Six-Day War. Despite a somewhat ragged appearance these soldiers are well armed with FN rifles and Israeli-produced Uzi sub-machine guns.

A typical arrangement of web equipment worn by Israeli soldiers in 1967; most items are local adaptations of US and British fittings. Attached to the belt are two British-type ammunition pouches and in between them is a US water bottle and first aid pouch. The entrenching tool attached to the pack is also of US origin.

Ever since the creation of the Israeli state in 1948 the Israeli Army has been kitted out with a diverse collection of arms and equipment, and this soldier of the Six-Day War is no exception. Uniform comprises a wool khaki shirt and French paratroop trousers, as well as a US M1 helmet covered with sacking and a helmet net. Webbing is of Israeli manufacture but based mainly upon British and American designs. Armament consists of the Israeli version of the famous 7.62mm FN FAL rifle, the standard Israeli infantry rifle used throughout the 1960s.

THE MIDDLE EAST

The Israeli Armoured Corps

Despite the pre-eminent position given to the tank by Israeli military theorists today, it was initially considered ineffective by the Israeli Defence Forces (IDF). In Israel's War of Independence (1948) the IDF deployed only one tank battalion composed of obsolete French light H-35s with one Sherman M-4 and two Cromwell tanks. This battalion met with little success and Israeli strategists came to regard tanks as slow and unreliable. More importance was ascribed to fast-moving infantry who would make deep penetration attacks into enemy positions. Nevertheless a number of modified Shermans and French AMX-13s were acquired to equip three rather infantry-heavy armoured brigades in time for the 1956 Suez campaign. The Shermans were highly successful in breaching strong Arab positions, so opinions were revised.

In the build-up to the Six-Day War of 1967 Israel concentrated on the potential of main battle tanks (MBTs) and aeroplanes to achieve success. In the process Israeli commanders realised that the tank crews would need different standards of conduct from the rest of the army. Israeli soldiers combine their undoubted military abilities with a highly individual appearance and attitude. This ostensible absence of military discipline is in part due to the 'newness' of the IDF, which lacks the long historical traditions of its Western counterparts, but even more significantly results from the relationship of the armed forces to

Above: An Israeli tank commander directs operations during the fighting in Lebanon in 1982. Integral with his new-style helmet are a pair of binoculars which allow him steady vision while at the same time leaving his hands free for other tasks.

Israeli society. The dividing line between civil and military has always been blurred in Israel, and as a true 'citizen's army' the IDF has accepted – and even encouraged – the more unorthodox tendencies of its troops. In the Armoured Corps this was expressed in a cult of individual initiative, where junior commanders were given a level of responsibility unknown in other armies. This approach had its critics, however, and some senior Israeli military men suggested that it was responsible for a less than good maintenance record within the Armoured Corps. Thus in 1965 General Israel Tal rejected the casual approach to discipline and his Armoured Corps Regulations called for a more conventional military appearance and a renewal of traditional distinctions between officers and men. And while Israeli tank soldiers have remained individual in appearance to a foreign eye, they are in fact more conformist than other members of the IDF.

During the 1960s Israel built up her tank forces so that on the outset of the Six-Day War there were 800 tanks at the ready, including British Centurions and US M4s and M48s. The Six-Day War was a resounding success for the theory of MBT pre-eminence and for the high standards of training and ability of the Armoured Corps soldiers, but the Yom Kippur War of 1973 led to a re-evaluation of Israel's tank tactics. Although Israel won the war, due in no small part to the fine conduct of the tank soldiers in the defensive battles, there were sharp questions asked about the heavy losses incurred by the MBTs when counter-attacking. The absolute importance of the MBT as a decisive weapon was reviewed and the tank men were accused of being too inflexible (partly perhaps as a reaction against their greater apparent discipline).

Although the vulnerability of their heavily armoured tanks to anti-tank guided weapons surprised the Israelis, they did not give up their belief in the importance of MBTs. There was a realisation, however, that mechanised infantry and artillery were an essential part of an armoured division and these troops were brought in to form an integral part of MBT-dominated battle groups, sharing the black beret and discipline of the tank soldiers proper. Continued emphasis on tank design – epitomised by the production of Israeli-built Merkava tanks – and on the importance of tank personnel has ensured that the men of Israel's Armoured Corps remain a specialist elite to rival any other within the IDF. To back them they have a highly capable workshop service which returns damaged tanks to the battlefield with incredible speed and reclaims and alters captured enemy material. However, the basis of the Israeli Armoured Corps' success lies in a commitment to sheer military efficiency which provides its tank units with an unmatched *esprit de corps*. In the campaign against Lebanon launched in 1982 the Israeli Armoured Corps was once again in action, and with its new Merkava MBTs proved convincingly that it was as effective as ever.

Israeli Tank Commander
— Six-Day War 1967 —

This Israeli tank officer wears a simple olive-green uniform surmounted by the Israeli version of the US tank crewman's protective helmet. Hanging from his neck is a junction box for the armoured vehicle communication system. Rank is indicated by the two green bars on the khaki slide attached to the shoulder strap, and in keeping with his officer status a revolver is carried on the web belt.

Below: The Israeli tank crewman's helmet of the Six-Day War was the US World War II model, but considerably modified and improved. Constructed of fibre and leather with padded earpieces, it featured a boom microphone which could be folded sideways to allow access. This helmet was subsequently replaced by the US 'bone-dome' version.

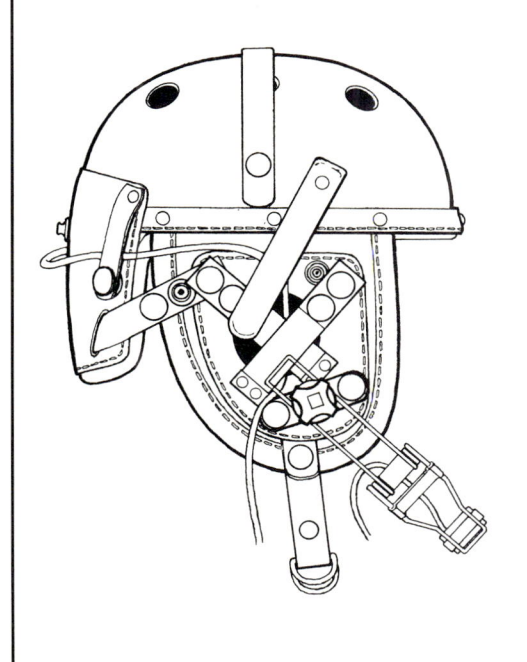

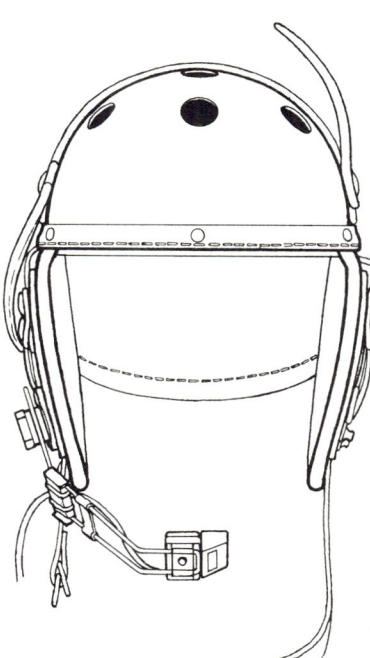

THE MIDDLE EAST

The Egyptian Army 1954-80

The character of the Egyptian Army has changed a great deal since the election of Colonel Gamal Abdel Nasser as president in 1954. Nasser and his successors Anwar Sadat and Hosni Mubarak have all had a military background and been, in effect, authoritarian military rulers of the country. Although the power of modern Egyptian presidents has rested in the last analysis on the army, their political orientation and military policy have differed widely. Nasser's regime was cloudily socialist and maintained exceptionally close ties with the Soviet Union while Sadat's was more conservative and initiated a serious break with Russia; Mubarak has moderated Sadat's line but still relies on the West for military support. All this has had much effect on the strength of the army, the type of equipment and tactics it uses, and on the political outlook of its commanders.

Nasser inherited armed forces with a fairly inglorious tradition of incompetence and pronounced social divisions. The main legacy of this era was a British rank and command structure with British-style uniforms. Nasser's reconstructed army after 1954 was very heavily armed with Soviet weapons and, whilst discipline was still harsh, the social gulf between officers and men was much reduced. This force had three main objectives: to maintain the regime in power, to destroy the state of Israel and to support Egypt's Arab allies in military disputes. While it performed reasonably satisfactorily in two of its roles, it suffered a disastrous reverse in the 1967 conflict with Israel. The inferiority of Soviet equipment, the unsuitable tactics advocated by Soviet advisers and the overwhelming success of the Israeli air attack were much to blame for the defeat but there was no disguising the fact that the Egyptian Army was not as good a fighting organisation as the Israeli Defence Forces. Many Israeli soldiers were particularly scathing about the quality of Egyptian officers.

After 1967 the quality of the Egyptian Army showed a considerable and growing improvement. The army was produced by conscription but since it was only 350,000 strong and many more conscripts became eligible each year than the 100,000 needed to maintain its strength, the annual intake was virtually composed of picked men. As military service was attractive to Egyptians in terms of pay and status many conscripts became regular soldiers at the end of their three-year term of duty and so Egyptian NCOs were increasingly experienced and professional. Training and education of all ranks was fairly thorough so that the human material fit to face the Israelis was quietly assembled from the ashes of the defeat in 1967.

By the early 1970s Egyptian commanders knew that their Soviet equipment was still inferior and, after President Sadat's rift with Russia in 1972, it was also in less fulsome supply, but they planned to fight the next war against Israel on their terms by using surprise. They had the advantage of being rid of Soviet tactical advisers and were able to retrain the army to adopt a more offensive outlook and to practice for a limited battle in which missiles would offset Israeli armoured and air superiority. The resulting 1973 attack on the Israelis was an initial success and the Egyptian Army performed very creditably until it was forced to reach out from its missile cover; then it was decisively defeated by Israeli armoured formations.

Above: By the early 1980s the Egyptian Army had severed its links with the Soviet Union, and its troops were even engaged in working alongside US soldiers in combined desert warfare exercises.

The Yom Kippur War of 1973 proved that the army had become much better than the Soviet-dominated and rather casual force of 1967 in terms of fighting ability but at the same time it was also, strategically, a weaker force. At odds with the Soviet Union there was no way in which Egypt could acquire the huge quantities of heavy weaponry needed to match the Israelis; the unsubsidised weaponry of the European powers was not affordable and the USA was always too deeply committed to Israeli security to arm a rival. But by the late 1970s the Americans were far more friendly and prepared to supply second-rank weaponry, and the Egyptian Army made the best of the situation by abandoning its threat to Israel and becoming a regional African power. Instead of being a heavy, armoured force prepared for blitzkrieg warfare it has shifted emphasis to possessing an ability to intervene decisively to aid the regimes of nearby states.

These more recent developments may not have been well received by Egyptian soldiers. Patriotic and well motivated as they may be, a proportion of them have an allegiance to the Arab cause which is wider than national interest. These men may regret the inability to challenge Israel and, as the army is the real guardian of the regime, their disaffection could be dangerous. To take care of this, every president since 1956 has had the services of a very large security service whose agents penetrate all ranks and departments of the armed services. This in itself is one of the distinguishing characteristics of the Egyptian Army: it is not only a military force but also a political one which must be carefully controlled by the regime.

Egyptian Commando
— Six-Day War 1967 —

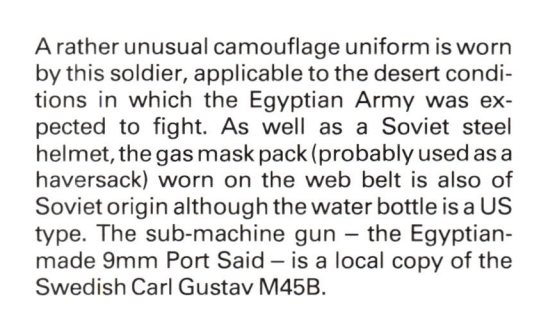

A rather unusual camouflage uniform is worn by this soldier, applicable to the desert conditions in which the Egyptian Army was expected to fight. As well as a Soviet steel helmet, the gas mask pack (probably used as a haversack) worn on the web belt is also of Soviet origin although the water bottle is a US type. The sub-machine gun – the Egyptian-made 9mm Port Said – is a local copy of the Swedish Carl Gustav M45B.

Right: Egyptian recruits simulate a charge into a trench shortly before the outbreak of the Six-Day War. Their youthful optimism was to have little effect against the professionalism of the Israeli Defence Forces.

121

THE MIDDLE EAST

The Jordanian Army

The Jordanian Army traces its roots back to the Arab Legion set up by the British in the 1920s. At first little more than a paramilitary security force the Arab Legion was expanded after the 1948 Arab-Israeli War when the new state of Israel was considered to be a threat to Jordan. The Legion grew into an all-arms force and after the expulsion of the British from the Legion in 1956 it became the Jordan Arab Army.

In 1956 the strength of the Jordanian Army stood at around 27,000 men and over the next 10 years its size was doubled and large sums of money spent on arming and equipping the force. Strong armoured units were correctly judged to be a key element for any Middle-Eastern army and by 1967 there were nearly 100 Centurion and about 300 M47 and M48 tanks within the Jordanian Army.

During the 1948 conflict with Israel the Jordanians had gained a reputation as resolute infantry fighters and when the Jordanian Army went to war again in 1967 it was confident of success. This optimism was to prove misplaced, however. The hardest fighting of the campaign took place in Jerusalem where the Jordanian garrison fought a pitched battle against the attacking Israelis for over 30 hours until it was overwhelmed by superior Israeli firepower. Jordanian positions within the West Bank were tactically faulty, with insufficient forces in reserve, so that once the Israelis struck they were caught off-balance. In addition, total Israeli air-superiority was the death-knell of Jordan's armoured units, shot-up before they could be committed against the Israeli ground forces. Jordanian problems were compounded by the lack of resolute leadership at the highest level so that within three days Jordan's badly mauled units were forced to retire across the River Jordan leaving the West Bank and Jerusalem in Israeli hands.

Jordanian troops stand alongside a dug-in Centurion tank during the dispute with Syria in 1970. Like their sometime Israeli opponents the Jordanians found the Centurion a highly effective battle tank, its powerful 105mm gun combined with good armour protection and a reliable powerplant. A feature of this tank is the US 0.5in Browning machine gun mounted on the turret in an anti-aircraft role.

The loss of the highly prosperous West Bank and the destruction of much of the army was a great blow to Jordan, but this was made worse by the influx of Palestinian refugees into Jordan. Owing little allegiance to King Hussein – who traditionally drew support from the semi-nomadic Bedouin tribesmen of the interior – the Palestinians constituted the majority of the population after 1967 and saw the Palestine Liberation Organisation (PLO) as their legitimate authority rather than the Jordanian government. Throughout the late 1960s armed PLO guerrilla units mounted operations against Israel from the East Bank which in turn invited ruthless Israeli reprisal actions against Jordan. The growing confidence of the PLO was seen as a direct threat to Hussein and in 1970 the army was called in to crush the PLO guerrillas. When the Jordanian Army moved against the PLO, Syria intervened in favour of the PLO but the army held out, repulsing the Syrians and defeating the Palestinian fedayeen who were expelled from Jordan.

The defeat of the PLO removed the threat of the Palestinians to Hussein and since then the army has played an important role in ensuring the security of the country against any internal or external threat. The army still draws upon the Bedouin for its men; few Palestinians enter its ranks and then only in the technical services where there is a shortage of suitably qualified personnel. The Jordanian Army played little part in the 1973 Yom Kippur War, and as offensive operations against Israel would be foolhardy Jordan has withdrawn from an overtly anti-Israeli position.

By the early 1980s the Jordanian Army had a strength of just over 60,000 men organised into two armoured divisions and two mechanised infantry divisions plus an independent tank brigade and four self-propelled artillery regiments.

Jordanian Infantryman
— Six-Day War 1967 —

The Jordanian Army has always been equipped and armed from a combination of two sources, American and British. This soldier wears a British steel helmet, webbing (1937 pattern) and anklets, while the US influence is represented by the 0.3in M1 rifle slung over his shoulder. The sets of web pouches fixed on the waist belt are for holding clips of M1 ammunition. An interesting indigenous feature are the khaki herring-bone twill fatigues, an item of uniform unique to Jordan.

Below: Jordanian troops stand alongside an American truck. While the uniforms display a predominantly British influence the weaponry is of US origin: the soldier on the right is armed with an M1 carbine and on the truck is a 0.5in Browning machine gun.

THE MIDDLE EAST
Dhofari Guerrillas

The Omani province of Dhofar is ideal guerrilla country. Situated in the extreme west of the sultanate and some 800km (500 miles) from the capital, Muscat, it is bordered in the west by broken terrain leading into the People's Democratic Republic of Yemen (PDRY), in the south by the Arabian Sea and in the north and east by a huge expanse of inhospitable desert known, appropriately, as the Empty Quarter. Within these boundaries the province is dominated by the jebel, a belt of mountains which act as backcloth to a thin coastal strip around Salalah, isolating it behind steep sided escarpments and virtually impassable wadis. Even the weather favours the guerrillas: between June and September much of the province is subject to the southwest monsoon, producing plant growth to mask guerrilla movement; for the rest of the year the high temperatures hamper counter-guerrilla operations.

The population of Dhofar is divided between those who live on the Salalah plain, enjoying the agricultural benefits of the monsoon, and those who inhabit the mountains; it was among the latter – tough, nomadic and intensely religious tribesmen, collectively known as jebalis – that resistance to the rule of the sultan, Said bin Taimur, emerged in the early 1960s. Their grievances were understandable – Said governed his country with heavy-handed repression, refusing to sanction any policies of modernisation or reform – and their aims, initially, were strongly nationalistic, specifying independence for Dhofar and an end to foreign (predominantly British) interference. Formed in 1962 from among exiled Dhofaris in the Gulf States, the Dhofar Liberation Front (DLF), led by Mussalim bin Nufl, instigated a low-level campaign of sniping, sabotage and ambush, but despite a weak response from the poorly-equipped Sultan's Armed Forces (SAF), they failed to make much impact. Outside support, principally from Saudi Arabia, was spasmodic and, by the mid-1960s, there were fewer than 200 DLF fighters active on the jebel.

In late 1967 the situation changed dramatically, for when the British withdrew from Aden Protectorate, the newly-emergent PDRY offered support to the DLF and sent its own 'advisers' into Dhofar. At a special congress in June 1968, they ousted the nationalist leadership, replacing it with a communist-dominated General Command under Muhammad Ahmad al-Ghassani, dedicated to the spread of Marxism. Renamed the Popular Front for the Liberation of the Occupied Arabian Gulf (PFLOAG – amended in 1971 to denote Popular Front for the Liberation of Oman and the Arabian Gulf), the new movement strengthened its hold on the jebel, often by means of intimidation, and it initiated a guerrilla campaign which by 1970 succeeded in forcing the SAF to withdraw.

In July 1970 Said was deposed by his son, Qaboos, who immediately introduced reforms, but it was to take another five years of hard fighting before the SAF, led and inspired by British officers well-versed in the minutiae of counter-insurgency, could claim a victory. During that period the PFLOAG (renamed yet again in 1974, this time as the Popular Front for the Liberation of Oman) achieved a maximum strength of about 2000 guerrillas, organised rather loosely into three 'regiments', one in each of the western, central and eastern sectors of Dhofar. Equipped from the PDRY with Soviet or Chinese weapons – the ubiquitous AK-47 assault rifle, plus RPG-7 anti-tank missiles, 75mm and 82mm recoilless rocket-launchers, 81mm and 82mm mortars, 122mm Katyusha rockets and even, in the later stages, SA-7 anti-aircraft missiles – the guerrillas (known to the SAF as the 'adoo') exploited their local knowledge and perfected the techniques of ambush, hitting SAF units at long range before melting back into the jebel to escape air and artillery response.

Fortunately for the SAF, the communist leadership, following policies which undermined both the Muslim religion and the tribal system, alienated many jebalis, while government 'civil development' centres, offering advantages of water, medicine, education and protection, attracted tribal settlement. Moreover, as guerrillas surrendered they were recruited into British-organised 'firqat' and sent back into the mountains to track down their erstwhile colleagues. It was a successful exercise in the exploitation of the natural fighting abilities of tribesmen in ideal guerrilla terrain.

Below: A guerrilla of the PFLO (Popular Front for the Liberation of Oman) poses for a Western cameraman. He is armed with an AK series assault rifle which has a permanently fixed bayonet, here folded back.

Dhofari Guerrilla
—Dhofar 1973—

This guerrilla from the latter stages of the conflict in Oman is kitted out in a mixture of European and indigenous uniform and equipment. The camouflage jacket is probably of East German origin, and a British 1958-pattern web belt holds a Soviet ammunition pouch. Armament comprises a Soviet 7.62mm AKM rifle. The rest of his clothing is of local origin.

Above: Blending into the desert a Dhofari soldier stands guard armed with an FN self-loading rifle. The harsh environment of the jebel provided the guerrillas with ideal terrain for conducting an insurgent war against the Omani authorities.

THE MIDDLE EAST

Egyptian Armoured Forces in the 1973 War

At the beginning of the Yom Kippur War on 6 October 1973 the Egyptian Army contained about 1750 main battle tanks (MBTs) of Soviet design (1650 T54/55s and 100 T62s). The majority were grouped into armoured divisions which initially remained to the west of the Suez Canal; the rest were organised into armoured brigades which accompanied the five infantry divisions tasked with crossing the Canal into Israeli-occupied Sinai. The Egyptian strategy was well thought out: as the infantry (having negotiated the Canal) infiltrated through the Israeli defensive positions of the Bar-Lev Line, they would remain beneath the protective umbrella of surface-to-air missiles (SAMs) and deploy a screen of Sagger anti-tank guided weapons (ATGW), before coming to a halt about 10km (6 miles) inside Sinai. Israeli counter-attacks, denied close air support, would be broken against the defensive shell of Egyptian positions and, as the war degenerated into attritional stalemate, the inherent Israeli economic weaknesses (made worse by sustained mobilisation) would be exploited to force a negotiated ceasefire on Arab terms. If this proved difficult, the main Egyptian armoured reserve could be deployed into Sinai against the weakened and demoralised Israeli Defence Forces (IDF) to achieve the decisive victory the Arabs wanted.

Above: Seated in front of a T54 tank, Egyptian troops learn how to strip a 7.62mm DPM tank-mounted machine gun. These men are all wearing the field cap introduced with the new uniform of 1955. The man on the left is wearing an olive drab sweater under his uniform, useful for the cold desert nights.

The plan came close to success, for between 6 and 13 October Israeli commanders in Sinai found it almost impossible to counter the SAM/ATGW combination and were forced largely onto the defensive, with all the attendant implications of long-term confrontation. Egyptian units to the east of the Canal could be defeated if they were tempted beyond the slant range of SAMs on the west bank, but so long as the armoured reserve remained uncommitted nothing more elaborate could be attempted. What the Israelis wanted was a set-piece battle on ground of their choosing, under conditions in which their airpower and armour advantages could be brought to bear.

The Egyptians made changes in their strategy, partly because local Israeli successes against units in Sinai threatened the security of the Canal bridgeheads, but mainly because, with the defeat of the Syrians on the Golan Heights, the full weight of the IDF would soon be available to force a decisive engagement. On 13 October, in an effort to pre-empt such a development, Anwar al Sadat ordered his armoured divisions across the Canal. On the following day the set-piece battle occurred as nearly 1000 Egyptian MBTs advanced on three main axes into Sinai, leaving the protection of the SAMs and rapidly outpacing the Sagger operators, most of whom were on foot. It was an ill-considered move, made worse by the inferiority of Egyptian equipment. Soviet tanks were poorly suited to desert warfare: their engines over-heated, requiring the crews to open ventilation louvres which exposed the tanks to counter fire; the tracks proved unable to cope with the rocky floor of the Sinai desert and the guns lacked both the range and sophisticated ammunition required to take out Israeli armour. In addition, the Egyptians found the tanks extremely cramped, adding to the fatigue of combat and leading many crews to abandon their vehicles at the first sign of trouble. By the end of the day, for the loss of only 10 MBTs, the Israelis had destroyed or captured over 250 Egyptian tanks and Sadat's armoured divisions had lost all coherence.

The battle – with nearly 2000 MBTs deployed it was described as the biggest tank battle since Kursk in July 1943 – was decisive. Once the enemy armour had been destroyed, the IDF was free to carry out the plan suggested by Ariel Sharon as early as 7 October – to counter-attack across the Canal into Egypt itself. The fighting was still to pose problems, particularly as Egyptian forces to the west of the Canal continued to enjoy SAM protection, but by the time of the ceasefire on 24 October the Egyptian armoured formations had virtually ceased to exist. Although the Israelis reported that Egyptian tank crews had displayed greater determination and bravery than in earlier wars, this was small comfort to men who, through a combination of poor strategic direction, Syrian ineffectiveness and inferior Soviet equipment, had been forced to fight an unequal battle and one for which they had hardly been prepared.

Egyptian Tank Crewman
— Sinai 1973 —

This tank crewman is wearing the type of sand-coloured field service uniform first issued in 1955 and still worn today. The padded helmet is of Soviet origin and made of black canvas with an internal headset; the white fur-lining indicates that it is the winter-issue version. Also of Soviet origin is the harness for a throat microphone around his neck and the jack for the RT/1C internal tank communication radio hanging down his shoulder.

Below: A T54 tank of the Egyptian Army moves rapidly through the Sinai in 1973. The majority of the Egyptian tanks in service were either T54s or the nearly identical T55, both armed with the 100mm anti-tank gun. In combat, these tanks proved inferior to their contemporaries, the Centurion and the M47/48 Patton. This particular tank has a 12·7mm DShKM machine gun mounted on the cupola.

The Syrian Army in the 1973 War

Prior to October 1973 the reputation of the Syrian Army as a fighting force was poor. It was deeply divided along ethnic and religious lines – many of its officers were drawn from the minority Alawite sect while its soldiers were predominantly Sunni Muslims – and had been heavily politicised through a succession of coups (over 20 since 1949) which had led to the creation of a radical Ba'athist government dominated by military men. It had an appalling record of weakness in battle, having been badly mauled by numerically inferior Israeli forces in 1948 and 1967 and defeated by fellow Arabs in 1970 when it had tried to lend support to the embattled Palestinians in Jordan. To the Israelis in 1973, secure in their positions on the Golan Heights overlooking the Damascus plain, the Syrians did not seem to constitute a particularly serious threat when the record of their army was considered.

But this was to ignore a number of factors that had come into play since 1970. In that year Lieutenant-General Hafez al Assad, head of the Syrian Air Force, came to power in another coup, and he spent the next three years gradually enhancing the potential of his army. He purged the officer class of those men who had been promoted because of their political beliefs and replaced them with officers of some military merit, and although many were still Alawites, their new sense of professionalism led to better relations with the soldiers and boosted morale. At the same time, Assad re-equipped his divisions with Soviet-supplied main battle tanks (MBTs), armoured personnel carriers, missiles and artillery of modern design, and accepted Soviet advisers to train the army in their use. Finally, by means of elaborate deceptions he exploited Israeli complacency, lulling them into a false sense of security while preparing a surprise attack, designed to recapture the Golan Heights, break through to the Jordan River and threaten northern Galilee. Coordinated with a simultaneous Egyptian assault across the Suez Canal into Sinai, this attack began at 1400 hours on 6 October 1973.

The Syrians conducted a two-pronged advance which caught the Israelis largely unprepared. In the northern sector of Golan the 7th Infantry Division, backed by part of the 3rd Armoured Division, drove approximately 500 MBTs (T55s and T62s) against positions held by the Israeli 7th Armoured Brigade, which fielded less than 100 tanks. Further south, in the main thrust, the 5th and 9th Infantry Divisions, supported by the 1st and elements of the 3rd Armoured Divisions, used 600 MBTs against the 57 tanks of the Israeli 188 Brigade defending the Rafid Opening. The assault was conducted in classic Soviet fashion, its intention being to achieve the breakthrough by weight of numbers and concentrated firepower.

But the Syrians still could not achieve success. The narrow front and broken, hilly terrain of the Golan proved unsuitable for mass armoured manoeuvre, channelling the tanks into predictable lines of advance which the Israelis could block, making full use of their superior training, morale and weapons to inflict disastrous losses on the attackers. Although some Syrian vehicles did break through to the Jordan River, they were unsupported and unable to advance any further, chiefly because they lacked the reinforcement of a second wave dedicated to exploitation. Over 800 of their tanks lay destroyed or abandoned on the Golan, many having simply run out of fuel or spare parts as the fragile Syrian supply chain cracked under the strain of war; there was little coordination as command and communications networks collapsed and there were no signs of the flexibility and initiative which might have enabled the remnants of the breakthrough force to carry on regardless.

Top: The crew of a Syrian BMP-1 atop their vehicle in Lebanon. Above: A Syrian commando practises his bayonet drill at a training camp.

Even so, the fighting had been hard, demonstrating that the Syrian Army was no longer a force to be lightly dismissed. Individual Syrian soldiers had fought well, officers had led their men forward in a manner unknown in 1967 and, as the Israelis counter-attacked, an effective defence had been set up around Sassa.

Syrian Soldier
— Golan Heights 1973 —

The Syrian Army is one of the most security-conscious in the world, and information on details of its uniforms is hard to find. This man's camouflage fatigues suggest that he belongs to an elite unit (Syrian regular troops wear olive drab or dark khaki), possibly commandos or paratroopers, but this is not certain. The fatigues appear to be based on a French pattern, although made in East Germany, and, like much Syrian equipment, have also been supplied to members of the Palestine Liberation Army. The helmet is of Soviet design as is the 7·62mm AKMS rifle.

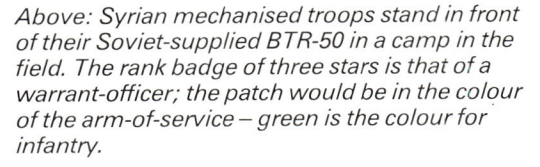

Above: Syrian mechanised troops stand in front of their Soviet-supplied BTR-50 in a camp in the field. The rank badge of three stars is that of a warrant-officer; the patch would be in the colour of the arm-of-service — green is the colour for infantry.

The Palestine Liberation Organisation

The Palestine Liberation Organisation (PLO) is a 'government-in-exile', dedicated to the aim of establishing an independent Palestinian state in territory now under Israeli control. Formed in 1964, after a 16-year period in which resistance to Israel had been fragmented and largely ineffective, the PLO was designed to coordinate and command the nationalist movement. Politically, much has been achieved – since 1964 over 100 states have recognised the PLO as the official voice of the Palestinian people and, since 1974, the organisation has enjoyed observer status at the United Nations – but militarily the PLO has failed to have a decisive impact.

One of the main problems has been a persistent lack of consensus about the most effective use of military force. The first chairman of the PLO, Ahmed Shuqairy, favoured the creation of an 'army-in-exile', organised along conventional lines and allied to the armies of other Arab states intent upon the physical destruction of Israel. But as the 1948-49 war had already shown, that was a questionable approach, implying a dependence upon ineffective non-Palestinian forces and an acceptance of PLO subordination in military terms. As early as 1965 Yassir Arafat's Al-Fatah group mounted selective 'hit and run' raids into Israel, indicating the potential of guerrilla warfare, and after the crushing failure of the conventional war approach in June 1967 (the Six-Day War) this became the favoured strategy. Arafat was elected chairman of the PLO in February 1969, but he could not unite the movement behind a single approach. Already George Habash had declared his preference for terrorism, founding the Popular Front for the Liberation of Palestine (PFLP) in 1968, and this triggered the creation of a number of splinter groups, each one progressively more extreme. When it is added that the conventional units of the earlier period – notably the Palestine Liberation Army (PLA) and the Syrian-controlled Saiqa – continued to exist, the degree of confusion may be fully appreciated.

But even if coherence had been achieved, success would probably have remained elusive, for despite the existence of a large, predominantly pro-PLO refugee population within which guerrillas could be raised, trained and supported, the Palestinians have lacked the benefits of unassailable 'safe bases'. In the early 1960s, this may not have been an acute problem – refugee camps in the Gaza Strip, the West Bank, Syria and Lebanon provided bases close to the Israeli borders – but since 1967 the Palestinians have been gradually pushed back. During the Six-Day War the Israelis captured Sinai, the West Bank and the Golan Heights, forcing the PLO to withdraw deeper into Egypt, Jordan and Syria. This obviously lessened the impact of the guerrillas as they had to travel so much further through hostile terrain to reach their targets in Israel (a factor which contributed to the growing preference for international terrorism), but more importantly it created intolerable strains between the Palestinians and their host nations. As 'front line'

Above: Well-equipped Palestinian troops prepare to leave the war-torn city of Beirut following the Israeli invasion of 1982. Although capable of spirited actions on a small scale the Palestinians were no match for the Israeli Army in conventional warfare. And yet despite the Israelis' military victory the PLO remains a political force in the affairs of the Middle East.

Arab states suffered the effects of Israeli retaliatory raids in response to guerrilla attacks and faced the emergence of PLO-controlled enclaves inside their own territory, the Palestinians lost significant support. In 1970 King Hussein forcibly ousted the PLO from its bases to the east of the Jordan River, while both Egypt and Syria imposed close controls upon the Palestinians within their boundaries. A PLO move to bases in southern Lebanon enabled the guerrillas to regain a degree of effectiveness, but the subsequent civil war in that state (1975-76), followed by an Israeli invasion (1982), had the effect of weakening them still further.

The result was an undermining of PLO independence, particularly in the aftermath of Arafat's enforced withdrawal from Beirut in 1982, for the humiliation of defeat, coupled to the effects of both Israeli and international counters to guerrilla and terrorist activity, drove a deep wedge into the Palestinian movement. A virtual civil war between Arafat's supporters and a Syrian-controlled faction led by Abu Musa in northern Lebanon in late 1983 reinforced this division, leaving the PLO militarily a spent force. Arafat survived, exploiting the political strengths of the PLO, but the Syrians assumed the power to dictate Palestinian strategy, destroying the military initiative of the PLO and subordinating its aspirations to those of a wider Arab world.

PLO Guerrilla
—Golan Heights 1974—

Above: PLO troops at work on the maintenance of a Soviet-built 73mm RPG-9 recoilless rifle at a PLO base in southern Lebanon.

Although PLO troops usually wear military uniform this guerrilla fighting on the Golan Heights is kitted-out in civilian clothes, which include the famous shemagh head scarf. Armament comprises an automatic pistol, worn at the waist, and a Degtyarev RPD light machine gun. The RPD entered Soviet service shortly after World War II and has since been exported worldwide to friendly nations and political groups. Capable of a practical rate of fire of 150 rounds per minute it is fed by two 50-round ammunition belts held in a drum magazine.

THE MIDDLE EAST

The Iranian Army

Although the army of the Islamic Republic of Iran is a highly radical institution brought into being by the revolution of 1979, it nevertheless owes much to the imperial legacy of the previous Shah's regime.

When the Shah achieved real control over Iran after the coup of 19 August 1953 he set about a comprehensive, though autocratic, modernisation programme for the nation. The army played a key role in the process, as well as guaranteeing Iran's internal and external security. Enjoying a new found power as an oil-producing nation Iran drew predominantly upon US military resources for the supply of its armed forces.

During the 1960s and into the next decade the army increased in size considerably, reaching a figure of 150,000 regular forces with 400,000 in reserve by 1979. Armament was provided on a lavish scale, weapons coming from a variety of sources, including British Chieftain and Scorpion tanks, US M48 and M60 tanks, APCs, artillery, anti-tank and anti-aircraft weapons, and helicopters.

Despite the fact that the Shah had raised up the army to its highly prestigious position within the state it did not save him during the 1979 revolution. The Shah's reforming measures had outraged the religious establishment and alienated the conservative masses while his autocratic methods turned the emerging middle classes against him, so that an alliance of these powerful forces – fuelled by Islamic fundamentalism – brought about his downfall in January 1979.

After the expulsion of the Shah, command of the army was vested in the president but real power was exercised by the religious leader Ayatollah Khomeini whose fundamentalist vision was the directing force in the Iranian Army after the revolution. Quite what effect the revolution had upon the army is hard to establish but certainly numbers fell and the loss of many officers through anti-army purges and desertion reduced basic military efficiency. More serious for the army's effectiveness as a military force was the pronounced anti-Western line adopted by the new regime which, especially after the take-over of the American embassy in Tehran, denied the army the essential logistic support facilities for its highly advanced weapon systems.

The Iraqi invasion – designed to exploit the confusion in Iran's armed forces – was a severe test of the army's ability. Fortunately for Iran, the Iraqi armed forces were of indifferent quality and poorly led so that after some initial setbacks the Iranians were able to hold the Iraqi advance. The invasion was, in fact, a unifying force in Iran and a holy war was instigated by the Mullahs to repel the invaders. The fundamentalist spirit which pervaded most of Iran transformed the army into a popular military force where conventional military doctrine was largely replaced by religious fervour.

In the vanguard of this religious/military enthusiasm was the Pasdaran or Revolutionary Guard Corps, a force of around 150,000 men organised to spearhead the costly frontal offensives that characterised the Iranian counter-offensive. Formed into battalions, the Revolutionary Guard Corps either served independently or were attached to regular army brigades. Despite their bravery, a lack of tactical expertise and suitable support weapons ensured high casualties for only limited gains. Typical of their approach to military matters were the preparations for the 1984 spring offensive: thousands of plastic keys were sent to the front-line to be distributed to the troops as symbolic reminders of the fact that if they were killed in action the keys would open the gates to heaven!

The regular troops have a more prosaic attitude towards combat which is compounded by logistic shortages and a considerable level of confusion as to how the war should be waged. Precise details of the strength and organisation of the Iranian Army are impossible to ascertain but estimates can be made: some three or four armoured divisions are committed to the struggle; there are four infantry divisions of varying quality and Iran's elite forces consist of three paratroop brigades and three airmobile brigades, all of whom are used in an infantry role.

Above: A blood-spattered Iranian soldier rests in his emplacement following an engagement with Iraqi forces. The Iranian Army is well equipped with smallarms – such as the 7.62mm G3s carried here – but lacks heavier support weapons. Tactics are rudimentary and Iranian disregard for human life has led to heavy casualties.

Iranian Revolutionary Guard
—Gulf War 1980—

Unlike their Iraqi opponents who normally wear khaki drill uniform, the Iranian armed forces often wear olive green fatigues even though much of the fighting takes place in semi-desert regions. The helmet is the US M1 pattern while the webbing seems based on British models, although the immediate source is unclear. Armament comprises the West German H&K 7.62mm G3 assault rifle, which alongside the Belgian FN FAL, the US M16 and the Soviet AK series is one of the great export successes in modern smallarms manufacture.

Unchanged since the days of the Imperial Iranian Army, this set of webbing equipment comprises two web ammunition pouches, a bayonet for the G3 rifle and a water bottle.

THE MIDDLE EAST

The Iraqi Army

By the early 1980s the Iraqi Army's position within the state of Iraq was in grave danger. The immediate threat to its existence came from Iranian forces, putting it under considerable pressure after years of war. Besides this there were the threats of internal disunity which were stirred up by lack of success in the war; the Sunni Muslims who are the nation's rulers and who make up virtually the entire officer corps of the army are a minority in the population. Even more threatening is the fact that divisions within the Sunni Muslims themselves could be reopened because the most obvious way of ending the war would involve toppling the ruling group of Sunnis who dominate political life and form the officer corps of the army's most effective units. All in all a bleak future that was set in motion by the Iraqi attack on Iran in 1980.

The war itself has revealed that the army's apparently imposing strength was not as great as it seemed. Oil wealth had allowed Iraq fully to equip the soldiers brought to the forces by universal two-year conscription. This had given the state an army of 180,000 with 250,000 reserves organised in a standing force of four armoured, two mechanised and four infantry divisions with an independent armoured brigade, two independent infantry brigades, one special forces brigade and the Republican Guards brigade. In the autumn of 1980 it seemed that a brisk campaign would resolve the border dispute with Iran, then in turmoil following the fall of the Shah, particularly as the large Iraqi forces were well equipped and possessed nearly 2000 Soviet-built main battle tanks.

The Iraqi invasion did not go according to plan, however: the Iranian forces had not disintegrated as far as had been imagined and the Iraqis had to fight long and costly battles before they were able to gain the disputed territory. Once on Iranian soil the obvious defect of their battle plan became apparent: there were no strategic objectives in Iran that were within easy reach and so no way in which the Iraqi Army could deal a hard enough blow to end the war. In addition, the Iranian Army was still in being and was backed by a fanatically determined religious government, reinforced by suicidally brave Revolutionary Guards. A series of costly offensives by the Iranians pushed the Iraqis back to their starting line in most places by mid-1983 so that the Iraqi Army was forced on the defensive everywhere. Bereft of military success, the Iraqi hopes of making peace foundered on Iranian demands for the downfall of Iraqi President Saddam Hussein.

Despite the fact that Iraq was well supplied by the Soviet Union, its poor performance in the war against Iran demonstrated the many weaknesses of the army as a fighting institution. The officer corps lacked both proficiency and elan, and its rigid adherence to Soviet tactical doctrine during the fighting revealed the army as a clumsy and ultimately brittle instrument of the state's ruling elite.

Although far distant from the power struggles in Baghdad, the ordinary Iraqi soldier is not without some political influence. Most conscripted men come from the majority Shi'ite Muslim population which has been dominated by the Sunnis for centuries. There is also a significant minority of Kurds who are potentially hostile to central authority. These men may have become less than enthused with the prosecution of the war which has resulted in heavy casualties. Although they cannot pose a direct danger in themselves their disaffection might allow the Iranians sufficient success that factions within the Sunni officer corps would be compelled to act to 'save' the army and the state. Two such attempted coups were snuffed out in 1983 but the crisis is growing.

The essential fact is that the Iraqi Army must have an end to the war. The most satisfactory end would be through military victory which would destroy the Iranian threat; but reports indicate that the Iraqi Army seems to have abandoned hope of this and is concerned mainly to defend Iraqi territory. While this dangerous situation persists the Iraqi Army cannot be regarded as a totally reliable political instrument because all Iraqi history indicates that a coup would be mounted by officers of the armed forces.

Above: Armed with AK assault rifles Iraqi soldiers take cover during an engagement alongside the Shatt al Arab. Below: Iraqi troops celebrate a tactical advantage over their Iranian enemy while displaying a portrait of Iraqi leader President Saddam Hussein.

Iraqi Army Corporal
—Gulf War 1980—

Reflecting the climatic conditions of the Iran-Iraq war, a lightweight khaki uniform is worn, as are canvas and rubber desert boots. The two stripes pinned to the sleeve indicate rank while the Iraqi national symbol is represented in a gold eagle badge on the beret. As Iraqi weapons are largely Soviet-supplied, a 7.62mm AKMS assault rifle is carried with AK magazine pouches attached to the waist belt.

Below: An Iraqi soldier prepares to fire an RPG-7 rocket launcher at an Iranian position by the Shatt al Arab waterway. The fighting in this area marked the opening of the Iraqi offensive against Iran.

THE MIDDLE EAST

Israeli Airborne Forces

Above: Armed with Uzi sub-machine guns a section of Israeli paratroops prepares to go out on patrol on the Golan Heights. Left: Although Israel's paratroops act mainly in an infantry role, parachute training is taken seriously and five of Israel's mechanised infantry brigades have a basic paratroop ability.

Israeli paratroop forces came into being in 1954 when Moshe Dayan brought together the Independent Paratroop Battalion with Unit 101, a crack fighting unit whose main function had been to launch reprisal raids against Israel's Arab opponents. Known as the 202nd Parachute Brigade, the new formation faced its first major test two years later during the Sinai Campaign of 1956. Led by their commanding officer, Lieutenant-Colonel Rafael Eitan, 395 men of the 1st Battalion of 202nd Brigade made a daring parachute drop to secure the eastern end of the Mitla Pass, and hold it until relieved by a force of motorised infantry led by Colonel Ariel Sharon. Although the brigade suffered heavy casualties the position was secured and the paratroops earned for themselves the reputation of first-class combat troops.

In keeping with their Unit 101 ancestry Israeli paratroops have been employed in cross-border raids and have become expert in close-quarters fighting. Indeed, like many other paratroop units throughout the world, Israeli paratroops are mainly used as elite infantry, spearheading assaults on key enemy strongholds. The paratrooper's role as a vanguard of the Israeli Army was demonstrated during the Six-Day War of 1967 when the 55th Parachute Brigade stormed the heavily fortified Jordanian positions in the Old City of Jerusalem, and during the 1973 Yom Kippur War when the 31st Parachute Brigade helped hold the Syrian onslaught on the Golan Heights and were prominent in the subsequent counter-attack.

Perhaps the most audacious feat performed by Israel's paratroops was the Entebbe raid of 3 July 1976 when a select band of paratroops and special forces flew across Africa to Uganda and rescued over 100 Israeli hostages held captive by PLO guerrillas.

The success of the paratroops during the Sinai Campaign ensured their future as part of the Israeli Defence Forces and after that campaign their numbers were steadily increased. During the early 1980s five of Israel's 10 mechanised infantry brigades were paratroop-trained.

Israeli paratroops are all volunteers and the 18-month training programme is exceptionally rigorous. Commando-style skills of weapons use, demolition and night fighting are emphasised as part of their preparation for the clandestine cross-border raids that certain of the paratroop units – especially the 269 Counterterrorist Unit – are called upon to carry out. Since the Yom Kippur War most paratroop activity has been against PLO bases in southern Lebanon where small groups of paratroops have been dropped in secrecy using HALO (high-altitude low-opening) techniques. Whether in war or in ostensible peace Israel's paratroops have an important role to play.

Israeli Para Corporal
— Lebanon 1982 —

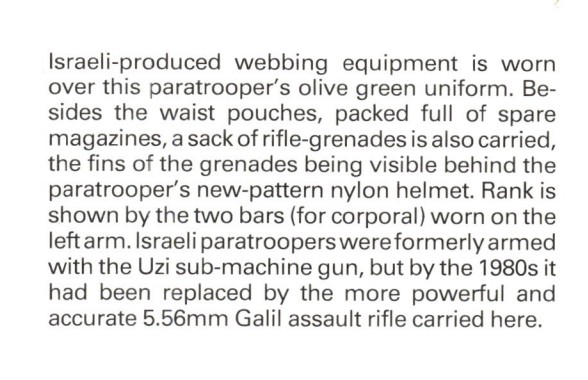

Israeli-produced webbing equipment is worn over this paratrooper's olive green uniform. Besides the waist pouches, packed full of spare magazines, a sack of rifle-grenades is also carried, the fins of the grenades being visible behind the paratrooper's new-pattern nylon helmet. Rank is shown by the two bars (for corporal) worn on the left arm. Israeli paratroopers were formerly armed with the Uzi sub-machine gun, but by the 1980s it had been replaced by the more powerful and accurate 5.56mm Galil assault rifle carried here.

Below: A distinctive feature of Israeli paratroop equipment is the broad nylon shoulder straps attached to the main belt with laces. On the belt are attached a number of pouches for ammunition and combat-survival equipment.

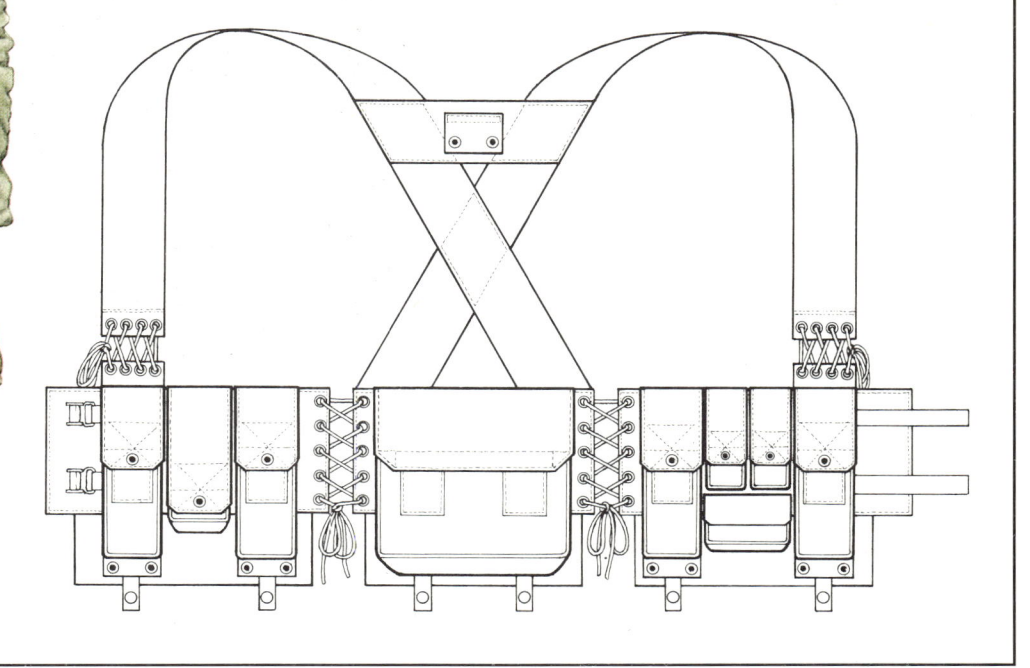

THE MIDDLE EAST

The Lebanese Army

The Lebanese Army played a brief role in the 1948 Arab-Israeli War, but thereafter was largely concerned with internal security, and was regarded as virtually a private militia by the country's dominant Maronite Christians, who under the 1943 National Pact held the presidency and command of the armed forces. Lebanon tried to stand aside from the Arab-Israeli conflict, but was embroiled by the presence of large numbers of Palestinian refugees in camps in Beirut and southern Lebanon. Palestinian attacks on Israeli targets led to Israeli reprisals, which the Lebanese Army was powerless to prevent. This failure to protect the largely Muslim population of the south, combined with a change in the population balance in favour of the Muslims and a general economic crisis, fuelled discontent, and in April 1975 Lebanon erupted into civil war. Maronite attempts to use the army against their leftist, Muslim, and Palestinian opponents led to its dissolution into its constituent religious factions, and throughout the course of the whole war it played only a negligible role.

A sort of peace was imposed after Syrian intervention in 1976, but the preservation of the status quo did not resolve the causes of the conflict, and prevented the rebuilding of the army. In March 1978, therefore, when Israel invaded southern Lebanon to destroy Palestinian bases there, the Lebanese Army was unable to offer any opposition.

From 1978 the United States assumed responsibility for improving the training of the Lebanese soldiers and supplied them with equipment, although not enough of the heavy weapons they needed to outgun the well-armed militias. In addition, so-called 'virgin battalions' were formed from officers and men who had not been too closely involved with any of the country's warring factions. Attempts to impose conscription, however, are not successful in Lebanon, as many groups and sects resist it, and the country is too fragmented for effective enforcement. Despite the efforts of the United States, therefore, the armed forces remained under-strength, and when Israel invaded again in June 1982 the Lebanese Army was still an irrelevant factor. The crisis provoked by the 1982 invasion showed the Lebanese Army to be still deeply divided, with three brigades loyal to the Maronite Phalange, two made up of a mixture of Sunni Muslims and Christians, and a sixth largely Shi'ite.

The Israelis pulled back from the Chouf Mountains, a stronghold of the Druze minority, in September 1983. The Phalangist militia and the Lebanese Army tried to move in, but were repulsed by the Druze, despite support from the guns of the US battleship *New Jersey*, stationed off the Lebanese coast. In the spring of 1984 the Lebanese Army suffered a further defeat, and practically ceased to exist as a unified force, when the Shi'ite Amal militia took over west Beirut. During subsequent fighting,

Above: Lebanese conscripts undergo basic drill. In April 1983 universal military service was introduced but in many Muslim areas conscription was impossible to enforce. Left: A Lebanese soldier stands guard holding a 5.56mm M16 rifle.

in which Amal broke the power of the rival Sunni Mourabitoun militia and attacked Palestinian refugee camps in Beirut, it had the backing of the army's Sixth Brigade, which by the summer of 1985 was practically indistinguishable from Amal. Without a genuine reconciliation of Lebanon's divided communities, there seems no prospect of a reconstruction of the Lebanese Army to turn it into a unified national force.

Lebanese Infantryman
—Lebanon 1982—

A member of the hard-pressed force fighting in Beirut in 1982, this soldier is kitted-out in the standard olive-green fatigues of modern combat, and wears high black leather boots. A 10-pocket web bandolier for holding ammunition magazines is worn around the waist. Carried over the right shoulder on an improvised sling is a US 5.56mm M16A1 assault rifle with the curved 30-round magazine.

Left: Trained by US Marine instructors and armed and equipped from US sources Lebanese recruits are taught the art of marching.

South Asia

The countries of South Asia – India, Pakistan, Burma, Bangladesh and Sri Lanka – are all former colonies of Britain and the British left a greater or lesser mark on the armed forces of these countries when they withdrew in 1947–48. Since Independence, however, the armies of the region have developed in their individual ways in response to the conflicts that have bedevilled the region since 1947.

Even as the British withdrew they left behind a region already in the throes of conflict and with a potential for further outbreaks. The fundamental cause of the violence was religion, and this had been manifested in communal riots of horrific proportions during the final months of British rule. Although an attempt was made in the sub-continent to defuse the situation by the creation of Hindu India and Muslim Pakistan the chances of a lasting peace were slim. From the start, conflict between India and Pakistan was firmly on the cards.

It was made inevitable by the arbitrary way in which the new states were established, for neither accepted the territorial boundaries imposed, particularly in Kashmir, where clashes took place between units of the Indian and Pakistani armies as early as 1947. The pattern was to be repeated in 1965 and 1971, producing full-scale conventional campaigns in which armour, mechanised infantry, artillery and airpower (including airborne forces) were deployed. In this particular case, India eventually prevailed, defeating the Pakistanis in a blitzkrieg-style attack in 1971. She was not necessarily the most powerful state in the region, however: in 1962 her forces had been badly mauled by the Chinese in a border conflict fought in the inhospitable terrain of the Aksai Chin and North East Frontier Agency. Further problems derived from the 1947 division of India were resolved when the new state of Bangladesh, created by means of a guerrilla campaign conducted by the Mukti Bahini and assisted by an Indian invasion, became independent in 1971.

Bangladesh had been known previously as East Pakistan, and its secession highlights yet another strand in the web of South Asian violence: that of minority or ethnic pressure for self-determination. All the states of the region have suffered from this problem at some time since independence, and while Bangladesh represents a major success for self-determination (coming after years of repression, electoral fraud and massacre by the West Pakistan authorities), other similar movements have not been totally ineffective. In Burma the Karen revolt of 1948–50 caused problems for the central authorities, while in Sri Lanka (Ceylon) the Tamil minority has conducted a campaign of growing violence against the Sinhalese-dominated government since independence in 1948. But the chief sufferer from such pressure has been India, reflecting the disparate nature of the state. Since 1947 she has had to respond to guerrilla and terrorist attacks carried out by Tamils, Naxalites, Azad ('Free') Kashmir forces and, most recently, extremist Sikhs in the Punjab. In June 1984 elements of the Indian Army were used to seize the Sikh Golden Temple at Amritsar, headquarters of a growing revolt, and this triggered a fresh wave of communal violence throughout India, which was aggravated by the assassination of Prime Minister Indira Gandhi by vengeful Sikhs in October 1984.

Such a wide range of conflict has inevitably affected the organisation and development of the region's armed forces. The rivalry of Pakistan and India is reflected in terms of military strength, and although the Pakistani forces are smaller than their Indian counterparts, they strive to maintain a balance by fielding the most modern weapons available. Since the mid-1950s, when Pakistan was persuaded to contribute to Western policies of containing communism, joining both the Baghdad Pact/Cento (Central Treaty Organisation) and Seato (Southeast Asia Treaty Organisation), the main source of weapons supply has been the United States, providing M47/48 main battle tanks (MBTs), M113 armoured personnel carriers (APCs), guided anti-tank missiles and, in a deal negotiated in 1984, ultra-sophisticated F-16 fighter-bombers. This last represents part of a deliberate US policy of treating Pakistan as the frontline against supposed Soviet aggression in the region, but at the cost of alienating India. With its main rival firmly in the US camp and its fear of China still apparent, it is hardly surprising that India has turned to the Soviet Union for support, receiving T72 MBTs, BMP-1 APCs, a range of artillery pieces and, in the latest deal, permission to build MiG-27 fighter aircraft under licence. Neither Pakistan nor India is totally dependent upon its respective superpower sponsor and neither has adopted the politics of its main supplier, but the fact that what had been a purely regional rivalry is now seen as important in terms of the Cold War must be a cause for concern, particularly since India tested a nuclear device as long ago as 1972 and Pakistan is likely, in the near future, to acquire a nuclear capability.

The situation is equally worrying at lower levels of military activity, for all the states of South Asia have been affected by their need to conduct counter-insurgency or policing operations. There were army-backed coups in both Burma and Pakistan in 1958, and although the Burmese Army has since reverted to a more passive political role, its counterpart in Pakistan has regarded it as a duty to intervene whenever a crisis occurs, as happened most recently in 1977. Neither India nor Sri Lanka has yet suffered a coup, but the potential is undoubtedly there, particularly when the army is used more and more as a blunt instrument of government policy against ethnic minorities. With internal pressures mounting, coups an established pattern and outside interference the norm, the potential for future conflict for the armies of South Asia is awesome.

Right: Indian troops, sporting a wide variety of headgear but all equipped with ex-British .303in Lee Enfield service rifles, wait on board a truck during the advance on Dacca in East Pakistan (Bangladesh), December 1971. Members of II Corps, the men have just contributed to the capture of Jessore, a potential strongpoint abandoned by the Pakistanis.

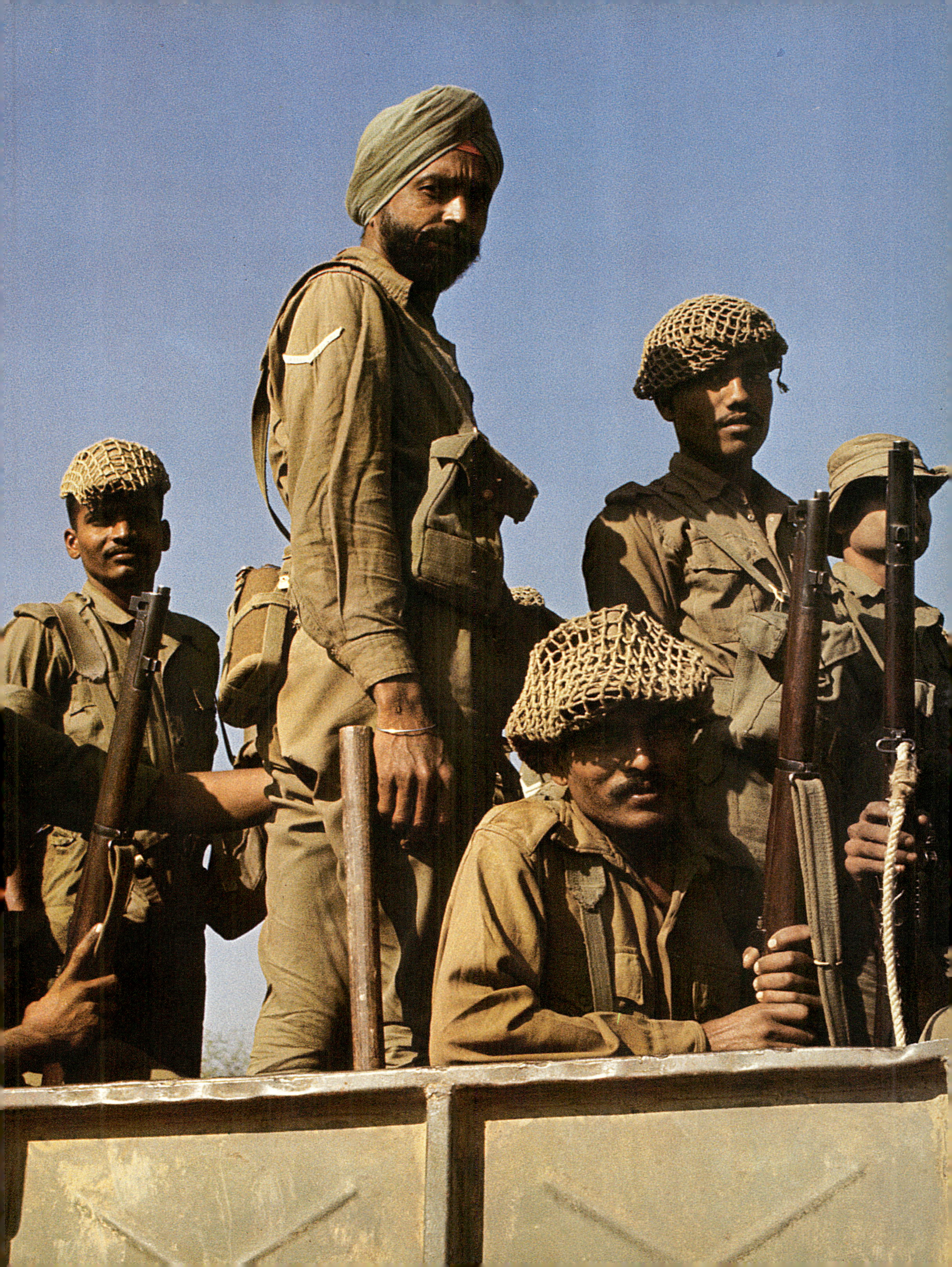

Azad Kashmir Forces

When the British withdrew from their Indian empire in 1947, leaving the sub-continent split between Hindu India and Muslim Pakistan, the northwestern Principality of Kashmir, which included the provinces of Jammu, Gilgit, Baltistan, Ladakh and Punch, was plunged into chaos. Ruled by a Hindu maharaja, Sir Hari Singh, yet containing a predominantly Muslim population, it was torn between its emerging neighbours, both of whom wished to control its resources and communications routes. Singh's initial response was to expand his state forces and aim for independence, but this produced confrontation with Muslims who had no desire to continue under his autocratic rule. In July 1947 a popular revolt occurred in Punch, led by Sardar Mohammed Ibrahim and, as Singh's forces moved in to quell the disturbances, Azad ('Free') Kashmir emerged as a politico-military movement.

Ibrahim favoured the establishment of an independent Azad Kashmir state, but it was apparent from the start that this would never be strong enough to stand alone. Despite its undoubted popularity in Punch and the steady addition of Muslim deserters from Singh's army, Azad Kashmir lacked the means to create or equip its own conventional army for the defence of the nation. Only small amounts of arms and ammunition could be imported across the Jhelum River from Pakistan, and there were few military leaders capable of moulding a disparate collection of deserters, ex-servicemen and enthusiastic amateurs into an effective force. This was shown in October 1947 when, in response to an unofficial 'invasion' of Kashmir by 2000 Muslim tribesmen from Pakistan, Singh unexpectedly acceded to the Indian federation in exchange for military aid; once the Indian Army had been deployed to protect Srinagar, the capital of Kashmir, Azad forces were outnumbered and outgunned. When the city of Punch fell in November, Ibrahim had to abandon his base and pull back towards the Pakistan border.

The fact that Azad Kashmir survived at all may be credited to two interrelated factors. First, Azad leaders recognised the potential that existed for guerrilla warfare: their soldiers were physically tough, well-motivated and familiar with the terrain of Kashmir, and it did not take long to exploit these advantages in a campaign aimed at cutting Indian lines of communication and supply and destroying isolated Indian outposts in the 'occupied' areas of Jammu and Punch. Second, as Ibrahim set up a new base in Muzaffarabad, close to the Pakistan border, that country became more interested in Azad Kashmir. This was perhaps inevitable – the Pakistanis could not avoid responding to the Indian advance of October 1947 – but it did boost Azad potential at a crucial time. In late 1947 and early 1948 heavier weapons and increased supplies were ferried across the Jhelum, Pakistani officers and technicians were granted indefinite 'leave' which they spent in Azad training camps, and Pakistani regular army units were deployed to the rear of Azad positions.

Unfortunately, these developments did little to enhance the Azad forces' capabilities, for as Indian and Pakistani regular army units clashed in Kashmir in 1948, Ibrahim's guerrillas became nothing more than pawns in a larger game. Although they continued to attack Indian positions, particularly around Muzaffarabad where 'General Tariq' (Brigadier Akbar Khan) proved to be an able leader, they were not consulted over the ceasefire on 1 January 1949 and were forced gradually to accept Pakistani control. By the 1950s seconded Pakistani officers were monopolising Azad command positions, and although extra weapons and supplies were being channelled into the Muzaffarabad base, Azad military actions were invariably subordinated to those of Pakistan. The fact that this was not an ideal arrangement was shown in 1965 and 1971, when Azad Kashmir shared in the ignominy of Pakistani defeat. By the late 1970s all pretence at separate military development had disappeared: Azad forces are now integrated with the Pakistani Army, constituting the 12th and 23rd Infantry Divisions. The dreams of a separate Azad Kashmir state, free from outside interference, have been dashed. As with so many other politico-military movements of the post-1945 world, Azad Kashmir lacked the self-sufficiency to protect itself, not just against its enemy, but also against the interests of 'friendly' states intent upon control of the disputed territory.

Above: Azad Kashmir soldiers advance through a field of crops. Although they fought for an independent Kashmir, difficulty in obtaining supplies led the Azad Kashmir forces to accept Pakistani sponsorship, and they have now been incorporated directly into the structure of the Pakistani Army.

Azad Kashmir Soldier
— Kashmir 1950 —

The armed forces of the Azad Kashmir movement were almost totally reliant on military supplies from Pakistan. The uniform worn by this man bears a strong resemblance to the cavalry uniforms of the pre-independence Indian Army from which Pakistan received most of its military equipment after partition. The bandolier holds rounds for his Lee Enfield .303in Mark III.

Below: Azad Kashmir leaders confer about plans for an attack on Indian troops. The forces of the Azad (Free) Kashmir movement fought for an independent republic against the reigning maharaja of Kashmir and Indian soldiers intervening on his behalf.

SOUTH ASIA

The Indian Army

Recruits in the Indian Army move onto the firing range for the first time, after 14 weeks of training. Their uniforms and equipment obviously owe much to the British inheritance, particularly the Lee Enfield No. 1 MkIII rifles.*

After the partition of British India in 1947, the new Indian state was left with numerous regiments – Sikhs, Gurkhas and Rajputs for instance – which had a long and glorious military history as part of the British Empire. The new rulers of India were unwilling to destroy the worthwhile parts of their inheritance from the Raj but there were reasons for feeling that the character of the army was unsuitable for the new state. Far from being a symbol of unity in a country which was always struggling against separatist forces, the old Indian Army had been recruited from only a small section of the overall population and had maintained a reputation for exclusivity. It was agreed that things would have to change.

Yet forcing change on the army was always difficult because war, or the prospect of war, was always on the horizon and in those circumstances there was little chance of a thorough overhaul of the armed services. Nevertheless, the government in Delhi was determined that the army should have more in common with the nation and be less of a reflection of the military attitudes of the British, so that any new units which it raised – such as the Parachute Regiment – were not to be the exclusive preserve of the 'martial races' but were to be open to enlistment by any Indian regardless of race or creed.

While the Indian Army performed creditably during the Indo-Pakistan dispute of 1948-49, its failures in the border war with China in 1962 came as a surprise. India had complacently believed that her army would be a match for the Chinese, but the Indian forces were easily brushed aside by the Chinese who then promptly reclaimed the disputed border areas. After the end of recriminations between army and politicians as to their respective responsibilities for India's humiliation, a new interest in army reform gathered momentum. Considered by many to be too small for its task, the army was doubled in size but it remained a professional force and ideas of introducing conscription were soon abandoned. The increase in size provided an opportunity to change the composition of the army by making it more of a mix of the peoples and sects of India.

The changing nature of the army meant that it could be joined by any Indian citizen but certain regiments were, and remained, reserved for certain classes. The British influence continued, especially in the officer corps which was drawn from the upper social classes, and misgivings remained that the new mix might prove fragile in war. However, the reorganisation came of age in the 1965 war with Pakistan, and was aided by a policy to ensure that minorities were well represented in awards lists. On the public relations front, much favourable mention was made of the prowess of the newly recruited units.

After the baptism of fire in 1965 the Indian Army proved sensationally successful against a divided and strategically unbalanced Pakistan in 1971. The campaign demonstrated not only that its morale was as high as ever but that it was a modern army: speed of movement, flexibility and the frequent use of helicopter-borne assaults underlined the message that the Indian Army was a highly developed institution possessing the latest skills and weapons.

Indian Infantry Lance-Corporal
—Indo-Pakistan War 1965—

Although a Sikh, this infantryman is a member of an ordinary Indian line regiment. Nevertheless, he wears the traditional Sikh steel band on the right wrist as well as an olive green Sikh turban with a red band underneath, called a 'fifty' after the fiftieth turn of the turban. An olive-green uniform is worn, over which is British 1937-pattern web equipment, anklets and 'ammunition' boots. Reflecting the still important British military legacy within India, the rifle is a Lee Enfield No. 1 MkIII*, with bayonet fixed.

Below: Based on the British 'officer's set' this 1937-pattern webbing consists of a revolver holster (probably holding a .455 Smith and Wesson) with an ammunition pouch above, small haversack, water bottle and a binoculars case, above which is a compass pouch.

The Pakistani Army

The army is a popular and respected institution within Pakistan and as such it has come to be seen as the embodiment of the state. Although the army has intervened in politics on several occasions, it remains generally untainted by the corruption endemic to much of Pakistani political life. Despite a poor performance in 1965 and defeat in 1971, the Pakistani Army remains reliable and well organised.

This reliability and high standard of training have been with Pakistan's army since its origins in the break up of the British Raj. At the partition of India in 1947 the new Muslim state of Pakistan was allocated the Muslim units of the old Indian Army. There were obvious disadvantages to this dismemberment of a force which had been designed to serve the entire subcontinent but there was also the great advantage of having an inheritable tradition. Famous regiments such as the Guides cavalry, Probyn's and Watson's Horse live on in Pakistan as does the cement of the regimental tradition. The result bears the stamp of British influence in the importance accorded to rank and the minute observance of military courtesies.

Unfortunately for Pakistan it has not been easy to equip the army with the modern weaponry it requires. This had always been a problem because Pakistan's alliances with America and Britain place the country within the Western sphere of influence where a vacillating foreign policy uses weapons supply as a political lever. Until the 1965 war British and, above all, American equipment was in fairly lavish supply but both allies introduced an arms embargo at the outset of hostilities. Resulting efforts to diversify have made life difficult for the Pakistani soldier. Procurement of Chinese, French, Soviet and Swedish equipment has resulted in complication of weapons training and maintenance.

The quality of the human material owes its origins to the nature of Pakistani society as well as to army training. All servicemen are volunteers and there has never been a need for compulsory national service although the army is a large one – 450,000 men with half a million trained reserves. Some of the enthusiasm to enlist may come from widespread unemployment but it also comes from a strong military tradition. Even before Pakistan was shorn of its eastern wing, which was to become Bangladesh in 1971, the vast majority of its soldiers came from the west; from the Punjab and the North West Frontier areas where the population had been recognised by the British as 'martial races'. Recruits from these people have an interest in military life instilled into them long before they join the colours. The darker side of this coin has been a certain arrogance, particularly among senior officers, which has marred both the 1965 and 1971 campaigns.

The Pakistani Army today comprises 16 infantry and two armoured divisions; four independent armoured and five independent infantry brigades, and seven artillery brigades, as well as anti-aircraft and other auxiliary units. Armament and equipment reflect the diversity of Pakistani military sources: US M48, Soviet T54-55 and Chinese Type-59 tanks; US and West German APCs; British and US artillery; US anti-tank weapons and French anti-aircraft missiles.

Below: Pakistani troops engage an Indian position at long range in the Khen Karan sector, a few hours before the ceasefire of 24 September ended the 1965 war. Armament consists of a Bren LMG, a Lee Enfield rifle and a 0.3in Browning machine gun.

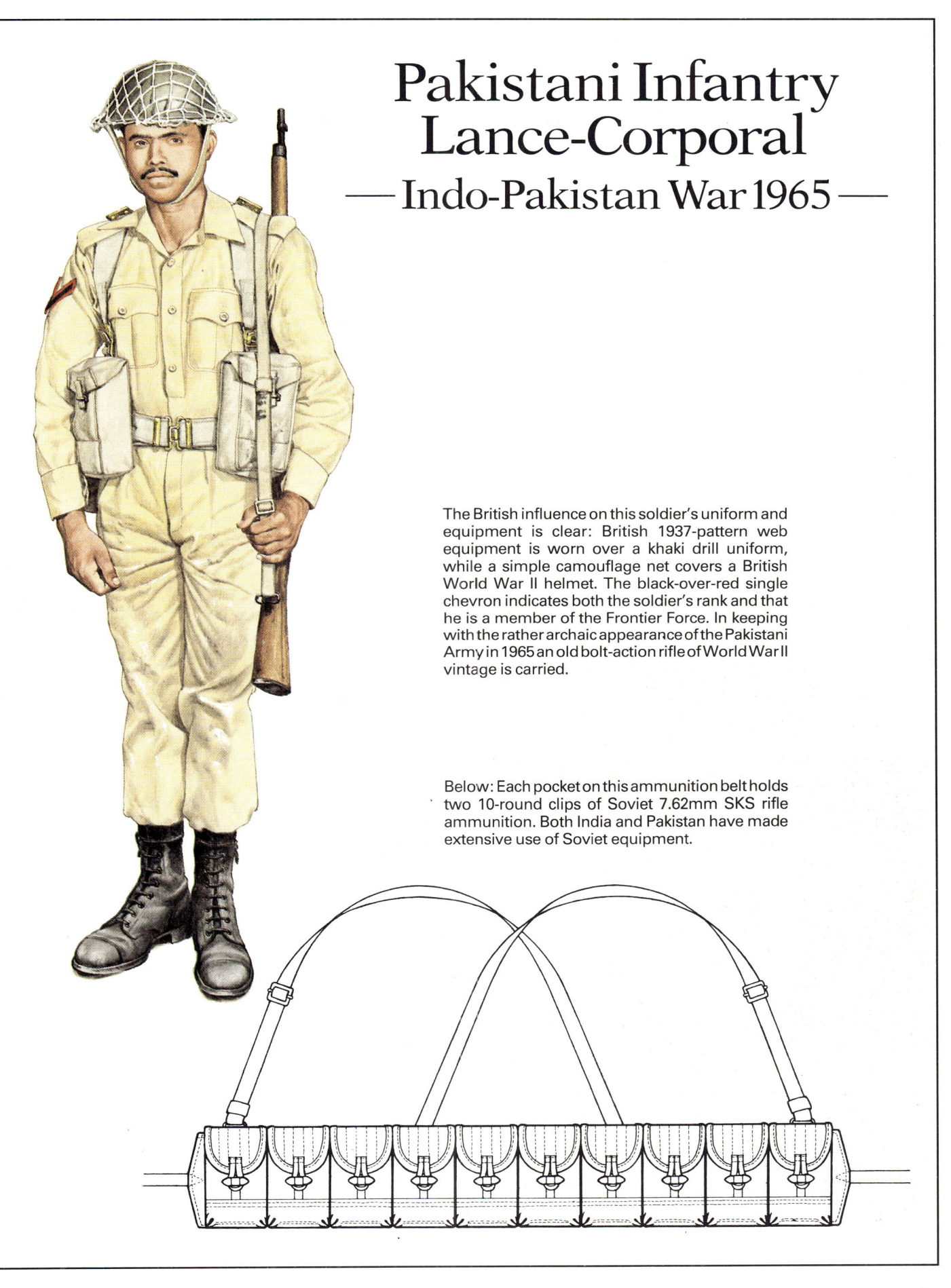

Pakistani Infantry Lance-Corporal
—Indo-Pakistan War 1965—

The British influence on this soldier's uniform and equipment is clear: British 1937-pattern web equipment is worn over a khaki drill uniform, while a simple camouflage net covers a British World War II helmet. The black-over-red single chevron indicates both the soldier's rank and that he is a member of the Frontier Force. In keeping with the rather archaic appearance of the Pakistani Army in 1965 an old bolt-action rifle of World War II vintage is carried.

Below: Each pocket on this ammunition belt holds two 10-round clips of Soviet 7.62mm SKS rifle ammunition. Both India and Pakistan have made extensive use of Soviet equipment.

SOUTH ASIA

The Indian Army in 1971

As the Indian government committed itself to a policy of neutralism in foreign affairs in the period following independence in 1947, the Indian Army was one of the more neglected of the country's institutions. But the shock of the army's defeat at the hands of the Chinese in the Sino-Indian border dispute of 1962 changed this state of affairs and a long-term programme of army reform and expansion was instigated. Incompetent generals were removed from their positions and the lot of the common soldier was considerably improved. In addition, as the government injected greatly increased funds into the army, new divisions were raised so that regular army strength was doubled to 750,000 men supplied with modern weapons and equipment from many nations.

The inconclusive 1965 war with Pakistan came too early to act as a real test of the reforms, but the 1971 conflict was a successful proving ground for the Indian Army; its lightning campaign in East Pakistan caught worldwide attention and led to the complete defeat of the Pakistani Army in only 12 days. The terrain the Indian Army had to fight across was particularly difficult – East Pakistan being laced by a vast interlocking system of rivers and waterways – but the flexibility of Indian tactics, which included a parachute drop at brigade level and the extensive use of heliborne troops, ensured a spectacular victory.

Despite the reforms of 1962, the Indian Army remained in 1971 – and continues to remain – much as it had been during the period of colonial rule, namely a highly-trained conventionally-organised force whose prime role was the defence of India's borders. Although there have been periodic moves to reorganise the armed forces on other foreign models – the Chinese militia system, for example – it nonetheless reflects the Imperial legacy in uniforms, rank structure, organisation and general military philosophy.

The army accordingly maintains the old 'regimental' system so that older units can trace a common ancestry back to the 18th century and the old East India Company. The forces of continuity remain a powerful factor for conservatism within the army and this is most forcefully expressed in the caste system which still applies throughout the armed forces. Traditionally the army recruited from the high-caste peoples of northern India and despite government efforts in the 1960s to extend the area of recruitment the Indian Army of 1971 continued this tradition.

While there is a problem in recruiting officers of the required standard there is no such problem for other ranks. India has a relatively small army for the size of her vast population and as the prestige of the soldier is high in Indian society there are as many as 10 men applying for each vacancy. This provides the Indian Army with the advantage of highly motivated volunteers who can be moulded into a professional force.

During its period of British rule the Indian Army had obviously been supplied with British weapons and equipment and this relationship continued until the 1965 war when Britain curtailed shipments in the interest of 'neutrality'. Following this move India rapidly diversified her sources of weapons supply and in particular began to take large amounts of Soviet equipment. By 1971 the army's weapons inventory included Soviet T54/55 and British Centurion tanks, a combination of British, American and Soviet field guns and a wide variety of infantry support weapons including British Sterling sub-machine guns and SMLE rifles, Belgian FN rifles and machine guns, and British and French mortars. In order to obviate the dangers of relying on foreign supplies and to encourage her home industries India has stepped up her own arms manufacturing capacity, which now includes such advanced items as tanks and fighter aircraft.

Below: An Indian soldier shelters in a dug-out ready to fire his 7.62mm FN rifle. Bottom: Sikh troops of the Indian Army prepare to form up. Armament comprises FN rifles and a Sterling sub-machine gun. As Sikh troops are bound to wear turbans by their religion these men are unable to wear the standard helmet.

Indian Army Para
—Indo-Pakistan War 1971—

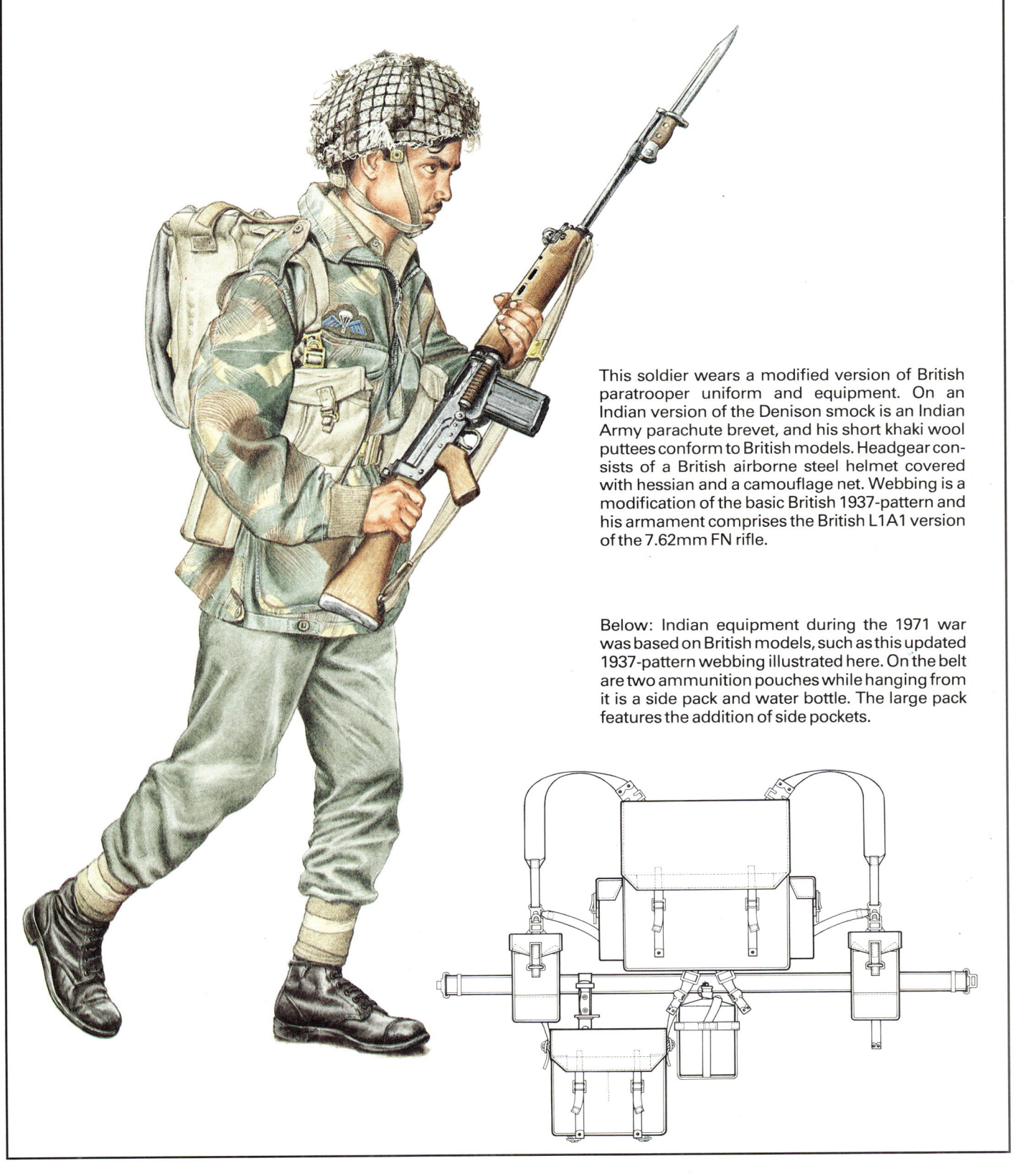

This soldier wears a modified version of British paratrooper uniform and equipment. On an Indian version of the Denison smock is an Indian Army parachute brevet, and his short khaki wool puttees conform to British models. Headgear consists of a British airborne steel helmet covered with hessian and a camouflage net. Webbing is a modification of the basic British 1937-pattern and his armament comprises the British L1A1 version of the 7.62mm FN rifle.

Below: Indian equipment during the 1971 war was based on British models, such as this updated 1937-pattern webbing illustrated here. On the belt are two ammunition pouches while hanging from it is a side pack and water bottle. The large pack features the addition of side pockets.

The Pakistani Army in 1971

In the 1947 division of the Indian sub-continent into a Hindu India and a Muslim Pakistan (itself divided into two parts separated by India) lay the seeds of the 1971 war. Although East and West Pakistan shared the same religion they were divided by culture, race, language and not least by geographical distance. West Pakistan was the dominant partner and held almost complete power, which in turn led to the political and economic exploitation of the East, so much so that it was a virtual colony of the West. The Pakistani Army was drawn predominantly from the West and in the East it acted as an army of occupation.

East Pakistan's dissatisfaction with this state of affairs led to general unrest in March 1971, and the Pakistani Army was ordered to suppress any signs of dissent. This it did with a vengeance, going on a rampage of systematic slaughter that led to around one million deaths. The reign of terror instigated led to a mass exodus which saw tens of thousands of refugees fleeing into India. Tension between India and Pakistan was already high but the events of 1971 made matters worse. When Pakistani troops crossed into India in hot pursuit of East Pakistani resistance fighters border clashes resulted. India decided upon military force to resolve the situation.

The Pakistani Army was in an extremely difficult position in a conflict against India, its forces divided by 1600km (1000 miles) of enemy territory. Once war was declared in December 1971 all the Pakistan High Command could realistically expect was to delay defeat in the East and hope to make territorial gains in the West which could be transformed into bargaining counters once a ceasefire was declared.

In West Pakistan the army deployed 10 infantry and two armoured divisions plus various independent brigades. In East Pakistan the army had only four infantry divisions (plus a number of independent units) and two light armoured units. This small force had to hold a border nearly 2250km (1400 miles) long and control an area with a hostile population of about 70 million people against a numerically superior Indian force. Such a task would have been impossible if it had not been for the fact that East Pakistan was criss-crossed by many large rivers and their tributaries so that strongly defended positions could be utilised to hold the Indian advance.

Despite being outnumbered and suffering the grave strategic disadvantage of fighting separately on two fronts the Pakistani Army was seriously weakened by other factors. The quality of the officer corps left much to be desired, being over-confident in its abilities against an Indian Army that had improved considerably since the inconclusive war of 1965. Equipment and weapons posed problems too. Denied sufficient quantities of British and American weapons Pakistan had turned to China for help and in 1971 there was considerable confusion within the Pakistani Army as it tried to deploy incompatible Western and Chinese weapon systems.

In the West the Pakistani Army's offensive thrusts came to little: territorial gains made were more than offset by corresponding gains made by the Indian Army which revealed itself as the better organised army, combining air power and armoured thrusts to good effect. But it was in East Pakistan that the war was to be decided.

Once the autumn monsoons had ended the Indian Army prepared to invade East Pakistan and the offensive began in earnest on 4 December. The Pakistani commander, General Niazi, deployed his forces in static forward positions intended to deny the Indians access into the interior of the country. Although his fortress defence policy was effective in so much as it controlled the main towns and river crossings, the Pakistani positions were not mutually supporting and there were insufficient reserves to counter any Indian breakthrough. No arrangements were made for a fighting withdrawal so that this policy of attempting to deny the Indians territory proved tactically disastrous; Indian armoured forces were able to by-pass Pakistani strong points leaving them isolated and useless. The Indian troops were resolutely led and as their armoured columns moved on the capital of Dacca Pakistani morale began to crumble. Realising their hopeless position and fearful of the wrath of the East Pakistani people the Pakistani Army surrendered to the Indians on 16 December after less than two weeks of fighting. Pakistani losses were estimated at 8000 men killed plus, of course, the loss of East Pakistan which achieved independence as the state of Bangladesh.

Above: Pakistani troops man a position near Indian lines at Dangapora at the outbreak of the war. The diversity of Pakistan's weapon supply is hinted at in this photograph. The soldier in the background is armed with an American 3.5in M20 rocket launcher – commonly known as the Bazooka – while the others are armed with Chinese copies of Soviet weapons: a Type 56 assault rifle (a copy of the AK-47) and a Type 56 light machine gun (a copy of the RPD).

Pakistani Infantryman
—Indo-Pakistan War 1971—

This soldier deployed around Chhamb in West Pakistan wears khaki drill uniform, over which is worn a woollen pullover with a buttoned opening and chest pockets which was exclusive to the Pakistani Army. The helmet is a US M1 with a sacking cover and camouflage net, while the web equipment is of British origin. Armament consists of a US 0.3in Garand which was used alongside the British .303in SMLE by Pakistani infantry.

Below: Wearing their distinctive camouflage nets over British steel helmets the crew of a Pakistani light mortar prepares to bombard Indian positions.

SOUTH ASIA

The Mukti Bahini

The Mukti Bahini emerged in early 1971 as an Indian-backed partisan group, dedicated to the elimination of West Pakistani rule over East Pakistan and the creation of an independent state (Bangladesh) governed by Sheikh Mujibur Rahman's Awami League. India's invasion of East Pakistan at the end of the year was clearly the key factor in eventual success but, rather like the French Resistance in 1944, the Mukti Bahini contributed to the liberation of their country, tying down the enemy and loosening his military grip through a policy of escalating guerrilla violence.

Armed opposition to West Pakistani rule was an inevitable outcome of General Yahya Khan's decision to crack down on the Awami League after its landslide electoral success of December 1970. On 25 March 1971 Lieutenant-General Tikka Khan, martial law administrator in the East, initiated a programme of deliberate repression which swiftly degenerated into genocide, and although he tried to pre-empt organised opposition by interning the bulk of the locally-raised East Bengal Regiment (EBR) and East Pakistan Rifles (EPR), sufficient numbers of officers and men escaped to act as a focus for spontaneous guerrilla action. Roads and railways were hit and Pakistani military outposts attacked, but the groups (know collectively as the Mukti Fauj) lacked co-ordination and were easily contained. What was needed was foreign backing, safe bases, effective central leadership and a supply of arms: all the attributes that were essential for successful modern guerrilla warfare.

These were provided by India. As the remnants of the EBR, EPR and East Pakistan Police (up to 10,000 men) withdrew across the border into eastern India in April, they were kept together in special camps, placed under the command of a retired Indian Army colonel, M.A.G. Osmani, and allowed to recruit from among the thousands of refugees fleeing from Tikka Khan's repression. Many of the latter were members of the educated middle classes and proved relatively easy to train in the rudiments of military skill; backed by the EBR/EPR regulars, they were organised into guerrilla groups for use in East Pakistan. Renamed the Mukti Bahini, they gradually grew in size (from August about 2000 recruits emerged from the training camps every six weeks), although it took time for them to be prepared for a sustained campaign. To begin with, therefore, they concentrated on small-scale actions, designed to make continued West Pakistani rule as unattractive and expensive as possible, principally by killing soldiers (and taking their weapons) and by disrupting the lucrative jute and tea crops of the East. Guerrilla groups, exploiting their local knowledge and support, infiltrated the border but rarely penetrated deep into the country. The Pakistanis found little difficulty in absorbing such attacks, generally leaving the process of counter-insurgency to specially-raised and exceptionally brutal Razakars, recruited from the Bihari minority which opposed the creation of an independent state.

Operations continued at this level throughout the monsoon (June-September), but once the ground dried out escalation occurred. By October it was estimated that the Mukti Bahini had a potential strength of over 100,000 men, backed by units of the Indian Army which guarded the border and maintained an increasingly concerned watch over events in the East. This enabled larger and deeper guerrilla penetrations to be organised, concentrated against road and rail networks, power plants and even shipping in the estuaries or off the coast of East Pakistan – the latter in an effort to prevent the export of jute and tea. As confidence grew, direct clashes with the Pakistani Army were no longer avoided, particularly in areas close to the border where Indian artillery and air support could be guaranteed. By late November 'liberated zones' had been carved out, chiefly around Jessore, and the Pakistanis were finding it difficult to move outside their fortified zones.

The growing intensity of the guerrilla war proved a significant advantage to the Indian Army when it invaded East Pakistan on 4 December 1971; and the Mukti Bahini continued to aid their ally as the campaign progressed, providing intelligence, disrupting enemy communications and attacking rear-area targets. Once Bangladesh had been created, the bulk of the guerrilla force was disbanded, although a hard core was retained to form the nucleus of the new state's army. The fact that within four years that army had overthrown Sheikh Mujib and formed its own government, should not detract from its very real contribution to the partisan-guerrilla campaign of national liberation in 1971.

The Mukti Bahini were armed and equipped from a diverse range of sources, although the Indian Army was the major supplier. Below right: Mukti Bahini commander Major Jaffar Iman supervises a guerrilla operation armed with a Soviet-designed AK assault rifle and a belt of machine gun ammunition draped over his shoulders. Below: Wearing a Pakistani Army pullover and webbing this guerrilla carries an old British Sten sub-machine gun.

Mukti Bahini Guerrilla
—East Pakistan 1971—

This somewhat strangely attired individual wears indigenous civilian clothes surmounted by a British steel helmet, camouflaged for fighting in the marshes of East Pakistan. The five-pocket bandolier slung over his left shoulder is for carrying clips of smallarms ammunition, although, in fact, he is armed with a West German 7.62mm MG3 machine gun captured from the Pakistani Army. The MG3 is a descendant of the World War II MG42, a highly influential weapon that served as a model for the development of the modern general purpose machine gun.

Below: A Mukti Bahini mortar detachment bombards Pakistani Army positions near Sylhet. An interesting range of armaments are carried by these troops including FN rifles and Sterling sub-machine guns.

Southeast Asia

Before the Japanese invasion and occupation of Southeast Asia in 1941–42, the region was ruled almost exclusively by European colonial powers, dependent for their authority upon the contrast between their military prowess and the weakness of the native peoples. The myth of European invincibility was shattered, however, by the ease with which the Japanese took over, and resistance to the occupation reawakened a sense of national identity among the colonial subjects, often, ironically enough, fostered by the very Allied powers that were intent upon a restoration of their prewar rule. The imperial cause was not advanced by the fact that few of the states involved were actually liberated by victorious Allied armies. With the exception of the Philippines and parts of the Dutch East Indies (Indonesia), where full-scale military campaigns did take place, Southeast Asia was still under Japanese control when the atomic attacks forced a sudden surrender.

This left the nationalists in a curious position, for although some groups were well-placed to take over power from the defeated Japanese, they were forced to recognise that the Europeans had no intention of meeting demands for immediate independence and that resistance activities would have to continue. Thus, when British troops moved into Indonesia in late 1945, they faced armed opposition, and had to fight to establish control preparatory to the Dutch returning to their colony. Moreover, between then and 1949 the Dutch experienced the full force of a nationalist campaign, finally relinquishing colonial control as casualties mounted and domestic support for the war diminished. It was a pattern that was to be repeated in northern Indochina (Vietnam), where returning French troops, intent on re-establishing colonial rule, met well-organised and experienced nationalist guerrillas who gradually outmanoeuvred and outfought the European army. In May 1954 Vietnamese nationalists under Ho Chi Minh defeated the French in open battle at Dien Bien Phu, forcing them to accept the reality of independence for Vietnam north of the 17th Parallel.

A key factor in Vietnamese victory was the adoption of tactics and techniques associated with Mao Tse-tung and the Chinese communist forces. With the emphasis firmly on political subversion, persuading the mass of the people to support the revolution, all military activity was geared towards a gradual undermining of enemy armed strength, preparatory to a seizure of political control, and it was this politico-military combination that the French were unable to counter. They treated the campaign as a colonial uprising, using technology and firepower in a vain attempt to overwhelm the insurgents, and although they enjoyed occasional successes they did nothing to prevent the spread of communist ideas among the people.

Similar mistakes were made by the Americans between 1965 and 1973, when they supported the South Vietnamese against mounting pressure from Viet Cong revolutionaries backed by North Vietnamese Army (NVA) regular units. Once again, the defenders – US armed forces and the Army of the Republic of Vietnam (ARVN) – ignored the steady progress of political subversion, preferring to concentrate on the more tangible military threat. As US ground troops fought the NVA on the borders, other units backed the ARVN in a series of massive (and generally unproductive) 'search and destroy' operations designed to swamp the Viet Cong with firepower. The ARVN inevitably developed into a modern, technological army, dependent upon US-supplied armour, artillery, helicopters and aircraft, and soon proved incapable of carrying out a counter-insurgency campaign in which political awareness and low-level tactical responses were the keys to victory. With the withdrawal of the Americans and a reduction in supplies of weapons and ammunition, even the ARVN's technological advantage was undermined. In 1975 the NVA took Saigon.

This was a major victory for the communists, and similar success was achieved by the Pathet Lao in Laos and Khmer Rouge in Cambodia at much the same time. Mao's revolutionary warfare was not unstoppable, however, for elsewhere in Southeast Asia the communists had been contained. In the Philippines between 1946 and 1954 the Hukbalahaps failed to achieve their aims in the face of a strong central government that was prepared to grant political concessions to undermine popular support to the insurgents; in Malaya between 1948 and 1960 the Malayan Races Liberation Army was forced to abandon its anti-British campaign when the latter adopted a politico-military response to guerrilla subversion. Indeed, so successful were the British techniques that many of them were used in the 1960s to counter Indonesian communist-style guerrilla attacks on Brunei and Borneo, designed to prevent those colonies joining the Malaysian Federation.

The Borneo 'Confrontation' was the last of the anti-colonial campaigns in Southeast Asia, and although guerrilla activity continues at a reduced level in the Philippines and Malaysia, most armies of the region now face the more conventional threat of attacks from neighbouring powers. In 1978 the Vietnamese used their experience, Soviet support and captured US/ARVN equipment to invade Kampuchea (Cambodia), aiming to overthrow the repressive regime of Khmer leader Pol Pot. By the mid-1980s they had gained control of most of the country, but had clashed with the Thais in the west and, in 1979, had been forced to respond to a punitive attack by the Chinese, who were fearful of Vietnamese expansion and the spread of Soviet influence into Indochina. In the event, the Vietnamese were able to push the Chinese back, but if, as seems likely, Southeast Asia is to become the battleground for Sino-Soviet rivalry, the local armies, conceived as anti-colonial guerrilla forces and used primarily for internal policing, may not be able to cope.

Right: A member of the Army of the Republic of (South) Vietnam (ARVN) rests on board his jeep, Mekong delta area, 1972. He is armed with a US M60 machine gun, while the jeep itself mounts a 106mm recoilless gun. The soldier is equipped entirely from US sources, from his helmet and flak jacket down to his boots – a dependence that was to prove a major weakness once the Americans withdrew from Vietnam in 1973.

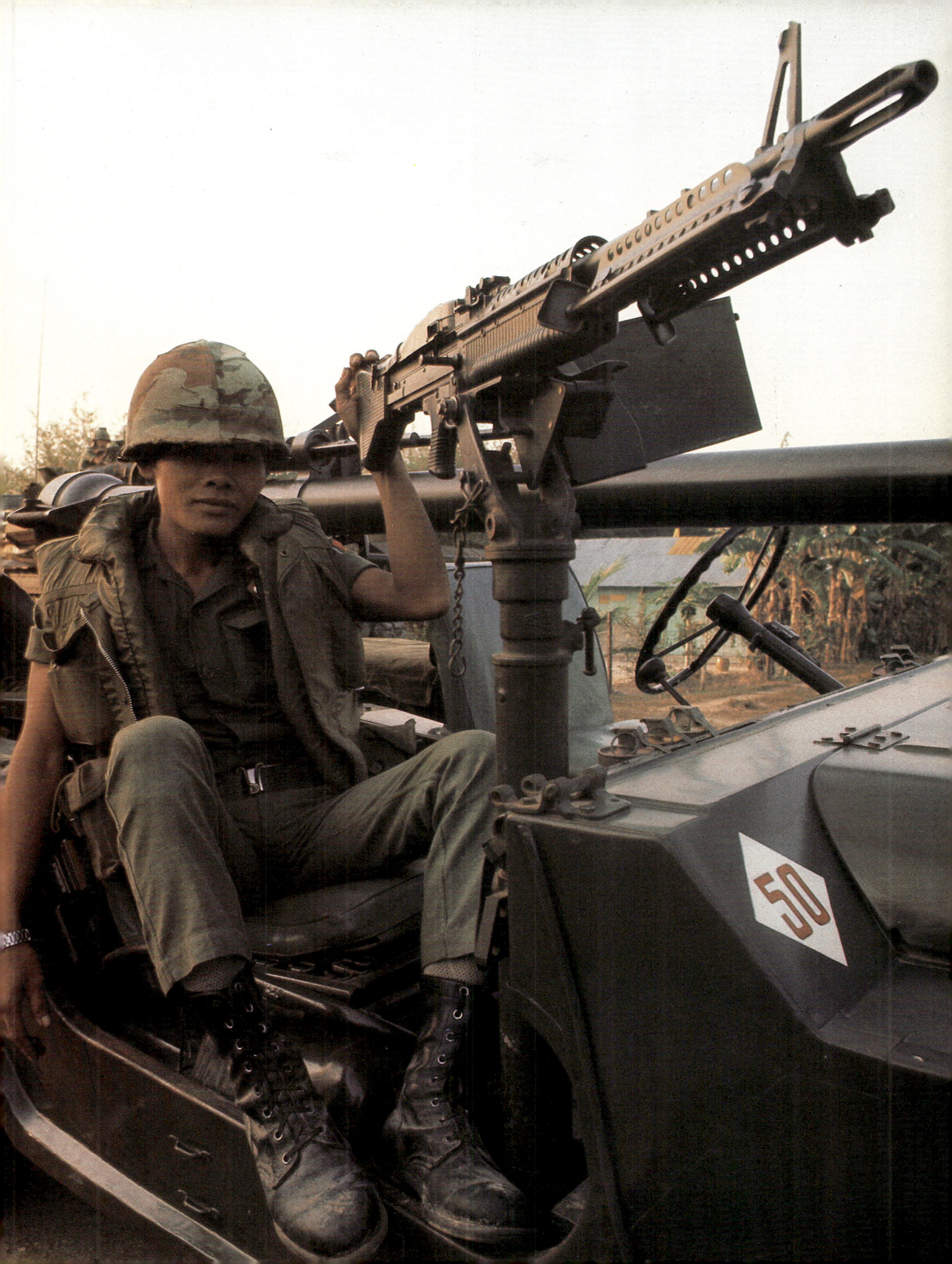
50

The Malayan Races Liberation Army

The communist-led Malayan Races Liberation Army (MRLA) came into being in 1948 as the military arm of the Malayan Communist Party's (MCP) attempt to oust the British from Malaya and gain control of the peninsula. As a guerrilla organisation the MRLA had the great advantage of being able to recruit men who had gained valuable military experience when acting as part of the communist Malayan People's Anti-Japanese Army (MPAJA). Although disbanded in 1945, MPAJA commanders had ensured that caches of arms and ammunition were safely stored away should the need for armed struggle again arise. Despite this, however, the MRLA was forced to operate within a complex politico-military and racial situation which, when faced by determined British resistance, was to ensure that the communist insurrection would ultimately fail.

Following a campaign of civil unrest by the MCP in the urban centres, the struggle was extended into the military sphere in July 1948. Able to raise and equip some 3000 guerrilla fighters the MRLA was organised on conventional military lines with a structure that ranged from the platoon up to units at battalion and regimental level, though the latter were more an organisation on paper, being clearly unable to take on British forces at the level of full-scale operations. Nonetheless, like many guerrilla organisations before and after them, the MRLA made the initial mistake of attempting to mount relatively large military operations which played into the hands of the British who could then locate the guerrillas (the hardest part of counter-insurgency warfare) and destroy them in open combat.

Once the error of this strategy was realised the MRLA adopted the traditional guerrilla approach of isolated ambushes, assassination of key figures, and the carrot-and-stick policy of intimidation and aid to the local population. On the organisational side, units were correspondingly reduced in size, typically to raiding parties of less than a dozen men, although the base camps remained skilfully hidden in the Malay jungle. Winning over the people to the revolutionary cause proved to be especially difficult; the fairly even divide of the population into Malays and Chinese was not necessarily a problem but as the vast majority of the MRLA were of Chinese stock the ordinary Malays failed to identify with the guerrillas and consequently had little interest in the MCP's aims.

At its peak the MRLA had a strength of around 10,000 men but it was faced by well-organised and numerically superior government forces which amounted to some 60,000 police and auxiliary units and 30,000 regular troops. The type of war waged by the MRLA was cat-and-mouse attack and counter-attack fighting where ambushers could easily find themselves ambushed. Long, strenuous marches along winding jungle tracks, setting up ambushes and avoiding them in turn, conducting surveillance operations and assassinations and the sabotage of Malay industry formed the tactical background to the MRLA guerrilla. The overall strategy was to terrorise the peasant population, alienate them from their masters and bring about the destruction of Malaya's economic wealth, based largely on its extensive rubber plantations. That the MRLA did not succeed was mainly due to the generally intelligent counter-measures adopted by the government forces in preventing the guerrillas from subverting the loyalty of both the urban and rural populations.

The MRLA soldier was a hardy fighter often operating under the most difficult physical circumstances for long periods of time. Altogether nearly 7000 MRLA guerrillas were killed in the conflict, which lasted 12 years from July 1948 until July 1960 when the State of Emergency was officially ended. That the MRLA – grossly inferior in men and materials and lacking any realistic hope of victory – held out for so long was testimony to the grit of its soldiers.

Above: This guerrilla wears standard MRLA 'uniform' of khaki-drill shirt and trousers and the distinctive five-pointed cap. Right: A diminutive soldier of the MRLA is led away for interrogation by a member of the security forces.

MRLA Guerrilla
—Malaya 1953—

When the Malayan People's Anti-Japanese Army re-formed itself to become the Malayan Races Liberation Army (MRLA), the guerrillas were unusually well-uniformed and equipped. The typical Malay guerrilla shown here is wearing a five-pointed peaked cap in khaki drill with the ubiquitous communist red star to the front. The uniform is also khaki drill and the puttees are worn in the style of the Japanese Army. In contrast to the heavy-duty leather boots worn by the security forces, this guerrilla is wearing basketball-type rubber and canvas lightweight boots. The webbing would probably be British 1937-pattern, while the water bottle is of Japanese origin. Armament consists of a British .303in SMLE Rifle No.1 Mk III*, and a five-pouch canvas ammunition bandolier is worn round the waist.

SOUTHEAST ASIA

The North Vietnamese Army

Above: Camouflaged against US aerial observation North Vietnamese troops rush forward to their battle positions. Above right: Grouped around a destroyed bridge in North Vietnam men of an NVA unit display their weaponry, including SKS carbines and an AK-47 assault rifle; both types are of Soviet design.

During the Vietnam War the North Vietnamese Army (NVA) was always more impressively and heavily equipped than its leaders acknowledged: it is a popular misconception that the 30-year long struggle for communist victory in Indochina was waged by lightly-armed guerrilla forces because major battles were fought by very large regular formations between 1951 and 1975. Indeed the communist authorities have obscured the role played by regular units in the victory over the American and South Vietnamese armies in favour of presenting the war in Vietnam as a conflict waged by the indigenous population against the colonial oppressors.

This bland outward show of an inevitable progression by the peasant masses towards victory also provided concealment for the defeats which the NVA suffered. In fact the first action by large regular formations of the NVA – an advance on Hanoi by five divisions in 1951 – resulted in a particularly bloody defeat at the hands of the French. Again, between 1965 and 1967 US forces badly mauled NVA formations, although the complete lack of North Vietnamese reaction to heavy losses among their units was a weapon in itself, because it denied the Americans any taste of victory and induced the growing frustration that in part led to US withdrawal.

Despite the inauspicious beginning for NVA regular forces in 1951, they were always maintained to be used in conjunction with guerrilla formations. Throughout their existence they were as heavily armed as possible. The great victory over the French at Dien Bien Phu in 1954 was gained by the enormous weight of artillery that the NVA was able to concentrate upon the besieged garrison. By the 1960s NVA weapons were very largely provided by the Soviet Union which was also the manufacturer and donor of most of the other heavy equipment – from mortars and anti-aircraft missiles to tanks and armoured personnel carriers – which entered the inventory of the NVA. The Chinese also provided equipment but their scantier resources and, perhaps, a latent animosity towards the Vietnamese made them very much the secondary supplier of weaponry. The artillery and anti-aircraft weapons were very useful in fighting the Americans but the total US air superiority precluded much use of armour. Once the Americans had withdrawn, however, the NVA was able to mount a full-scale armoured assault, spearheaded by hundreds of T54-55s, in 1975.

On the other hand it is possible to over-emphasise the importance of NVA regular forces in that the guerrillas were crucial to communist victory in Vietnam. Even in recruitment the pool of soldiers provided by the guerrillas was the reservoir from which regular forces were drawn. The system was one of total mobilisation of the populace: the pick of each village's guerrilla forces was sent to the mobile regional guerrilla force and the pick of this was inducted into the main force or regular army. After the establishment of the North Vietnamese state in 1954 conscription was introduced but a drive to find volunteers was mounted and this was alleged to have produced 1,500,000 signatures. Military training was universal so that conscripts to the NVA would already have received some training in their local militias before joining the regular forces.

In the matter of ranks and uniforms the NVA has chosen a path somewhere between that of the Chinese and Soviet armies: it maintains a hierarchical structure with conventional titles of rank for officers, although there are no badges of rank in the NVA and officers wear the same uniform as their men. It is a typically North Vietnamese arrangement: an outward show of equality balanced by an adoption of the most effective method of organisation. There can be no doubt that the present Vietnamese domination of Indochina is largely due to the strength of its army, a strength which shows no sign of diminishing.

NVA Infantryman
—Vietnam 1963—

This simple and functional green field uniform features trousers gathered at the ankle and fastened by a button and loop, while headgear consists of a woven reed sun helmet with cloth cover. A water-bottle cover is utilised as an ammunition pouch for the French 7.5mm MAS 1936 rifle, and a machete-type knife is worn on the soldier's waist belt.

Top (left and right): The old French colonial influence can be discerned in this NVA sun helmet; usually green in colour but occasionally white. The insignia – gold star on scarlet ground with gold rim – was rarely worn, however. Above (left and right): The soft field cap was a popular form of NVA headgear; made from dark green cloth the earflaps could be folded together over the head.

The Indonesian Marines

Because Indonesia comprises a myriad of islands spread over a vast expanse of ocean, it is inevitable that its armed forces should contain amphibious capability. By the 1980s this was reflected in the existence of two regiments (six battalions) of Marines – Korps Komando Operasi (KKO) – equipped with light tanks and armoured personnel carriers and backed by various support units (a total of 12,000 men), and by the fact that such forces enjoyed an elite status. Under the nominal command of the navy, which provided the necessary amphibious landing and fire support, the Marines constituted an integral part, together with other elements of the Tentara Nasional Indonesia (Indonesian armed forces), of a National Strategic Command, assigned to the defence of the home islands. Renowned for their tough training and aggressive fighting spirit, they would appear to be crack troops, capable of swift and decisive action.

As with Marine units elsewhere, however, the amphibious role has tended to be overlaid by a more general responsibility for combat ashore, particularly offensive operations in difficult conditions. In most countries this comes naturally from a lack of suitable opportunities for seaborne landings, although in the case of Indonesia it may reflect something more fundamental. Because of the dominant position of the army in Indonesian politics, particularly since the coup of 1965 which ousted President Sukarno from office, the navy has rarely been afforded the priority it deserves, often coming a poor second in terms of both funding and new equipment. This has clearly affected the Marines who, despite their undoubted fighting capabilities, have not been used in the amphibious role even when the campaign involved such operations. In wars against both the Dutch in West Irian (1962) and the Portuguese/Fretilin forces in East Timor (1975), the initial island assaults were carried out by army paratroopers, with Marines appearing, if at all, at a later stage, while the army itself has retained its own amphibious capability, the paracommandos, totally separate from that of the navy.

This was further reflected during the Confrontation with Britain and Malaysia in Borneo (1963-66), even though the nature and scale of the fighting were different. The campaign took place in thick jungle, many miles from the sea; this was perhaps an area in which the Marines were not the natural choice, but small numbers were deployed from the start, passing on their fighting skills to groups of 'volunteers' whose task it was to mount cross-border raids into the British colonies of Sarawak and North Borneo (Sabah). Despite an initial advantage of surprise – the first such raid, on Tebedu in Sarawak on 12 April 1963, caught the British largely unawares – the volunteers were soon contained, forcing the Indonesians to commit their own regular troops. The majority of these came from army units, but some Marines found themselves responsible for leading reorganised volunteer groups in a new wave of incursions and raids, particularly after Sukarno's decision to escalate the fighting in September 1963 in response to the formation of the Malaysian Federation. The Marines' task was by no means an easy one. The volunteers were drawn from a wide range of ethnic groups and not all were willing participants; the training time allowed was often pitifully short and the men were unsuited to the harsh conditions of jungle fighting. By all accounts, the Marines themselves were tough opponents, but their losses to the superior tactics and mobility of British and Malaysian forces were disproportionately large. In one raid into Sabah in late December 1963, for example, a force of volunteers led by 35 Marines was isolated and destroyed by Gurkha troops: only 14 Marines survived. Indeed the whole involvement of the Indonesian armed forces in the Confrontation with Malaysia was a sorry episode and few of the small-scale raids were successful.

Such incursions declined in importance and impact after April 1964, and thereafter the Indonesians shifted the emphasis of their campaign away from Borneo, initiating a series of landings on the coasts of Singapore and Malaya. The fact that the Marines were not used at all in this phase of the war – the landings were carried out by groups of volunteer and army personnel – merely reinforces the point that their amphibious potential has not been fully exploited. There is no doubt that the Marines are crack troops, but to a large extent they seem to have adopted the role of elite land forces, with the specialised skills that their name implies occupying a subordinate position.

Below: During the 1965 coup that overthrew Sukarno, a member of the Indonesian armed forces stands by as Muslim youths assault a Chinese student suspected of being a communist. The resemblance of the Indonesian armed forces to those of the United States is apparent; the helmet and M1 carbine are of US origin and the fatigues are cut in the US style. Since the 1965 coup, Western military equipment has been provided in larger quantities as Indonesia has improved its relations with the United States.

Indonesian Marine
— Borneo 1963 —

Despite Indonesia's non-aligned, nationalist stance, the Indonesian Marines of the early 1960s had a very American appearance. This man's uniform is made from US Marine camouflage cloth, although the cut is different from the US Marine uniform. His helmet and its camouflage cover are also of US design, being the M1-pattern steel helmet with a World War II US Marine-surplus camouflage cover. On his sleeve, he wears the emblem of the Korps Komando Operasi – the Indonesian Marine Corps. His rifle is a Czech 7.62mm Vz52, and he carries its ammunition in a US-pattern pouch belt and webbing.

Above: A member of the Indonesian armed forces on patrol in Medan on the island of Sumatra. This man is armed with a US-supplied M3 'grease gun' and equipped with a US helmet and jungle boots.

SOUTHEAST ASIA

The Viet Cong

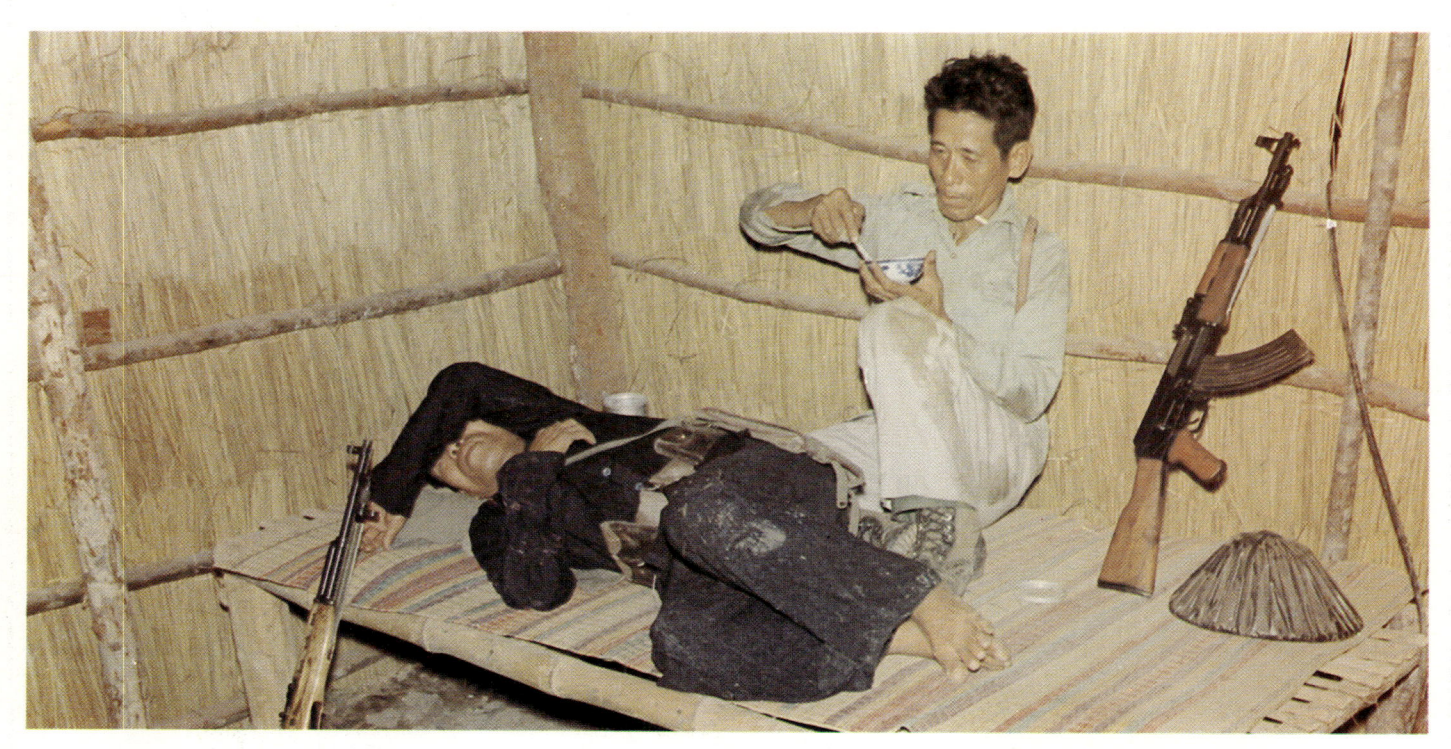

The Viet Cong (Vietnamese communists) traced their origins back to the Viet Minh who had fought the French during the first Indochina War. The Viet Cong were those communists and their sympathisers who had remained in southern Vietnam following the partition of the country into North and South in 1954.

Guerrilla activity against the government of the South was instigated in the late 1950s when the strength of the Viet Cong stood at about 5000 armed activists supported by some 100,000 sympathisers. Recognised as the National Liberation Front (NLF) by the North, the Viet Cong began to build up strength and influence in the rural areas until the early 1960s when, with an active strength of 40,000 men, it instigated large-scale guerrilla action against the unstable South Vietnamese government. Commanding widespread support from the peasantry and the poorer town-dwellers, the well-trained and iron-disciplined Viet Cong were able to mount a real challenge against their US-backed opponents. The South was saved, however, by the arrival of American ground forces in 1965. Over the next three years while the main battles were fought between the US forces and the regular North Vietnamese Army (NVA), which infiltrated into the South, the Viet Cong increased their control over the countryside.

The Viet Cong were organised in a number of different ways, which in the military sphere included companies and battalions. A main-line battalion could have a strength of up to 600 men divided into three infantry companies, a heavy weapons company (including mortars, anti-tank rocket-launchers and recoilless rifles) plus reconnaissance, engineer and signals units. Reasonably well-armed by guerrilla standards, they were a formidable force. Their real strength lay in the combination of excellent organisation at almost all levels (something rarely found in guerrilla formations) and the deeply held convictions of the individual fighters that enabled them to endure the most desperate privations.

The great test of the Viet Cong came early in 1968 with the opening of the Tet offensive. This was an all-out attack against the South Vietnamese government undertaken both in the country and in the urban areas (especially Saigon and Hue). Although the offensive was carried out with the utmost determination and ruthlessness, the Viet Cong misjudged the mood of the people – who failed to come over to the communist cause. By mid-summer it was clear that the Tet offensive had been a military disaster for the Viet Cong: over 30,000 of their best troops had been killed and the morale of many of the units was irreparably damaged. But for the communists Tet had one great advantage in that it shook the resolve of the American political establishment and from then on America began the process of disengaging her troops from the war.

As the influence of the Viet Cong declined after 1968, that of the NVA grew so that by the early 1970s the North supplied the guerrilla fighters who had once come from the South. This trend suited the communist leaders in Hanoi who wished to have a free hand in the South without any Viet Cong/NLF interference. The Viet Cong had done their job keeping the war going in the 1960s, and with the fall of the South in April 1975 they were disbanded.

Above: A Viet Cong soldier rests while an NVA regular eats his rice ration in a palm leaf hut in South Vietnam. Alongside the 'pyjama'-clad Viet Cong is a Soviet-made SKS rifle and on the bunk is a Chinese copy of the AK-47. The Viet Cong played an integral part in the North Vietnamese communists' bid to overthrow the South Vietnamese government, and were sacrificed to that aim in the Tet offensive.

Viet Cong Guerrilla
—Vietnam 1966—

The Viet Cong had no formal uniform, but many wore the black 'pyjama' outfits that were common amongst the peasantry of Indochina. As a reminder of the region's colonial past, this guerrilla wears a pith or sun helmet made of pressed paper covered by a layer of cloth. It was also popular with the NVA regulars. The 'Ho Chi Minh' sandals are improvised from cut-up lorry tyres, the soles from the tread and the straps from the inner tube. Equipment consists of a cloth tube worn over the shoulder and said to be capable of holding a month's supply of rice. Carried on the back would be a small pack, made from canvas or thin poncho material, while on the captured US M56 web waist belt is attached a sheet of plastic-covered material (possibly a poncho), a canvas bag and, obscured by the left arm, a water bottle. Over the right shoulder is slung a musette bag of Warsaw Pact origin (probably Polish). Replacing the almost standard AK assault rifle is an anti-tank rocket-launcher, either the Soviet RPG2 or the Chinese-made Type-56 copy.

Right: Operating in the field for long periods, the Viet Cong were often required to carry a considerable amount of equipment, as is illustrated here. Below the homemade pack is a 10-pocket SKS rifle cartridge belt, each pocket holding up to 20 rounds of 7.62mm ammunition. Underneath the cartridge belt is, from the left, a musette bag, a canvas pocket holding two NVA stick fragmentation grenades, a small (possibly first aid) pouch and a Chinese water bottle, based on a Japanese World War II design.

SOUTHEAST ASIA

The South Vietnamese Army

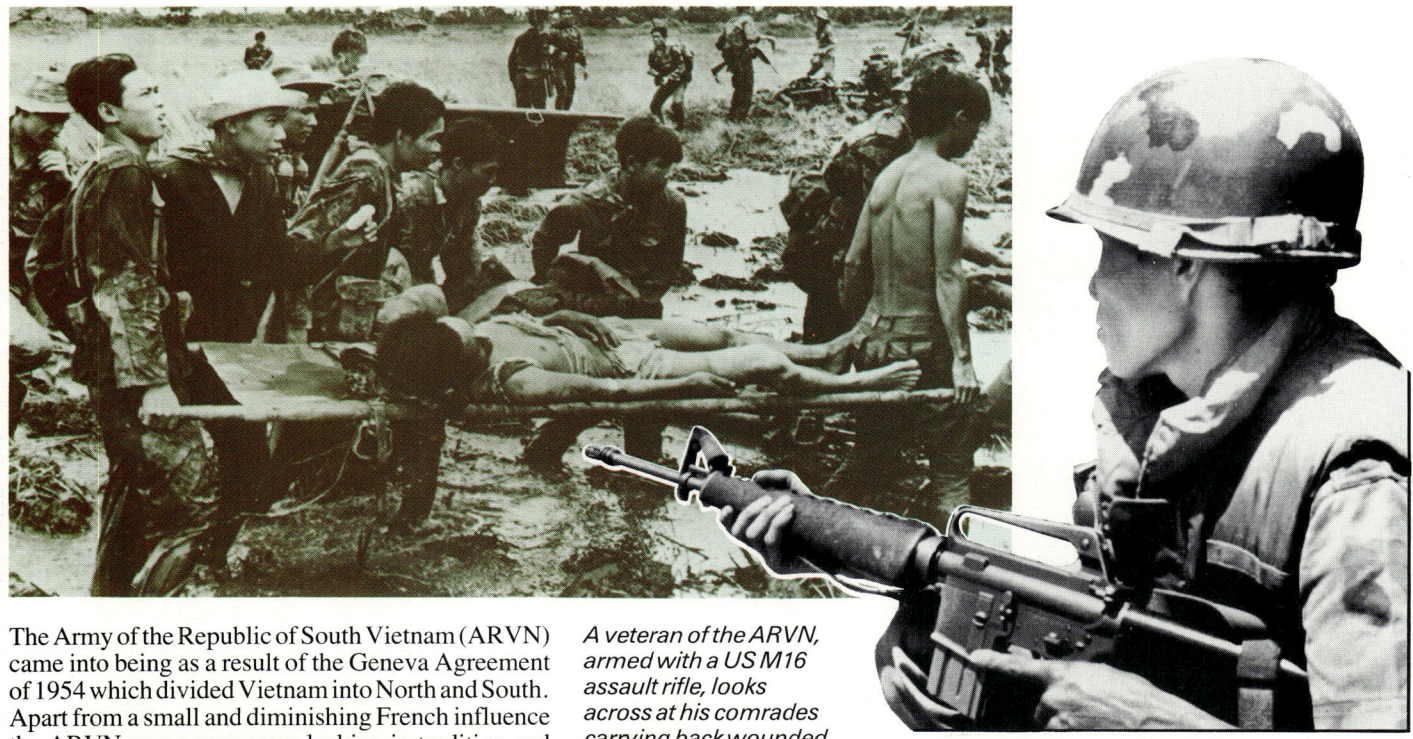

A veteran of the ARVN, armed with a US M16 assault rifle, looks across at his comrades carrying back wounded from an engagement with the North Vietnamese Army.

The Army of the Republic of South Vietnam (ARVN) came into being as a result of the Geneva Agreement of 1954 which divided Vietnam into North and South. Apart from a small and diminishing French influence the ARVN was a new army lacking in tradition and military experience, and as such it was beset by problems of trying to produce a modern fighting force while at the same time attempting to defend South Vietnam from battle-hardened Viet Cong.

During the early 1960s the tempo of conflict between North and South increased, and America, worried for the survival of the South, sent increasing amounts of aid – and later men – to shore up its wavering ally. ARVN arms and equipment were almost totally of American manufacture; and the American imprint on the ARVN was extended further as US military advisers tried to weld the army into an efficient fighting body along the lines of the US Army.

The massive injection of US aid allowed rapid expansion, from 220,000 men in 1964 to 416,000 in 1968. The ARVN was organised into 10 infantry divisions plus numerous combat support units, which received the majority of US resources. From 1965 to 1968 the main brunt of the fighting was borne by American troops, the intention being to give time to the ARVN to reorganise itself. After the Tet offensive of 1968 the ARVN was given a more prominent position in the firing line and, as American troops began to withdraw, a modernisation programme was instigated – the ARVN being supplied with surplus though modern US arms and equipment. By 1970 most units were armed with M16 rifles, M79 grenade launchers and M60 machine guns.

The ARVN was unable to fill the gap left by the Americans, however, and while holding the North Vietnamese during the 1972 Easter invasion, it succumbed to the communist forces in 1975. The weaknesses of the ARVN were many: corruption was rife and advancement within the service was based on favouritism; contact between officers and men was almost non-existent; and army organisation – based on a cumbersome territorial system – acted against mobility. And while the Americans provided the material to keep the ARVN in being, at the same time they removed the initiative from the South Vietnamese who were chronically lacking in offensive spirit. Not surprisingly, morale was often poor and desertion was rife – in 1965 alone some 113,000 men deserted.

Despite these serious (and eventually insoluble) problems the ARVN continued to fight, slogging it out with the Vietnamese communists in a bitter conflict that lasted over two decades. While the bulk of the ARVN was of only average standard or below, certain units were of the highest quality, capable of taking on crack North Vietnamese formations without US support. The 'Ranger' battalions and the Airborne and Marine Divisions were held in the highest regard and the 1st Infantry Division was considered to be on a level with US Airmobile and Marine units. The superior combat performance of such units was usually a consequence of inspired leadership by a few key officers; General Ngoi Quang Truong, commander of the 1st Infantry Division, raised the quality of his troops through careful integration with US forces whose combat experience rubbed-off onto the South Vietnamese soldiers. Unfortunately for the South, officers such as Truong proved to be an exception.

ARVN Lieutenant
—Vietnam 1970—

The reliance placed by South Vietnam upon America extended to the provision of uniforms and weapons; consequently this ARVN patrol leader is entirely US-equipped. The two-piece camouflage suit is in the 'tiger stripe' pattern worn by US Special Forces and popular with many South Vietnamese units. The waistcoat is of nylon mesh complete with integral pockets. The rank system is distinctly South Vietnamese and is depicted here by two gold plum blossoms on the hat, denoting the rank of 1st Lieutenant. Well armed, this officer carries a 5.56mm M16A1 assault rifle with two M26A2 fragmentation grenades and a pistol attached to his web belt. A further American feature – though strictly unofficial – is the peace sign tag worn at the neck, traditionally made from the ring pulls of beer cans.

Below: US M56 pattern equipment was widely used by ARVN forces and depicted here are, from left to right, a first aid pouch, plastic water bottle, 'butt' pack, .45 automatic pistol with black-leather holster, and an ammunition pouch for two spare pistol magazines.

SOUTHEAST ASIA

The Khmer Rouge

The Khmer (Cambodian) Liberation Army – dubbed the 'Khmer Rouge' by Cambodian head of state Prince Norodom Sihanouk in the late 1960s – was a peasant-based revolutionary force which established its political authority over all Cambodia in April 1975. Because its victory coincided with that of the North Vietnamese in Saigon, it is often seen as part of a closely coordinated Indochinese revolution, but in reality this was not the case. Despite common origins in the Indochinese communism of the 1930s and a measure of mutual support in the early 1970s, fundamental differences of ideology, leadership and experience existed between the two groups – differences which, when added to traditional territorial rivalries, led to a Vietnamese invasion of Kampuchea (as Cambodia was renamed after the Khmer Rouge victory) in December 1978 and a war which was still flickering on in the mid-1980s.

The split between Vietnamese and Cambodian revolutionaries dates back to 1954, when the new government in Hanoi, anxious to adhere to the terms of the Geneva Agreement, withdrew support from the Cambodian Communist Party and left the state to pursue a neutralist policy under the autocratic Prince Sihanouk. His widespread popularity and the relative prosperity of Cambodia, where few people starved and over 90 per cent of the peasants owned land, lessened the attraction of communism, and although an irreconcilable remnant, convinced that Hanoi had betrayed the revolution, went underground, they could achieve little on their own. Throughout the 1950s and much of the 1960s they scraped a precarious existence in the jungles and hills of the northeast and the Cardamom mountains of the southwest, setting up rudimentary 'safe base areas' on the Maoist pattern and organising occasional guerrilla attacks on Sihanouk's army, but to minimal effect. Although some new recruits (including intellectuals who were soon to assert overall leadership) drifted into the Khmer Rouge sanctuaries after 1960, they were still too few to be decisive.

A turning point occurred in 1967, when Sihanouk ordered his new prime minister, Lon Nol, to deal with a peasant uprising in Battambang Province (an uprising which seems to have owed nothing to Khmer Rouge activity), for his ruthless violence quickly alienated substantial elements of the population. A sudden influx of recruits enabled the communists to step up their activities and, as Sihanouk wavered, Lon Nol seized the opportunity to organise a military-backed coup in Phnom Penh (March 1970). Turning to the United States for aid, he initiated a campaign of deliberate repression and the war acquired a new vicious intensity. By 1973, with an estimated 4000 regular troops and up to 50,000 guerrillas available, the Khmer Rouge was strong enough to exert its control over the northern provinces of the state.

There followed a two-year campaign in which Khmer Rouge guerrilla groups, armed by the North Vietnamese and Chinese, infiltrated government lines, destroyed isolated military outposts and gradually drew a noose around Phnom Penh. The fighting was by no means one-sided – in late 1973/early 1974, for example, Lon Nol was able to defeat a major communist offensive against the capital – but by spring 1975, with US support halted by Congress and up to 60 per cent of Cambodia already in Khmer Rouge hands, Lon Nol was isolated and communist victory assured.

By this time the Khmer Rouge had made what seemed to be a smooth transition from guerrilla force to regular army but its new-found strength was dissipated by the bizarre actions of its leaders, particularly Saloth Sar (Pol Pot). Basing his policies on the views of Khieu Samphan, who advocated a return to the simplicity and self-sufficiency of rural life, Pol Pot forcibly removed the population of Phnom Penh to the countryside and introduced a campaign of terror and murder against those who would not contribute to the new utopia. By 1978 the Khmer Rouge had lost much of its military cohesion, and the Vietnamese invasion force found it surprisingly easy to advance as far as the Thai border. Sporadic guerrilla attacks continued into the 1980s, however, demonstrating the ability of the Khmer Rouge to survive at a basic level as an insurgent force.

Above: These three Khmer Rouge soldiers are wearing Chinese-style uniforms. The man in the centre is armed with an ex-US M79 grenade launcher, the grenades for which are suspended from his belt. The soldier on the left carries an AKMS, while the man on the right is armed with an RPG-7.

Khmer Rouge Soldier
—Cambodia 1975—

The black peasant clothes worn by this man were common among the irregular armies of Indochina; the Khmer Rouge have also been photographed wearing dark-brown or olive-green fatigues. The Khmer Rouge are the proteges of China in Indochina and this cap is almost identical to those worn by the Chinese People's Liberation Army. Chinese influence is also visible in the Type 56 7·62mm assault rifle, a copy of the Soviet AK-47, and the Chinese ammunition pouches. The scarf, shown here in blue and white, came in many variations including green and white, a pattern similar to the Royal Stewart tartan, and a combination of brown shades.

Below: Two Khmer Rouge on patrol in Kampuchea. The forested areas of western Kampuchea provide ample cover for the operations of the surviving elements of the Khmer Rouge in their struggle against the Vietnamese-backed regime.

East Asia

The emergence of a communist regime in China in October 1949 altered the strategic and political balance of East Asia, replacing a weak, essentially Western-orientated government with one of great potential strength, tied firmly to Marxist ideology. This had two immediate effects. First, the success of Mao Tse-tung's revolutionaries acted as a model for similar groups elsewhere, leading to a rash of communist-inspired insurgencies, particularly in the colonial areas of Southeast Asia; secondly, the sudden spread of communism into the most populous nation on Earth produced a new sense of Chinese identity, manifested in pressure to restore the 'ancient boundaries' of the state. Yet despite the fact that most of China's neighbours have experienced some sort of border conflict or intervention since that time – Tibet and Korea in 1950, India in 1962, the Soviet Union in the late 1960s and Vietnam in 1979 – the long-term impact of Mao's revolution has been muted. Far from developing into the 'Superpower of Asia', China is now facing problems of economic development and is effectively contained within a ring of rival states.

When the Second World War ended, however, none of this was apparent. The Kuomintang (KMT) nationalists under Chiang Kai-shek were in control in Peking, and China itself, although weakened by eight years of war against the Japanese, had a powerful voice in world affairs, sitting as a permanent member of the UN Security Council. But this was a façade, hiding the fact that the KMT, war-weary and dispirited, was facing the growing menace of a unique form of communist revolution propounded by Mao Tse-tung. He advocated a three-phase process of rural-based revolt, with the ultimate aim of seizing political power. Phase One concentrated on gaining popular support in remote 'safe bases', creating a solid, deep-rooted foundation upon which to build an unstoppable social force; Phase Two used guerrilla tactics to protect the safe bases and begin a long campaign of wearing down the resolve of government forces; Phase Three transformed the guerrillas into a conventional army, capable of defeating weakened government forces in open battle preparatory to a takeover of political power. Mao followed this pattern in China before 1949, establishing his safe bases initially in the Chingkang mountains and then (after the 'Long March' of 1934-35) in the remote northern province of Shensi, before initiating guerrilla subversion which forced the KMT to spread its units thinly to protect vital ground. By 1946 the People's Liberation Army (PLA) was ready to assume the offensive, advancing into Manchuria as a preliminary to all-out civil war against the Nationalists. When Peking fell to the revolutionaries in October 1949, forcing Chiang Kai-shek to withdraw to the island of Taiwan (Formosa), there seemed nothing to prevent the spread of communism into neighbouring states.

At first this appeared to be happening, for Mao's victory acted as a powerful boost to concurrent communist campaigns in Indochina (Vietnam, Laos and Cambodia), Malaya and the Philippines, and enabled the PLA to intervene in both Tibet and Korea. But the results were mixed. Despite eventual Vietnamese success in Indochina, the Maoist pattern of revolt was broken by determined government action elsewhere in Asia, while in Tibet the emergence of local resistance to Chinese rule tied down the PLA in a lengthy campaign of repression. Even in Korea, where PLA units intervened to prevent the defeat of their North Korean allies, hard-pressed by US/UN forces reacting to the invasion of South Korea in June 1950, the initial success of Chinese 'human wave' tactics was soon countered by heavy firepower and superior weapons technology. By 1953, after nearly three years of expensive self-sacrifice, the PLA adhered to an armistice that left Korea still split on the 38th Parallel. Nor did the problems end there, for the PLA fared badly against the vastly more experienced Vietnamese in 1979.

The reasons for this lack of long-term military success are not difficult to define. The ideological split with the Soviet Union, which emerged in the 1960s, has forced the Chinese to reassess their strategic priorities, looking northwards and devoting substantial parts of their defence effort to the creation of nuclear weapons designed to deter a full-scale Soviet attack. This in turn has left the PLA starved of funds for conventional weapons, and although it could be argued that the declared strategy of a 'People's War', with its emphasis on the mobilisation of the population to fight guerrilla-style campaigns against any invader, does not require the deployment of sophisticated weapons, the fact remains that available equipment is largely obsolete, acting as a constraint to the development of new tactics or military skills. Thus, although the PLA can field tanks, artillery, helicopters and jet aircraft, many of the designs are direct copies of those supplied by the Soviets in the 1950s.

At the same time, the regional balance of Asia is weighted against the Chinese. Some of the local states now have a far wider experience of war than their Maoist neighbour and are prepared to accept the impact of the Sino-Soviet dispute if this means they can have access to modern Soviet equipment. Both Vietnam and North Korea have adopted this approach, presenting the Chinese with the prospect not just of military defeat in the event of war, but also of gradual Soviet encirclement. Other states, outside the communist sphere, look to America, and although Sino-American relations have improved since the early 1970s, Peking cannot ignore the military potential of South Korea, Taiwan and even Japan. In every sense, China has been contained, and if the time should ever come when she feels sufficiently threatened to break out, using a revitalised PLA, East Asia will witness a war of catastrophic proportions.

Right: Soldiers of the People's Liberation Army (PLA), armed with Chinese versions of the Soviet AK-47 assault rifle, strike an aggressive pose. Despite its huge size, the PLA suffers from a lack of modern equipment and still depends largely upon locally-made copies of Soviet kit from the 1950s and 1960s.

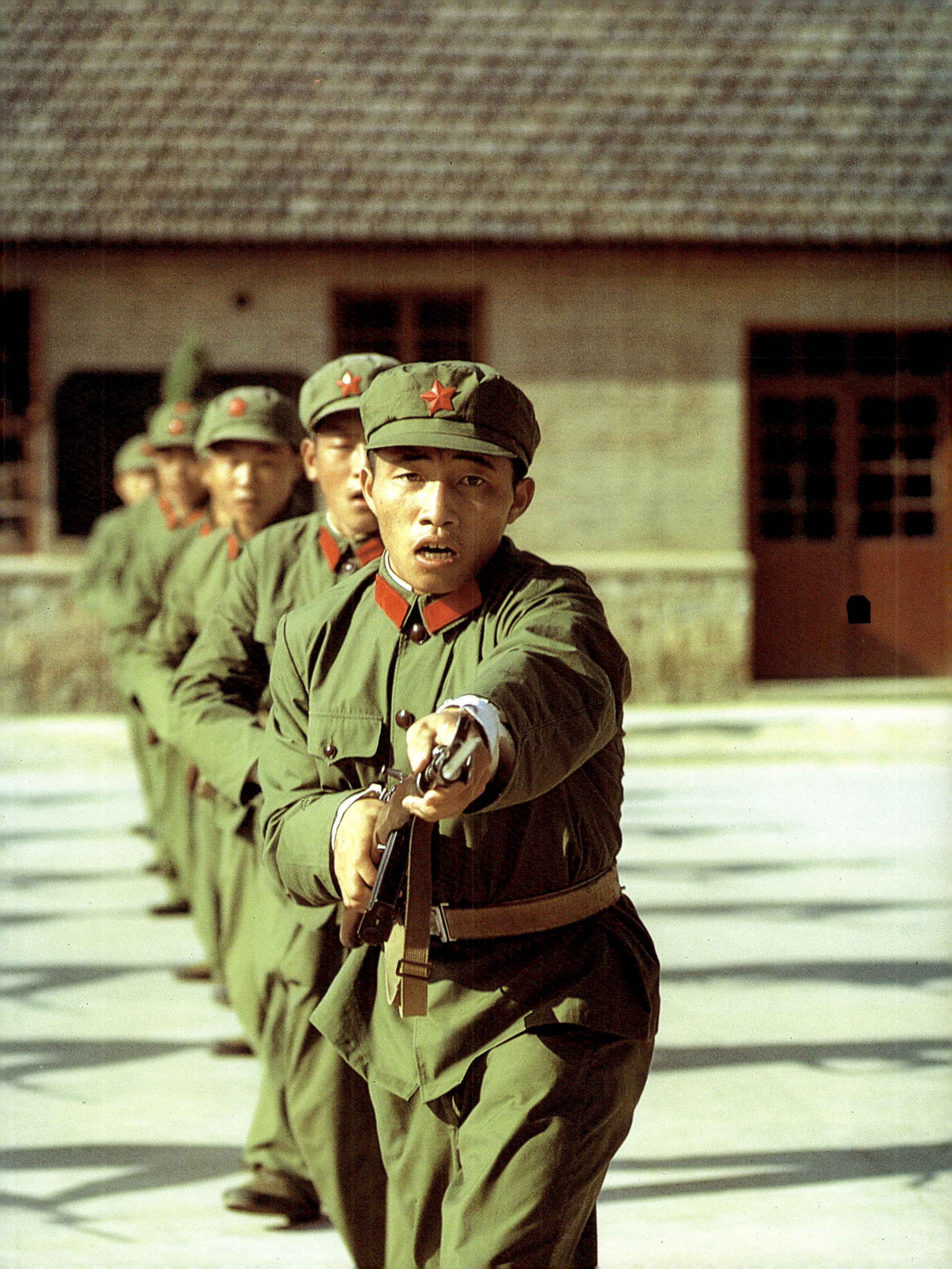

The Chinese Nationalist Army

The Chinese Nationalist Army originated from the need for a truly national, professional force to replace the warlord armies that dominated much of the nation during the confusion that reigned after the collapse of the Manchu dynasty in 1911. Dr Sun Yat-sen, the 'father of the revolution', was determined that the new republic would have effective armed forces at its disposal.

During the early 1920s, the example of the Bolshevik revolution in Russia inspired Chinese military planners and, indeed, there was at this stage some cooperation between the newly formed Chinese Communist Party (CCP) and the Kuomintang (KMT), as the Nationalist grouping was known. In 1926, however, Chiang Kai-shek took over the Nationalist movement. He seemed to be extremely successful in implementing direct, authoritarian rule over much of China, purging his erstwhile communist allies in 1927 and by 1928 bringing most of the local warlords under control.

Chiang wanted to restructure his army along modern European lines, and to this end placed great weight on the theories of his German advisers. As far as tactics were concerned the German instructors expounded the value of positional warfare as it had been practised during World War I – and the acceptance of this doctrine can perhaps be seen as the root of the Nationalist failure to overcome the communists, for it contrasted strongly with Mao's strategies of movement and flexibility. Throughout the 1930s, communist base areas were often attacked but never eliminated by Nationalist forces.

By 1937 the Nationalist Army had raised some 1.7 million troops, which initially seemed an adequate number with which to contain both the communists and the Japanese who had invaded in that year. However, increasing pressure from within, by the communists, was extending Nationalist resources, and as the Japanese took the most important ports and cities along the eastern seaboard, the problems of supply began to affect the general efficiency of the Nationalist forces.

America's entry into World War II and its recognition of China's problems in the war against Japan saw US aid flow towards Chiang in an increasing stream. A provisional truce with the communists helped the Nationalists, too. By the end of World War II, there were about four million Nationalist troops under arms, many supplied with good quality US equipment.

After World War II Chiang was convinced that he could launch a successful campaign against Mao's communist troops. The USA agreed to equip a 39-division core of the Nationalist Army and this was effected by early 1946. US trucks, heavy equipment, artillery and smallarms allowed the Nationalists to expand the army so that by early 1946 it was estimated that they had established a ground-force superiority over the communists of as much as three to one.

But ostensible superiority in numbers and equipment proved to be of little long-term value, for the Nationalist forces had suffered heavily – Chiang had lost many of his best officers – and the years under arms during the war against Japan had severely affected the morale of the rank and file. Inflation and corruption had gone hand-in-hand to create an army that had failed to live up to the expectations of the dynamic force of the late 1920s. Local commanders made bids to become virtually independent warlords again, and loyalty to the regime was at a low ebb. Added to this the new weapons themselves were sometimes misused, or at the least they presented many technical problems to the soldiery.

Finally, Chiang, anxious to demonstrate his control over all China, insisted on moving his forces into the main cities rather than pursuing the communist forces in the countryside. The biggest folly was the occupation of Manchuria, which led to large Nationalist garrisons being cut off and destroyed by Mao's forces.

By 1949, the Kuomintang soldiers had lost all stomach for the fight. It was estimated that over 2½ million deserted in late 1948 and early 1949 alone, and the unreliability and later, open treason, of Nationalist troops – especially their commanders – were the two biggest factors in the collapse of Chiang's regime. In January 1949, for example, General Fu Tso-yi gave Peking to Mao's forces by signing an agreement providing for the absorption of his 200,000 men into the communist armies. By early 1949 it had become quite clear that the Nationalist Army no longer constituted an effective fighting force.

Above: A horse-drawn artillery piece is brought up to the front during the final stages of the battle for Shanghai. Although much of their weaponry was antiquated by Western standards, the Nationalist forces were considerably better armed than their communist adversaries.

Chinese Nationalist Infantryman
—China 1945—

The uniform of the Nationalist forces remained the same as it had been during World War II, as is demonstrated by this soldier who wears khaki-drill summer uniform complete with archaic-looking puttees. On the cap is the distinguishing badge of the Nationalist forces, a white sun on a blue background. That the United States was a major supplier of arms and equipment to Chiang Kai-shek's armies is also evident: US webbing is worn (including the five-pocket magazine pouch) and his firearm is a .45 Thompson sub-machine gun.

Right: A detachment of Nationalist infantry is marched through the streets of Shanghai in February 1949, only a few months before the total collapse of the KMT at the hands of the communists.

EAST ASIA

The People's Liberation Army

The Chinese communist armed forces have always been distinguished by their close relationship with the Communist Party (CCP); from the formation of the Workers' and Peasants' Red Army in 1927 right through to the civil war in the 1940s and beyond, the political and military functions of the army have been virtually inseparable from those of the Party. The CCP leaders all performed military and political functions, and politburo members acted as field commanders.

The origins of China's Communist Army lay in the long protracted struggle against the Nationalists of Chiang Kai-shek, that had broken out into open warfare in 1927 and continued as a bitter guerrilla conflict until the temporary alliance made ten years later in order to defend China from the Japanese. Civil war between communists and Nationalists broke out again after the defeat of Japan, and in 1946 the communist forces were designated the People's Liberation Army (PLA).

During the war with Japan the communist forces had expanded in numbers – from 92,000 in 1937 to over three-quarters of a million by 1945 – and under the rigorous leadership of Mao Tse-tung had forged itself into an effective fighting force ready to take on the more numerous but ill-disciplined Nationalist armies.

As the PLA prepared to go over to the offensive in all out war against the Nationalists its greatest problem lay in shortage of arms and equipment, most notably the heavy weapons that had not been necessary when the communists had been undertaking simple guerrilla operations. The Soviet Army in Manchuria now came to Mao's help. During their destruction of the Japanese Kwantung Army in August 1945, the Russians had captured vast quantities of Japanese arms. Most of these arms were transferred, in one way or another, to Chinese communist forces during the winter of 1945-46. Other Japanese equipment was taken by communist forces in north and central China.

Moreover, as the PLA went over to the strategic offensive in 1947, ever-increasing quantities of military equipment were captured from the disintegrating Nationalist forces. By mid-1948, when the Nationalist armies numbered more than 2.5 million to 1.5 million deployed by the PLA, the two sides were equal in rifles and artillery.

While parity in equipment provided the PLA with its tactical cutting edge, more important was the superiority of its leadership and of the men on the ground. Unlike the quarrelsome Nationalist generals, the PLA was united by a common aim and ideology, and under Mao's undisputed control was able to impose a strategic unity over its disparate and far-flung forces. As a people's army the PLA drew its strength from the mobilisation of the masses, made possible by basic improvements to their standard of living and the promise of a united and prosperous China under communism. While the Nationalists ravaged the countryside, Mao's troops worked alongside and won over the peasants who provided a willing pool of manpower for the communist armies. The growing strength of the PLA was in direct contrast to the Nationalists whose power and influence waned, so that by the end of 1948 victory for the communists was assured.

Below: PLA infantry take up a defensive position amongst the crumbling stones of the Great Wall of China. The soldier in the foreground is armed with a Japanese Type 11 machine gun while his comrade carries a German 7.63mm Mauser C96 pistol. While the PLA had more or less standardised Soviet small arms for their troops by the end of the Korean War, during the Civil War of the late 1940s they were using equipment from a wide variety of sources. This included Japanese material captured by the Russians in Manchuria during World War II and American kit taken in battle from the Nationalists.

Chinese Communist Infantryman
—China 1945—

Both communists and Nationalists were uniformed very similarly and this soldier is fairly typical of the Civil War soldier. A khaki cotton uniform is worn with distinctly old-fashioned woollen puttees and a khaki field cap. Leather ammunition pouches are attached around the waist, the larger pouches capable of holding the 20-round magazines of the sub-machine gun carried by this soldier. The 9mm United Defense Model 42 was an American sub-machine gun developed in 1938; very well-made it was too expensive and complex to mass-produce and was only manufactured in small numbers, some of which found their way to China.

Below: Armed with a Type 41 Chinese version of the Bren light machine gun, a unit of the PLA stands firm against a Nationalist counter-attack during the Chinese Civil War.

EAST ASIA

The North Korean Army

Well trained, ably led veterans with superior equipment, the North Korean forces had things much their own way in the opening weeks of the Korean War. Even when faced with American soldiers and experiencing acute shortages at the end of over-extended lines of supply the North Korean soldiers displayed outstanding qualities of courage and endurance as they pressed home attacks around Pusan. Even the collapse which succeeded the UN counter-stroke at Inchon did not destroy morale utterly and many thousands of troops cut off in the South maintained guerrilla warfare or carried on the struggle as prisoners of war.

One key factor which made the initial North Korean success possible was the surprising extent to which the individual soldiers had seen combat before. Five of the ten divisions disposed of by North Korean leader Kim Il Sung in 1950 were partly or wholly comprised of veterans of the Chinese People's Liberation Army (CPLA). The 5th and 6th Divisions were simply the Chinese 164th and 166th Divisions which had always been composed of Koreans. The 7th Division was made up of Koreans released from the CPLA 139th, 140th, 141st and 156th Divisions while the 1st and 4th Korean People's Army (KPA) Divisions each contained an entire regiment of Koreans who had formerly served in the CPLA. It is noteworthy too that this massive infusion of experienced soldiers from the CPLA consisted of men who had already made their ideological commitment to communism before Kim Il Sung's regime came to power in the north; they were therefore deeply attached to their cause rather than being the shallow products of indoctrination.

If Chinese communism had schooled many of the soldiers of the KPA it was Soviet communism which trained and armed them. Russian officers had trained the KPA from its inception in February 1948; its formations were organised along Soviet lines and its tactical doctrine was recognisably Soviet in origin. Besides this its heavy weaponry was all supplied by the Soviet Union; not only the 120 rugged T-34 tanks which contributed so much to the drive south but also a lavish quantity (in itself typically Soviet) of artillery pieces – 12 SU-76 SPGs together with field and medium artillery in each division. All this was used according to Soviet principles so that the performance of the KPA provides a vivid contrast with that of the Chinese troops who burst into Korea in October 1950. The Chinese were forced to compensate for inferiority in war material by travelling light, moving at night and relying on weight of numbers to bring success. By contrast the KPA was more used to employing the blitzkrieg approach made possible by its superior level of equipment.

Just as the KPA preferred the Soviet way in war so it looked to Soviet methods to keep up political pressures on its soldiers. There was a political officer (commissar) at the army, division, regiment, battalion and company level while in each company there was a party cell which consisted of all platoon commanders and vice-commanders together with a few picked private soldiers. To maintain communist party control and heighten motivation about one quarter of military-training time was devoted to political education. North Korean soldiers accepted a frenetic cult of personality vested in the 'glorious leader' Kim Il Sung. Exaggerated statements of praise and devotion to Kim laced most KPA orders of the day. Unsubtle as the technique may seem it served well enough to blunt the critical faculties of the men of the KPA to the extent that Kim's position and prestige survived the disasters of September and October 1950 when the UN forces launched their successful counter-attack.

In contrast to the nearly fantastic level of devotion to the leader expected from North Korean soldiers, their command organisation was realistic enough. In contrast to the Chinese who experimented with abolishing ranks and badges of distinction, the KPA followed the Soviet example by having a rigid, orthodox military hierarchy. Terms of service for the lower ranks were always harsh: no real prospect of leave and virtually negligible pay. For officers – especially senior officers – it was a very different story with vastly greater pay and considerable emphasis placed on the deference owed by junior ranks to those above them. Soviet-style uniforms plainly displayed the insignia denoting differences in rank.

Above: Wearing camouflage uniforms two North Korean soldiers practise one of the most important elements of fieldcraft on the battlefield: cutting through barbed-wire entanglements.

North Korean Infantryman
—Korea 1950—

While North Korean soldiers were poorly equipped in comparison with their UN adversaries their uniforms and equipment were at least functional for the style of warfare fought in Korea. This soldier is dressed in winter uniform which consists of a simple quilted jacket and trousers plus a peaked cap with ear flaps. The sub-machine gun carried here is a Soviet 7.62mm PPSh, a typically robust short-range weapon fitted with a 71-round magazine.

Right: These two North Korean soldiers demonstrate the Soviet Union's influence on the KPA; their tunics and shoulder boards are of a Russian design which dates back to the Imperial Army of the Tsar's time.

EAST ASIA

The People's Liberation Army in Korea

Chinese military intervention in support of the embattled North Koreans in October 1950 was substantial. Over 200,000 soldiers of the People's Liberation Army (PLA), drawn from the 38th, 39th, 40th, 42nd, 50th and 66th Armies of XIII Army Group (part of General Lin Piao's Fourth Field Army), moved across the Yalu River on the border with North Korea to the west of the central Taebaek mountains to confront the American-dominated United Nations Command (UNC) which was in the process of driving north. Despite inferiority of weapons, tactics and operational procedures, this huge influx of manpower caught the UNC units unawares, forcing them back below the 38th parallel into South Korea. Although they were to recover sufficiently to prevent complete disaster, all hopes of an early UN victory disappeared as the war degenerated into a costly stalemate. When this ended in armistice in July 1953, the PLA had suffered enormous casualties – over a million according to some estimates – but had been forced to adapt to the demands of modern inter-state conflict.

When the intervention began the PLA was essentially a revolutionary army, dedicated to the ideals of Maoist communism and widely experienced in the art of insurgency. Most of the 'People's Volunteers' had fought Chiang Kai-shek's Nationalist Army during the civil war in China (1946-49) and many had conducted guerrilla operations in the 1930s and early 1940s against both the Nationalists and the invading Japanese. They were heavily politicised – commissars and political officers formed a core of Party control at every level of the PLA – and were made aware of the perceived dangers of a UN victory over North Korea. If anti-communist forces reached the Yalu, northern China and Manchuria would be directly threatened, while the growing links between the United States and remaining Nationalists in Taiwan (Formosa) could lead to a reopening of the civil war just when China desperately needed time to consolidate its recent victory on the mainland. Faced with such prospects, the motivation of the 'Volunteers' could only be high.

Nor was this their sole advantage, for the traditions of the PLA ensured a significant measure of shock and surprise against UN forces convinced that the war was won. The PLA soldiers were physically tough and capable of moving quickly across difficult terrain without the need for a sophisticated logistics 'tail' to betray their presence. The troops of XIII Army Group, joined in late November 1950 by men of IX Army Group to the east of the Taebaek mountains, were able to concentrate their forces preparatory to their assault despite the existence of unlimited UN air power by travelling largely at night and camouflaging their positions in the day. One army, for example, trekked over 450km (250 miles) in just 19 days across terrain regarded by the UN as impassable. The army's supply line, in common with that of other PLA formations, was subsequently attacked from the air, but was sustained by hordes of porters, each carrying

Above: These three Chinese prisoners were captured near Sudong-ni in South Korea. Prisoners were usually stripped of all their equipment and sometimes even of their clothes for fear of booby-traps. One of these Chinese was probably armed with a Type 88 rifle as the US Marine in the background is carrying one in his left hand.

35-45kg (80-100lb) of food or ammunition, who moved with equal speed and secrecy. Even if they had not delivered their supplies, the PLA units, true to their guerrilla roots, would certainly have attempted to live off the land. As infantry the PLA displayed great tactical flexibility and were able to deploy rapidly and effectively, and as individuals the first PLA troops committed to Korea proved courageous and tenacious in pursuit of their objectives.

These were strengths which could not ensure complete victory, for once the UN had recovered from the initial shock of Chinese intervention, the PLA faced an enemy whose technological and firepower advantages were considerable. The evolution of the 'meat-grinder' advance, whereby UN forces pushed forward behind an overwhelming display of artillery and air power, effectively countered the PLA 'human wave' approach which had swamped UN positions in late 1950. UN aircraft, concentrating on the supply choke-points of the Yalu river-crossings, gradually starved the Volunteers of their basic military needs. Massed infantry assaults, accompanied by trumpets, flares and a characteristic disregard for casualties, continued to be a feature of Chinese tactics throughout the war, but by 1952 they were achieving less success. In order to survive, the PLA was slowly forced to deploy artillery, armour and even its own air force, responding to the inherent strengths of its adversary by adopting the trappings of a modern conventional army and grafting them onto a force which owed its origins to a peasant-based revolutionary movement. In many ways the PLA is still affected by this dichotomy.

Chinese Infantryman
— Korea 1951 —

This man is well-dressed for the severe winters of the Korean peninsula, with a fur winter cap, the flaps of which can be lowered to protect the ears, and a uniform padded with cotton and quilted. He is armed with a Type 88 Hanyang rifle, a copy of the German M1888 (manufactured in China before World War II), probably captured from the Kuomintang forces. Over his shoulders are bandoliers for ammunition and tucked into his belt is a sack for rice. His light equipment highlights the emphasis placed on mobility of infantry.

Right: Captured soldiers of the Chinese Peoples' Volunteers who probably came from units of the Fourth Field Army commanded by Lin Piao. The 'meatgrinder' phase of the Korean War forced the PLA to abandon its guerrilla-style mobile tactics and become a more conventional army along Soviet lines.

The South Korean Army

The Army of the Republic of (South) Korea (ROK) is currently one of the largest in the world, fielding a total of 540,000 active soldiers, backed by a reserve of nearly one-and-a-half million. It is organised and equipped for large-scale conventional operations, based upon the use of tanks, mechanised infantry, artillery and even surface-to-surface missiles, is maintained by substantial American financial aid and a defence budget which absorbs up to a third of the country's gross domestic product and, perhaps inevitably, dominates the social and political framework of the state. Indeed, since the coup of 1961, the role of the military in directing policy has been crucial, despite a return to ostensibly democratic electoral processes.

Such a high level of militarism reflects the overriding fear of invasion from the North, where an even larger army is maintained, and draws its justification from the war of 1950-53, when ROK forces were patently incapable of defending the state without enormous United Nations (predominantly American) assistance. In retrospect, this was hardly surprising, for when the Soviet-backed North Koreans crossed the 38th parallel on 25 June 1950, the ROK Army was ill-prepared, lacking manpower, equipment and competent leadership.

The Americans, who had occupied the southern half of the Korean peninsula at the end of World War II, had shown a marked reluctance to raise a regular army for fear of provoking a Soviet reaction, and had been content to organise nothing more elaborate than a paramilitary Korean Constabulary of 50,000 poorly-equipped men, recruited on a regional basis and responsible for internal policing tasks only. When the Americans began to withdraw their forces in August 1948, handing power to the South Koreans under President Syngman Rhee, the Constabulary was merely expanded and renamed to produce the ROK Army.

By June 1950 the army comprised over 90,000 men in eight divisions, but officers were of low quality (many had been trained by the Japanese before 1945), most of the soldiers were raw recruits and the units were without tanks, medium artillery, air support and, in some cases, transport and ammunition. Small wonder, therefore, that within a month of the invasion the ROK Army had disintegrated, losing 40,000 men and most of its equipment in a series of chaotic retreats down the peninsula towards Pusan. In July, command of all ROK forces was delegated to the UN commander-in-chief – an American – by means of the so-called Taejon Agreement, emphasising the scale of the disaster.

In the light of this defeat, the Americans were initially wary of funding a ROK modernisation programme, preferring to depend on their own and allied units to conduct the war. In 1952, however, Syngman Rhee was granted the money, equipment and training facilities to modernise his army, which by the time of the ceasefire in July 1953 numbered over 500,000 men organised into 16 divisions, this force being large enough to occupy nearly three-quarters of the front line.

The reputation of ROK troops was reinforced in the late 1960s when, in response to American requests for aid, over 300,000 of them saw service in Vietnam, rotating through the Capital ('Tiger') and White Horse Divisions and conducting operations which were widely regarded as impressive, if sometimes rather brutal. Such experience, coupled with a high state of combat readiness – two-thirds of the army is stationed close to the border with North Korea at all times and frequently conducts exercises at corps level – undoubtedly enhances the deterrent value of the ROK forces, enabling them, with American backing, to maintain an uneasy peace along one of the flashpoint borders of Asia.

Above: South Korean troops watch a training exercise, well kitted-out in quilted winter uniforms and American M1 helmets. Once properly armed and equipped the South Koreans proved redoubtable combat troops.

South Korean Soldier
— Korea 1951 —

This soldier reflects the American domination of the ROK Army and he is accordingly uniformed and armed from US sources. The uniform is the US M43 combat pattern, with US cuff-top boots and a peaked cap worn under a hood (attached to the jacket) and an M1 steel helmet. He is armed with a US 0.3in M1 carbine to which is fixed an M4 knife bayonet. The M1 carbine was a World War II weapon which was nonetheless used extensively during the Korean War, especially by troops who needed a lighter weapon than the standard M1 rifle.

Right: Armed with a captured PPSh-41 sub-machine gun a South Korean volunteer prepares to go into action.

The Soviet Bloc

The Soviet Union has good cause to fear the consequences of war. Twice in the present century Russia has been invaded, on the second occasion losing an estimated 20 million of her citizens in the subsequent war. In more modern times, Soviet politicians have only to look at a map of the world to see what they believe to be well-armed, potentially aggressive enemies on every side: to the north, across the Polar cap, the United States, equipped with nuclear weapons of intercontinental capability; to the southeast the ideological enemy, China, similarly equipped and with an army of immense size; to the west the European members of Nato (North Atlantic Treaty Organisation), fielding technologically sophisticated armed forces; to the south the Muslim powers of the Middle East, opposed to atheistic communism. In Soviet eyes, it is an awesome display of antagonism, and although from a different perspective it may be felt that the fear of aggressive encirclement is overstressed, there is no escaping the fact that the fear is there, affecting the policies of the Politburo.

This has had a number of effects. One way to escape encirclement is to force the enemy powers to divert resources away from Soviet borders: hence Moscow's interest in Third World states and the creation of an ocean-going navy. Similarly, if the fear is of sudden attack, a logical answer is to create a buffer-zone of friendly states whose territory can absorb any enemy advance without risking damage to the Soviet homeland: hence the policy of maintaining (by force if necessary) the communist regimes in eastern Europe and, in 1979, the decision to move into Afghanistan. Finally, if enemies abound, the Soviets need to maintain the capability to survive militarily: hence the emphasis upon large and well-equipped nuclear and conventional armed forces, deployed to face any threat that might arise.

Unfortunately, none of this takes place in a vacuum, and Soviet policies as they have emerged since 1945 have created or fuelled international tension by awakening fears in other states. To the West, the Soviet takeover of eastern Europe was blatant expansionism and was considered a threat to future security; the expansion of the Soviet nuclear arsenal was a deliberate bid for 'first-strike' superiority. The process works both ways – the Soviets, for example, view Nato as an aggressive, expansionist alliance – and the result is a state of latent hostility that does nothing to calm fears or engender lasting friendships.

The final and, perhaps, crucial element in this state of Cold War is the ideological conflict that permeates the entire East-West relationship. One of the basic tenets of Soviet communism is that the capitalist states of the West are inherently warlike, while the West in turn cannot believe that the Soviet state would not use its armed forces to accelerate the process of world revolution if it had the opportunity.

The armies of the Soviet bloc reflect this state of fear and tension. Unlike the Western allies, the Soviet Union retained a large army immediately after the Second World War, partly to deter potential aggressors, but also to provide a means of establishing permanent control in eastern Europe, providing support to the new pro-Soviet governments. Once those governments were in power, elements of the army remained to ensure their survival, while new armies, ideologically sound and under Soviet supervision, were raised in the satellite states. In 1955, a defence pact was set up at Warsaw to guarantee Soviet rights of deployment and interference. Nor was this a passive policy: in 1953 Soviet tanks appeared on the streets of East Germany to put down rioting, and three years later armoured units, backed by artillery and airpower, quashed the regime of Imre Nagy in Budapest. In 1968, Soviet and Warsaw Pact armour poured into Czechoslovakia to halt the reformist direction of Alexander Dubcek's new government, and 11 years later Soviet airborne and ground troops swept into Afghanistan to set up a friendly communist government that would act as a buffer to the spreading Muslim fundamentalism affecting the Middle East. Each move was logical from Moscow's point of view, but only succeeded in exacerbating East–West tension, and this, in Soviet eyes, increased the need for armed vigilance and effective defence. It was (and still is) a vicious circle.

In such circumstances, it is only natural that the Soviets and east Europeans should try to maintain effective armies. So far as basic preparation is concerned, no one can doubt that this has been achieved. The Warsaw Pact as a whole has nearly three million ground troops available, backed by a further five million reserves, organised into a myriad of armoured, motorised rifle, airborne and support divisions and well provided with modern military equipment – but there have been doubts expressed about the ability of these forces in a future war. The Soviet bloc armies have had little combat experience since 1945, and although the Soviet campaign in Afghanistan since 1979 may have affected tactical doctrines (as the recent evolution of the more flexible Operational Manoeuvre Groups implies), it is still very much the case that command initiative is weak and fighting skills are dangerously stereotyped. At the same time, the satellite states may not be willing to act as sacrificial buffers in a Soviet security system: since 1955 Albania has left the Warsaw Pact, Hungary and Czechoslovakia have tried to, Romania has distanced itself from the Soviets, and Poland has suffered all the trauma of internal unrest. Of course, it could well be that the satellite armies, dominated by officers of strong communist convictions and under the ultimate control of Soviet commanders, would fight as well as the Soviets themselves, but there must be enough evidence available to Moscow to create doubts in the minds of the Soviet planners. If this is so, the elaborate security policies evolved since 1945 may be little more than a paper screen.

Right: Soviet Marines, armed with a mixture of AK-47 and AKS-74 assault rifles, take part in military exercises. The distinctive red 'flash' on the side of their berets shows that they are members of the Red Banner Black Sea Fleet; their camouflaged uniforms suggest some sort of specialised role.

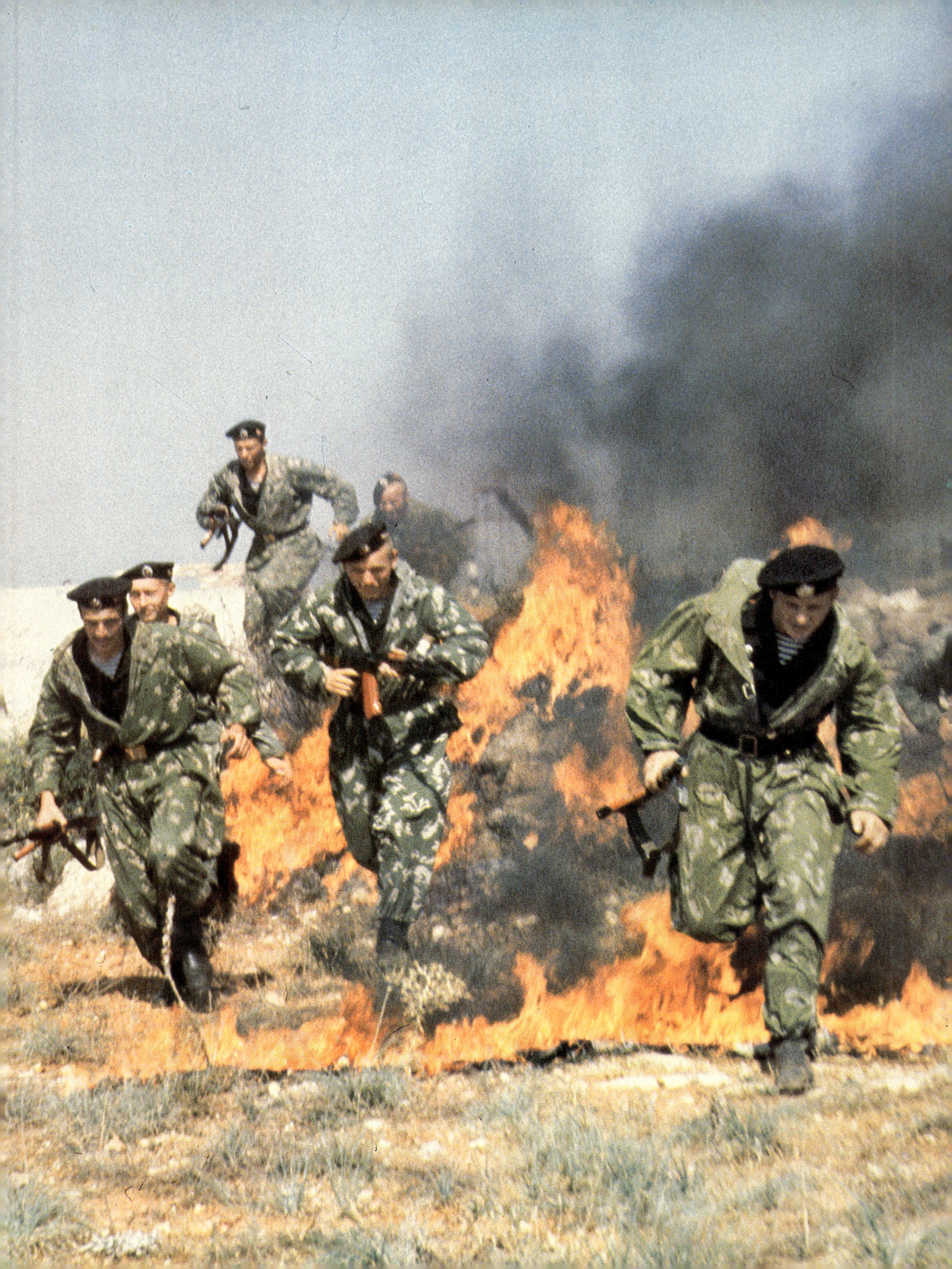

The Soviet Army in Hungary

Above: Soviet troops in Budapest. These men of a tank division are wearing their winter issue greatcoats and fur hats. The tanks are T54s and the armoured personnel carriers BTR-152s.

In the early hours of Wednesday, 24 October 1956, elements of two Soviet mechanised divisions, drawn from the normal garrison of Hungary, entered Budapest in a crude show of force designed to put a stop to popular demonstrations against the existing communist regime. It was an ill-prepared and poorly executed move, provoking a spontaneous armed response which the Soviets had clearly not expected and leading to a level of street violence that they found hard to contain – the army showing itself at its most inflexible, with its officers lacking initiative.

At a tactical level, the Soviets were surprisingly weak. Despite an awesome reputation for excellence in urban fighting, gained in the relatively recent advance from Stalingrad to Berlin, the troops committed to Budapest made a number of basic errors, chief among which was the rather naive presumption that their arrival in the city would intimidate the protestors and impose immediate order. It was felt that this could best be achieved by the deployment of tanks, sent in to protect key bridges, crossroads and administrative buildings without infantry support, but this took no account of armed opposition. As the tanks (mostly T34s) advanced into Budapest, therefore, they proved extremely vulnerable, running into a wide range of problems which could have been solved by accompanying infantry squads. As it was, insurgents were able to exploit their own intimate knowledge of the city to outflank, ambush and destroy enemy vehicles tied inextricably to the streets and unsure of what lay round the next corner. Molotov cocktails dropped from the upper floors of buildings set fuel tanks and engine compartments ablaze, snipers picked off any crew members foolish enough to leave the security of their armour and even small children attacked the tanks. Movement proved difficult against hastily-prepared barricades – ranging from elaborate structures drawn across the width of a street to the equally effective rows of upturned soup plates which, from the confines of a tank, looked like mines – and casualties mounted steadily. On 29 October, having lost an estimated 40 tanks, the Soviets began to withdraw.

A key factor in this decision must have been the morale of the battered tank crews. Most of them were conscripts, ill-prepared for the trauma of city fighting, and all had previously been stationed among the people they were now opposing. To begin with, on 24 October, some crews tried to fraternise with the demonstrators, displaying a marked reluctance to fight, and many found it difficult to understand the policy of their superiors that pitted communist against communist. Once the fighting began, they found themselves trapped inside their tanks in cramped conditions made worse by the constant fear of attack and the lack of clear directions about the purpose of their intervention. To this was added a very poor process of resupply – there is at least one case on record of a Soviet crew offering to hand over their tank to the insurgents in exchange for food – and an inadequate chain of command, leading inevitably to a situation in which military efficiency was dramatically undermined.

But the Soviet government could not allow the insurgents to win, and although some political concessions were granted as the tanks withdrew, it was soon apparent that this was merely a smoke-screen to hide more elaborate military preparations. By 1 November an estimated 12 Soviet divisions, drawn from the Carpathian Military District and commanded by General P. I. Batov, were massing on the Hungarian border, ready to invade. Four days later, the inevitable occurred, with simultaneous attacks on Budapest and a number of provincial towns. Soviet tactics were now more sophisticated and effective, for although up to 3000 tanks (mostly T54s) were deployed, they were closely supported by infantry in armoured personnel carriers, by artillery and even by airpower. Nor was there any sign of reluctance in the use of such overwhelming force: in Budapest whole buildings were destroyed, demonstrators shot down by machine-gun fire and rigid curfews imposed by troops ordered to suppress the 'fascist elements'. By 7 November the capital was quiet and the population, having suffered at least 3000 casualties, was cowed. Fighting was to continue in the provinces for another week, but it was already apparent that a ruthless use of coordinated armed force had ensured the restoration of a pro-Soviet regime in Hungary. It was a pattern of response that was to be repeated in Czechoslovakia 12 years later.

Soviet Army Soldier
— Hungary 1956 —

Were it not for his AK-47, this soldier could easily be mistaken for a member of the Red Army at the end of World War II. The side-cap, shirt, breeches (all in olive green) and boots are identical with the uniform worn during the Great Patriotic War, except for the absent breast pockets. The gas-mask case hanging over the right shoulder is also of World War II style, although the webbing pouches for the AK-47's 7·62mm ammunition are of post-war design. This cut of uniform continued in service with the Soviet Army until the new uniform of 1970-71 was issued.

Below: Soviet troops arrive outside Magyarovar town hall, used as a headquarters by Hungarian insurgents. Their transport is provided by a BTR-40 followed by a BTR-152 armoured personnel carrier.

THE SOVIET BLOC

Soviet Armoured Forces

Since the end of World War II Soviet military forces have experienced massive expansion and modernisation, and today the Soviet tank arm has become the main strike force of the Soviet land armies. Soviet doctrine is based on the offensive, centred on an armoured thrust supported by all other arms.

Soviet tank forces number some 47 divisions with a peacetime strength of 54,000 tanks. Of these approximately 127 tank regiments serve with motor-rifle divisions and about 500 battalions are deployed either in reserve or with motor-rifle regiments. The tank regiment consists of 95 tanks deployed in three tank battalions, plus extensive support units. A typical tank battalion will have a total strength of 31 tanks (three platoons of 10 tanks each and a further tank for the battalion commander). The independent tank battalions, which are more small regiments than large battalions, have a strength of 52 tanks (five platoons of 10 tanks each, a tank for the battalion commander and a tank for the divisional commander). Apart from its strengthened tank element, an independent battalion reflects its elite standing in the fact that not only is it the first to receive updated equipment, but it also has chemical, engineer, anti-aircraft and reconnaissance platoons attached. Yet despite this apparent superiority, these independent tank battalions are normally kept in reserve in order to protect the regimental headquarters and auxiliary divisional units, and to be prepared to exploit any front-line success.

A commander of a motor-rifle regiment will have at his disposal a tank battalion while the divisional motor-rifle commander has his own tank regiment. Further up the scale of command, an army commander controls a tank division and a front commander has a tank army.

Despite the proliferation of armour in the Soviet Union, training tanks are provided at the rate of one tank per platoon, or one tank per company in lower readiness categories. Those crews which do not use the training tanks are taught in classrooms, use wooden mock-ups of the controls, and are walked through tactical drills. The justification for this method of training is that it prevents deterioration of first-line equipment, though in Western armies such superficial training of the tank crew would be considered damaging to the tank arm as a whole.

Tanks were the most obvious aspect of the Soviet-led forces that moved into Czechoslovakia in 1968 to unseat the Dubček regime. Although tanks are not suited to urban warfare, the overwhelming presence of massed armoured units was sufficient to successfully intimidate the populace. Today, three Soviet motor-rifle and two tank divisions are deployed in Czechoslovakia.

Above: Soviet and Czech tank crewmen and infantry take a break during combined manoeuvres in Czechoslovakia in the late 1960s. The tank crew are easily distinguishable by their ribbed and padded protective helmets while the infantry wear standard issue forage hats and the Soviet officers, flat caps.
Right: A thoughtful Soviet tank man waits by his tank during the occupation of Prague in August 1968.

Soviet Tank Crewman
— Czechoslovakia 1968 —

The Soviet Union bases much of its military strategy upon the rapid deployment of tank units, and this is a typical Soviet T55 tank crewman of the late 1960s. The protective helmet is ribbed and padded (winter helmets are lined with white fur) and a plug for the RT/1C radio-to-vehicle transmitter socket hangs down his shoulder. A further communications device in the shape of a harness for a throat microphone is hung around the crewman's neck. Underneath the heavy black cloth protective overalls the crewman wears a shirt-type tunic. The high leather boots are a particular feature of Soviet military clothing. Personal armament consists of a Soviet 7.62mm AK-47 assault rifle, shown here with a lightweight folding metal stock which is standard issue to armoured forces troops. Although inaccurate at anything over a short range, the AK-47 combines simplicity of operation with reliability and has a sufficiently rapid cyclic rate of fire. This makes it an excellent smallarm for tank crews who are often forced to fight at close-quarters.

THE SOVIET BLOC

Afghan Guerrillas

Afghan tribesmen gained a fearsome reputation as guerrilla fighters in their many encounters with the British in the 19th century, and following the Soviet incursion in December 1979 the tribesmen have once again taken up arms. The control of central government has always been minimal in the remote countryside and the mountain tribesmen have led a semi-independent existence where tribal loyalties come first; and trained from an early age in the use of firearms they make natural guerrilla fighters. In addition, the rugged mountainous terrain that covers much of the country is ideal for guerrilla warfare and the long border with Pakistan – impossible for the authorities to control – provides the guerrilla with ready access to a means of sanctuary.

The Islamic revival of the 1970s fuelled the already fundamentalist religious tradition in Afghanistan so that the conservative tribesmen were fervently opposed to the Soviet-backed, atheistic government in Kabul. Recourse to arms was a natural response and since 1979 guerrilla warfare has been endemic.

The guerrillas are reasonably well armed with rifles which in the main consist of a heterogeneous mix of captured Soviet weapons, British-made Lee Enfields and a bewildering variety of home-made copies which, while lovingly made, lack reliability. The ubiquitous AK assault rifle is commonly used but far more useful in the mountains, forming the geographical background to the conflict, is the older Lee Enfield whose long-range accuracy is highly prized by the guerrillas. Given this diversity of weapon types ammunition supply is a problem but more serious is a shortage of modern anti-tank and anti-aircraft weapons. The guerrillas do have a few captured Soviet rocket-launchers and home-made mines are constructed, dangerously refashioned from unexploded Soviet bombs and shells, but these are clearly insufficient and as a result large-scale operations are usually out of the question. Guerrilla leaders have made successive pleas to the West for modern arms, but while sympathetic to the guerrilla cause in general, the Western powers have shied away from any such direct involvement. Not only do they fear an uncontrollable escalation of the conflict, but the resulting political and logistical problems would outweigh any possible embarrassment to Russia.

A second, more important, factor affecting the level and scope of military operations is that of organisation. The whole guerrilla movement consists of differing factions whose mutual rivalry prevents any nationally organised campaign of resistance. Even within the separate guerrilla bands themselves discipline is loose and organisation only rudimentary. Consequently even the simplest attacks on government or Soviet positions can degenerate into a complete shambles – as has been demonstrated on a number of occasions on specially mounted operations ostensibly designed to impress Western observers. Fortunately for the guerrillas the Soviet response to such raids is generally slow and unwieldy.

Despite these obvious weaknesses the morale of the guerrillas remains high and as fighters they are clearly superior to the unwilling conscripts that form the bulk of the government forces, a number of whom have in fact deserted to the rebels. In its turn the Soviet Army is subjected to an irritating series of ambushes and assassinations that are a constant reminder to the Soviet commanders that they have been unable to subdue the guerrillas, besides the fact that such attacks sap the morale of the Russian front-line troops. The war in Afghanistan is becoming increasingly unpopular with the soldiers themselves, and the parallels with the American involvement in Vietnam are becoming ever more apparent. The strategic stalemate that has developed suggests that the war will be a long one, but as in most such conflicts the initiative remains with the guerrillas; if they can hang on and continue the struggle they will without any doubt wear down the fighting will of the enemy and bring into question the whole value of the Soviet commitment.

An Afghan guerrilla leader stands with his men, armed with a valuable captured Soviet RPD light machine gun, an adaptation of the AK assault rifle but with an extended barrel, strengthened stock and a drum magazine capable of holding up to 75 rounds.

Mujahidin Guerrilla
Afghanistan 1980

Above: In a clandestine workshop an Afghan guerrilla prepares a home-made firearm for use against government and Soviet forces.

In appearance, the Afghan guerrillas fighting the Russians in the 1980s differ little from the tribesmen who fought the British in the late 19th century. Crude leather sandals in traditional Afghan pattern complement his baggy trousers and overjacket. The brown waistcoat, worn under the blue sash and musette bag, seems standard for the guerrilla forces. As modern smallarms remain in considerable demand and with supply limited at times, recourse is made to home-made adaptations of factory models, such as the bolt-action rifle carried here. The only really modern touch is the watch worn on the left wrist; such items of western technology are highly prized in Afghanistan.

THE SOVIET BLOC

The Afghan Army

Since its foundation in the 1870s the Afghan Army has consistently failed to assert the authority of government over the nation. In simple terms the explanation for this state of affairs lies in the fact that Afghanistan has never been a conventional nation state, rather a grouping of tribes in which divisive feuding has been the norm. Only at rare intervals has the army been strong or well equipped enough to suppress any serious tribal revolt. From 1953, however, this situation was remedied somewhat by Afghanistan's new interest in the Soviet Union as a military benefactor. The Soviet Union was generous with aid so that an army of 100,000 men could be maintained and equipped. This force, with its reserves of 150,000 men, was meant to provide a military buffer to Pakistan as well as to make internal security more of a reality. The new Soviet-backed army was unquestionably much stronger but Soviet training helped further the disastrous ideological and religious splits within the officer corps.

Before the Soviet connection the officer corps was riven enough by tribal enmities but several layers of complexity were soon added. Many young officers returning from training in Russia were Marxists but they usually kept their new loyalty secret siding with the progressive elements within the army. Another equally secretive officer grouping was the fundamentalist Muslim Brotherhood which was fanatically opposed to communism and social change of almost any kind. In 1973 the army staged its first military coup in favour of moderately progressive forces and in 1978 a second, Marxist-inspired, coup took place involving a pitched battle in the centre of the capital city Kabul, in which tanks, artillery and aerial bombardment helped bring the death toll into the thousands. Within two years this had been followed by the Russian invasion and complete success for the Marxists within the army.

The Marxist ascendancy produced disintegration, however. Staunchly Muslim officers and troops were disarmed but the new political line soon provoked a general tribal revolt throughout the country. When called into action to suppress this the army itself proved unreliable, so that desertions to the enemy were frequent. When combined with the widespread resistance to conscription that ensued, the army was believed to have lost half its effective strength by 1982 and was reportedly reduced to press ganging men of military age.

Few Afghans have any real sympathy for Marxist ideology; in addition most Afghans are devout Muslims and as the revolt has been proclaimed a Holy War their loyalty to the government has remained a matter of speculation. In summary, the Afghan Army can only be seen as an untrustworthy organisation involved in a struggle against a widespread revolt that it would certainly lose without the support of the Soviet Army.

Above: Reasonably well-equipped for the rigours of the Afghan winter, three government troops stand to attention at a command post in the capital of Kabul. The soldier on the right is armed with an AK assault rifle, with bayonet fixed, while his two comrades carry older PPSh sub-machine guns.

Afghan Infantryman
——Afghanistan 1980——

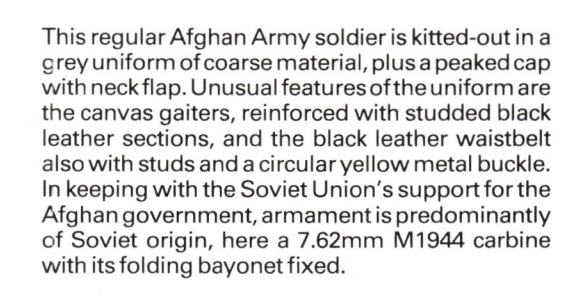

This regular Afghan Army soldier is kitted-out in a grey uniform of coarse material, plus a peaked cap with neck flap. Unusual features of the uniform are the canvas gaiters, reinforced with studded black leather sections, and the black leather waistbelt also with studs and a circular yellow metal buckle. In keeping with the Soviet Union's support for the Afghan government, armament is predominantly of Soviet origin, here a 7.62mm M1944 carbine with its folding bayonet fixed.

Below: Armed with Soviet 7.62mm M1944 carbines, a line of Afghan soldiers pose for a Western cameraman. The quality of conscripts in the Afghan Army leaves much to be desired.

THE SOVIET BLOC

The Soviet Army in Afghanistan

Prior to the invasion of Afghanistan in December 1979, the Soviet Army had seen little active service for over 30 years. Organised and equipped for conventional campaigns against China or the West, its only real experience had been occasional interventions in neighbouring communist states. This was apparent in Afghanistan: the initial seizure of power in Kabul, using airborne troops, was slick and professional, reflecting the experience of Hungary in 1956 and Czechoslovakia in 1968, but once the mujahidin guerrillas initiated active resistance, Soviet ground forces were quickly out of their depth. Lacking any tradition of small-unit fighting, low-level command initiative or tactical flexibility, the men of the invasion force, many of whom had been hastily mobilised and poorly prepared, found it impossible to do more than occupy the major towns, leaving much of the countryside and many Soviet supply routes in guerrilla hands.

Recognition of these shortcomings and the introduction of new techniques to rectify them has been a painful process, forcing the Soviets for the first time since 1945 to think beyond the demands of conventional war. During the early months of the Afghan occupation, the tactics employed were little different from those of the Americans in Vietnam – a combination of massive firepower and large-scale 'sweeps' of disputed areas – but since the disasters of 1980–81, marked by steadily increasing casualties and declining morale, certain changes have been made. The use of tanks was found to be inappropriate to the terrain of Afghanistan and they were gradually withdrawn, to be replaced by more flexible armoured personnel carriers, armed with automatic 30mm cannon. At the same time, anti-air and anti-tank weapons – clearly of little value against guerrillas – were shipped back to the Soviet Union, making way for extra manpower specifically trained in mountain warfare. Finally, the deployment of up-gunned Mi-24 Hind D helicopters has provided the Soviets with more accurate firepower, designed to take out specific targets rather than laying down indiscriminate fire.

But the Russians still find success elusive. The mujahidin continue to control vast areas of rural Afghanistan, leaving the Soviets to preserve an increasingly tenuous hold on the urban centres and supply routes. Guerrilla ambushes are frequent, implying a persistent Soviet reluctance to take the war beyond the roads; air and ground responses to guerrilla attack show a continuing dependence on firepower and, with the deployment of napalm and chemical weapons, a lack of concern for civilian casualties. There has been no serious attempt to conduct a 'hearts and minds' campaign, designed to persuade the Afghan population to support the Soviet-controlled government, and there are persistent reports of demoralisation among the Soviet troops. The pattern is familiar: like the Americans before them, the Soviets have discovered that large armed forces equipped with the latest technology can be resisted almost indefinitely by a determined insurgency campaign.

Below: Three Soviet soldiers, well protected from the cold, pose self-consciously for the camera in Afghanistan, 1980. They are armed with 5.45mm AKS-74 assault rifles, the new, lighter version of the AK-47, but they do not seem very sure of their role in a difficult and apparently endless war.

Soviet Army Sergeant-Major
—Afghanistan 1980—

The uniform of the Soviet Army has changed little since the end of World War II, and this example worn by an NCO of a motorised rifle battalion is no exception. The grey-brown overcoat and high leather boots are particularly distinctive, as is the grey, artificial fur cap. As a soldier in a motorised rifle unit, arm of service is indicated by the red gorget patches sewn onto the greatcoat collar, while rank is demonstrated by the red band running down the length of the shoulder straps. Armament consists of a 7.62mm AKM assault rifle and a pistol, most probably a Makarov PM, plus an AKM bayonet which also doubles as a wire cutter. One of the most famous smallarms to have been manufactured since 1945, the AKM is a development of the AK-47 and although not accurate at anything over short range it combines reliability and simplicity of operation with a high rate of firepower. Since the late 1970s the AKM has begun to be replaced by the AKS, a weapon very similar to the AKM but with the exception of having the smaller calibre of 5.45mm.

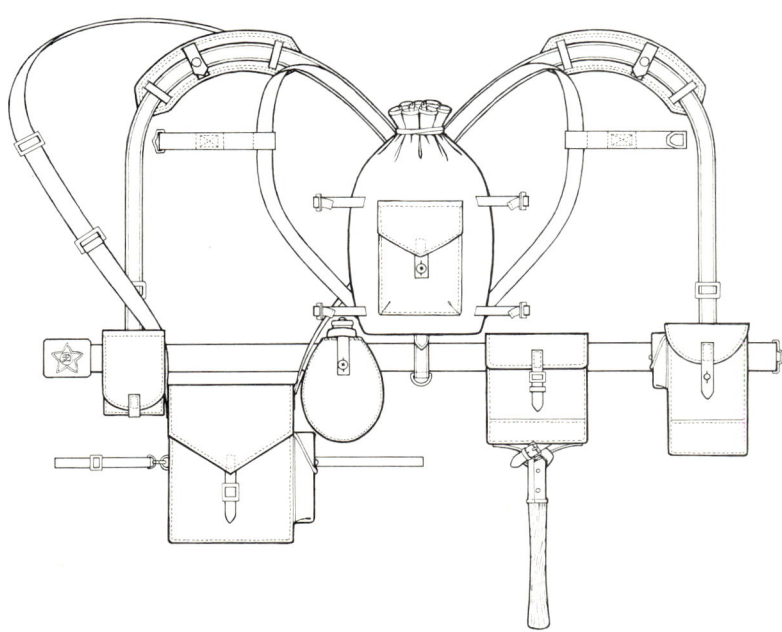

Left: As with his uniform, the equipment of the Soviet soldier has remained much the same over recent years. The pack is used to carry a ground sheet, foot cloths, rations and a field cooker, and is fitted with looped straps (on either side of the pack) capable of holding a rolled greatcoat or rain cape. On the main leather belt are hung – from the left – a grenade pouch, water bottle, entrenching tool, and an AKM ammunition pouch. Between the grenade pouch and the water bottle is a respirator case which holds the bulky Soviet gas mask and filter unit.

FURTHER READING

Beckett, I. and Pimlott, J. (eds.) *Armed Forces and Modern Counter-Insurgency* (Croom Helm, 1985)
Beckwith, C. and Knox, D. *Delta Force* (Arms and Armour Press, 1983)
Bergot, E. *The French Foreign Legion* (Howard and Wyndham, 1976)
Bonds, R. (ed.) *The Chinese War Machine* (Salamander, 1979)
Bonds, R. (ed.) *The Soviet War Machine* (Salamander, 1980)
Bonds, R. (ed.) *The US War Machine* (Salamander, 1977)
Cook, C. and Stevenson, J. *The Atlas of Modern Warfare* (Weidenfeld and Nicolson, 1978)
Dickens, P. *SAS: The Jungle Frontier* (Arms and Armour Press, 1983)
Ferguson, G. *The Paras: British Airborne Forces 1940-84* (Osprey, 1984)
Fowler, W. *Battle for the Falklands: Land Forces* (Osprey, 1984)
Frost, J. *2 Para Falklands* (Buchan and Enright, 1983)
Fullerton, J. *The Soviet Occupation of Afghanistan* (Methuen, 1984)
Gander, T. *Encyclopaedia of the Modern British Army* (PSL, 1982)
Hastings, M. and Jenkins, S. *The Battle for the Falklands* (Pan, 1983)
Heitman, H. *The South African War Machine* (Bison, 1985)
Herzog, C. *The Arab-Israeli Wars* (Arms and Armour Press, 1984)
Horne, A. *A Savage War of Peace* (Penguin, 1979)
Isby, D. *Weapons and Tactics of the Soviet Army* (Janes, 1981)
Jeapes, T. *SAS Operation Oman* (William Kimber, 1980)
Jeffery, K. (ed.) *The Divided Province* (Orbis, 1985)
Katcher, P. *Armies of the Vietnam War 1962-75* (Osprey, 1982)
Keegan, J. (ed.) *World Armies* (Macmillan, 1983)
Ladd, J. *Inside the Commandos* (Arms and Armour Press, 1984)
Laffin, J. *Arab Armies of the Middle East Wars 1948-73* (Osprey, 1983)
Laffin, J. *The Israeli Army in the Middle East Wars 1948-73* (Osprey, 1983)
Maclear, M. *The Ten Thousand Day War* (Thames/Methuen, 1981)
Mollo, A. *The Armed Forces of World War II* (Orbis 1981)
Pimlott, J. (ed.) *The Middle East Conflicts* (Orbis, 1983)
Pimlott, J. (ed.) *Vietnam: The History and the Tactics* (Orbis, 1982)
Porch, D. *The Portuguese Armed Forces and the Revolution* (Croom Helm, 1977)
Rees, D. (ed.) *The Korean War: History and Tactics* (Orbis, 1984)
Rottenberg, G. *The Anatomy of the Israeli Army* (Batsford, 1979)
Russell, L. *The US Marine Corps since 1945* (Osprey, 1984)
Strawson, J. *A History of the SAS* (Secker and Warburg, 1984)
Suvorov, V. *Inside the Soviet Army* (Hamish Hamilton, 1982)
Thompson, L. *Uniforms of the Elite Forces* (Blandford Press, 1982)
Thompson, L. *Uniforms of the Indo-China and Vietnam Wars* (Blandford Press, 1984)
Thompson, R. (ed.) *War in Peace* (Orbis, 1985)
Walmer, M. *Modern Elite Forces* (Salamander, 1984)
Weeks, J. *The Airborne Soldier* (Blandford Press, 1982)
Windrow, M. *French Foreign Legion* (Osprey, 1971)